CISCO NETWORKING

ESSENTIALS

CISCO NETWORKING
ESSENTIALS

Troy McMillan

WILEY

John Wiley & Sons, Inc.

Acquisitions Editor: Agatha Kim
Development Editor: Kelly Talbot
Technical Editor: Leslie Herron
Production Editor: Eric Charbonneau
Copy Editor: Sharon Wilkey
Editorial Manager: Pete Gaughan
Production Manager: Tim Tate
Vice President and Executive Group Publisher: Richard Swadley
Vice President and Publisher: Neil Edde
Book Designer: Happenstance Type-O-Rama
Compositor: Craig W. Johnson, Happenstance Type-O-Rama
Proofreader: Nancy Bell
Indexer: Ted Laux
Project Coordinator, Cover: Katherine Crocker
Cover Designer: Ryan Sneed
Cover Image: © Wayne Johnson/iStockPhoto

Copyright © 2012 by John Wiley & Sons, Inc., Indianapolis, Indiana
Published by John Wiley & Sons, Inc. Indianapolis, Indiana
Published simultaneously in Canada

ISBN: 978-1-118-09759-5
ISBN: 978-1-118-20383-5 (ebk)
ISBN: 978-1-118-20385-9 (ebk)
ISBN: 978-1-118-20384-2 (ebk)

For general information on our other products and services or to obtain technical support, please contact our Customer Care Department within the U.S. at (877) 762-2974, outside the U.S. at (317) 572-3993 or fax (317) 572-4002.

Wiley also publishes its books in a variety of electronic formats and by print-on-demand. Not all content that is available in standard print versions of this book may appear or be packaged in all book formats. If you have purchased a version of this book that did not include media that is referenced by or accompanies a standard print version, you may request this media by visiting http://booksupport.wiley.com. For more information about Wiley products, visit us at www.wiley.com.

Library of Congress Control Number: 2011939636

10 9 8 7 6 5 4 3 2 1

Dear Reader,

Thank you for choosing *Cisco Networking Essentials*. This book is part of a family of premium-quality Sybex books, all of which are written by outstanding authors who combine practical experience with a gift for teaching.

Sybex was founded in 1976. More than 30 years later, we're still committed to producing consistently exceptional books. With each of our titles, we're working hard to set a new standard for the industry. From the paper we print on, to the authors we work with, our goal is to bring you the best books available.

I hope you see all that reflected in these pages. I'd be very interested to hear your comments and get your feedback on how we're doing. Feel free to let me know what you think about this or any other Sybex book by sending me an email at nedde@wiley.com. If you think you've found a technical error in this book, please visit http://sybex.custhelp.com. Customer feedback is critical to our efforts at Sybex.

Best regards,

Neil Edde
Vice President and Publisher
Sybex, an Imprint of Wiley

*To my dear wife, Heike, who has supported me through
all the late nights working and missed weekends and who
has endured my ill temper throughout this process.
She is living proof there are angels among us.*

ACKNOWLEDGMENTS

I want to thank the entire editing and production staff that has helped to make this book as good as it can possibly be. That includes Kelly Talbot, my development editor, who gave me great advice beyond simply grammar and style. I took full advantage of all his years of experience as an editor. He was the conductor of this orchestra and ensured that everything was where it was supposed to be, when it was supposed to be.

I also would like to thank the technical editor, Leslie Herron, who saved me from myself a number of times. It is so comforting to know that someone with deep technical knowledge is looking over your shoulder. That also goes for Eric Charbonneau, who caught things that all of us missed, and the other members of the team, Pete Gaughan, Connor O'Brien, and Jenni Housh.

A special thanks goes to Jeff Kellum for recommending me for this book and to Agatha Kim, the acquisition editor, for selecting me for this book and helping to guide me through the entire process.

About the Author

Troy McMillan is a trainer and writer from Atlanta, Georgia. He began his IT career with IBM in 1999 supporting point-of-sale systems. After achieving his MCSE, he became a network administrator in the Atlanta office of a global manufacturer of electric motors. In 2000, he took his first job as a trainer, teaching MCSE classes to career changers at a local IT school in Atlanta.

In 2001, Troy started delivering corporate training for New Horizons in Atlanta. His concentration was in Microsoft, CompTIA, and Cisco classes. In 2002, Troy started his own training company while continuing with New Horizons on a contract basis and also teaching at various colleges and technical schools in the Atlanta area.

In 2003, Troy began traveling the United States and Canada, teaching Cisco, wireless (CWNA program), and Microsoft classes for training organizations such as Global Knowledge, New Horizons, PPI, and Knowlogy.

In 2005, Troy accepted a position with Kaplan IT Certification Preparation, creating practice tests and study guides for the Self-Test and Transcender brands. His work includes Microsoft, but he is the principal Cisco writer.

Troy's first book, *Change Your Career: Computer Network Security as Your New Profession*, was released in 2007. This guide provides resources and helpful hints for career changers considering this field.

Troy began contributing to and providing technical edits for Sybex books in 2009. He contributed to Todd Lammle's *CCNA Wireless Study Guide: IUWNE Exam 640-721* and *CompTIA Network+ Study Guide: Exam: N10-005*, provided technical edits and contributions to Todd's *CCNA Cisco Certified Network Associate Review Guide: Exam 640-802*, and was technical editor for Darril Gibson's *Windows 7 Desktop Support and Administration: Real World Skills for MCITP Certification and Beyond (Exams 70-685 and 70-686)*. He is currently providing technical editing on Toby Skandier's *Network Administrator Street Smarts: A Real World Guide to CompTIA Network+ Skills*.

In 2010, Troy coauthored *VCP VMware Certified Professional on vSphere 4 Review Guide* with Brian Perry, Chris Huss, and Jeantet Fields. He also created and edited textbooks for Penn Foster on Apple computers, basic troubleshooting, and mobile devices. Troy created classroom instruction materials for many of the Sybex titles already listed as well as for *MCTS: Windows Server 2008 R2 Complete Study Guide (Exams 70-640, 70-642 and 70-643)* by William Panek.

Prior to his career in IT, Troy was a professional musician. From 1968 to 1986, he recorded and performed with many of his own bands and as a backup musician for acts including Vassar Clements and Delbert McClinton. He worked for a number of years as a session musician and songwriter in Nashville as well. In 1983, he returned to school, earning a BBA in management from Georgia State University in 1986. He operated his own businesses after graduation as well as working several years in retail management. He began a self-study in IT in the 1990s, leading to his first IT job at IBM.

Troy lives with his wife, Heike, and a house full of dogs, cats, birds, and fish in Atlanta, Georgia. He enjoys running, music, and sports of all kinds, especially NASCAR.

CONTENTS AT A GLANCE

CONTENTS

INTRODUCTION

This book is designed to fill a gap that has existed for some time in technical books and instructional materials covering networking in general and Cisco technology in particular. As a trainer, I have struggled to find materials that strike a middle ground between basic networking texts and books that jump immediately into certification-level topics that many readers and students are not prepared to digest.

There will always be a market for books designed to present and review certification-level topics to those who are already familiar with the knowledge required to understand those topics. In today's economic times, however, there is a whole new breed of students who are either taking classes or operating in a self-study capacity but do not have this prerequisite knowledge and may not even realize this as they attempt to tackle certification-level classes and books.

I have seen these students in my classes over the years. They are no less intelligent or motivated than the students who have more background and experience. But at the pace at which these books and classes must move to cover all the material, they soon find themselves struggling. Some even give up entirely.

This book covers all of the basic knowledge required for you to really understand routing and switching. It provides the required amount of time for you to digest the fundamentals before moving on to actually setting up and configuring the routers and switches and seeing them operate. It does not attempt to cover every bell and whistle that these devices offer, nor does it cover every topic that is on a Cisco CCENT exam. What it does do is provide all of the basic network knowledge from a Cisco perspective.

The student who reads this book and works through these exercises or the student who takes a class using this book as its text will come away ready in every way to tackle books and classes targeted for exam prep for the CCNA. That is the goal of this book and was our guiding principle throughout its creation.

Who Should Read This Book

This book is designed for anyone wishing to gain a basic understanding of how networks operate and how Cisco devices in particular fulfill their roles in the process. This includes the following:

- ▶ Those who have been away from the IT industry for some time and are reentering the field

- ▶ Career changers with no previous experience

► Students who have struggled with certification-level prep materials

► Students who have had success with certification-level prep materials but came away from the experience with a shallow understanding of the core foundational knowledge

What's Inside

Here is a glance at what's in each chapter:

Chapter 1, "Networks," describes network components, classifies LANs and WANs by function, and compares and contrasts peer-to-peer and client-server networks.

Chapter 2, "The OSI Model," explains the purpose of reference models, introduces the layers of the OSI model, and describes how the layers relate to the encapsulation process.

Chapter 3, "TCP/IP," explains the TCP/IP reference model, compares it to the OSI model, and describes the function of the four layers of the model.

Chapter 4, "Protocols," describes the function of protocols in networking and surveys various protocols that operate at each layer of the TCP/IP model.

Chapter 5, "Physical and Logical Topologies," defines the meaning of a topology in networking and describes the main physical and logical topologies.

Chapter 6, "Numbering Systems," explains the main numbering systems of importance in networking, the binary and hexadecimal systems, and how they are converted to and from the decimal system.

Chapter 7, "Classful IP Addressing," explains the basics of IP addressing, identifies the types of IP addresses, introduces network troubleshooting tools, and describes the use of DHCP to automate the IP configuration process.

Chapter 8, "Classless IP Addressing," points out the shortcomings of classful IP addressing, explains the benefits of classless subnetting, and introduces the components of CIDR.

Chapter 9, "Media," begins with a brief description of media types, explains cable behaviors and characteristics, and ends with a survey of the types of cables and their proper use.

Chapter 10, "Network Devices," describes the functions of the various devices found in a network and explains design principles guiding their placement.

Chapter 11, "LAN Operations," explains both the routing and the switching process and describes how they fit together in end-to-end communication.

Chapter 12, "Managing the Cisco IOS," introduces the components of the Cisco operating system, describes the boot process of a router or switch, and describes how to navigate the command-line interface.

Chapter 13, "Configuring Routers," explains how to get a router operational, including cabling the router, logging into the IOS, securing the router, and configuring its interfaces.

Chapter 14, "Configuring Switches," explains how to get a switch operational, including cabling the switch, logging into the IOS, securing the switch, configuring its switchports, and creating and managing VLANs.

Chapter 15, "Configuring Static Routing," explains how routes are configured and verified at the CLI and how to configure inter-VLAN routing.

Chapter 16, "Configuring Dynamic Routing," introduces how dynamic routing functions, explains the types of routing protocols, and describes how to configure an example of each.

NOTE

Each chapter contains Additional Exercises and Review Questions. The answers to the Review Questions can be found in the book's Appendix. Please visit the book's companion website (www.sybex.com/go/ciscoessentials) to compare your answers to the Additional Exercises with the author's answers.

How to Contact the Author

I welcome feedback from you about this book or about books you'd like to see from me in the future. You can reach me by writing to mcmillantroy@hotmail.com or troy.mcmillan@kaplan.com.

Sybex strives to keep you supplied with the latest tools and information you need for your work. Please check their website at www.sybex.com, where we'll post additional content and updates that supplement this book should the need arise. Enter **Cisco Essentials** in the Search box (or type the book's ISBN—918-1-118-09759-5), and click Go to get to the book's update page.

CHAPTER 1

Networks

Computer networks are everywhere. It's impossible to escape them in the modern world in which we live and work. We use them at work, at home, and even in between, in places like our cars, the park, and the coffee shop. We have come to take them for granted in the same way we treat electricity and hot water.

But a lot is going on behind the scenes when we use these networks. Cisco routers and switches play a critical role in networks' successful operation.

This opening chapter lays the foundation required to understand all the details that make networks function. Specifically, this chapter covers the following topics:

▶ **Describing network components**

▶ **Classifying networks by function**

▶ **Defining network architectures**

Describing Network Components

To understand how networks work, it helps to have an appreciation of why they exist in the first place. As incredible as it may seem now, for a number of years, when computers first came into use, very few computers were networked. They operated as little islands of information with no connection to one another. Data had to be transferred between computers by copying it to a floppy disk, physically taking that floppy disk to the other computer, and copying the data to the destination machine. This process is now sometimes jokingly referred to as the *sneakernet*.

Modern networks can include many components. Some of the most basic components are computers, routers, and switches. Figure 1.1 shows some Cisco routers and switches. *Routers* are used in a network to transfer information between computers that are not on the same network. Routers are capable of doing this by maintaining a table of all networks and the routes (directions) used to locate those networks. *Switches* come in two varieties. Layer 2 switches simply connect computers or devices that are in the same network. Layer 3 switches can do that but are capable of acting as routers as well. Two models of routers are depicted in Figure 1.1, with a switch in the middle of the stack. Routers and switches are covered in depth in Chapter 10, "Network Devices."

FIGURE 1.1 Cisco routers and switches

In this section, the benefits of networking are covered as well as the components required to constitute a network.

Defining the Benefits of Networks

There are many benefits to networks, one of which was touched on in the introduction to this section: using a network makes sharing resources possible (without putting on your sneakers and leaving your seat). When connected by networks, users can share files, folders, printers, music, movies, you name it!

If it can be put on a hard drive, it can be shared. Additional benefits are included in the following list:

Resource Sharing   Resource sharing is less earthshaking at home, but in the workplace it was a key element that drove the adoption of PCs. Other computer types such as mainframe computers and dumb terminals were already in use, but were seen as specialized pieces of equipment to be used only by guys in lab coats and some other geeky types. There were other reasons for the PC revolution, but resource sharing helped to increase productivity. As an example, 10 coworkers could access a file on the network at the same time, which eliminated the time and effort spent burning, labeling, transporting, and storing 10 floppies.

Reduced Cost and Easier Installation of Software   Another advantage for business that didn't become apparent as quickly as resource sharing was a reduced cost of software. Many software products are sold to organizations on a network basis. For example, instead of buying 25 retail versions of word processing software, a single copy can be purchased for the network and then a number of seat licenses can be added to the bundle. The result is a significant savings to the company.

Taking that idea a step further, the network also makes it possible to place the installation files (from the CD containing the software) on a server and to then install the software over the network (as shown in Figure 1.2). This capability relieves IT staff from having to physically visit each machine with CD in hand to perform the installation. Moreover, the software could be installed on all five machines at once over the network by using those same files.

> The term *resource* is used extensively when discussing networking and simply refers to anything that a user on one computer may want to access on a different computer. Examples include files, folders, printers, and scanners.

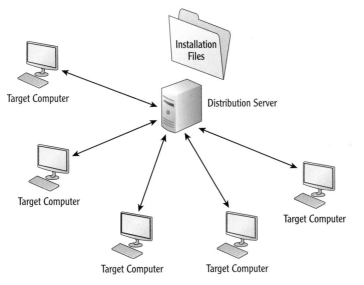

FIGURE 1.2 Network installation

Improved Security   All this peace, love, and sharing doesn't mean that everything is available to everyone. Shared resources can be secured with restrictions on who can access them and what exact access each individual possesses. So you can share a file on your computer but share it with only two of your coworkers, and not all of them. Moreover, you could allow one coworker to only read the document while the other could be allowed to edit or even delete the document.

This type of control was difficult when files were shared on floppies. After the floppy left your hand, it was out of your control. Computer networks can enforce security controls among the computers and users.

Improved Communications   It's hard to even imagine today's workplace without email, instant messaging, video chatting, and conferencing, but 25 years ago, these tools did not exist. In today's world, almost *no* communication can wait for regular postal mail (this service that we once depended on is now often called *snail mail*). Even more impressive is that distance is no obstacle. You can chat online with someone in India or China as easily as with a fellow worker sitting in the next cubical!

Now think of all the paper that is being saved that used to be consumed by companies sending regular mail to one another. The problem was multiplied by the need to keep multiple copies of the documents sent through the regular mail. Email systems can be configured to maintain a copy of every email sent, and documents that used to exist in multiple physical copies now reside as a single digital copy on a server (and probably also on a backup tape).

Meetings that used to require plane trips and hotel stays can now be held online with all participants able to see one another, share documents, view slides or documents from the presenter, and even hold votes and surveys. The only consideration is time zones!

Telecommuting means working from another physical location, usually from home. It saves gas, time, and in many cases results in more productivity on the part of the worker.

▶

More Workplace Flexibility   Users are no longer physically tied to the same computer. If resources are stored on servers, as they are in most organizations, a computer problem no longer renders a user unable to work. In a domain-based network (more on that later in this chapter in the section "Understanding Client-Server Networks"), the user can move to any other computer that is a member of the domain, access his files on the server, and continue to work while his computer is repaired or replaced.

Building on this idea, workers are increasingly telecommuting as they can use the Internet to connect to the work network and operate as if physically present in the office.

Reduced Cost of Peripherals   When users can share printers, scanners, and fax machines, usually fewer devices are needed. This reduces costs for the organization. Sharing these devices also offloads the responsibility for managing and maintaining these shared devices.

Centralized Administration   Although not possible in a peer-to-peer network, in a domain-based network, all computer administration is centralized. This means that the LAN administrator is responsible for maintaining the security of the network, and this work is done from a special type of server called a *domain controller*. Domain controllers do more than provide security. They also serve as the directory of the resources available on the network. This is why these services are called *directory services*. (Peer-to-peer networks, domain-based networks, and LANs are explained throughout the rest of this chapter.)

Peripherals **are any devices that operate in conjunction with the computer yet reside outside the computer's box. Examples include the display, mouse, keyboard, printer, camera, speakers, and scanners.**

DIRECTORY ASSISTANCE, PLEASE!

Directory services, such as Active Directory by Microsoft, help users to locate files, folders, and other resources in the network.

Identifying the Requirements for a Network

A network cannot be called a network if it does not meet certain requirements. At their simplest, those requirements include the following:

- ▶ At least two computers
- ▶ A resource that needs to be shared
- ▶ A transmission medium
- ▶ A communications agreement

Each requirement is detailed in the following list. The coverage of the last two bullet points is somewhat brief as transmission mediums are discussed in Chapter 9, "Cabling," and protocols (communications agreements) are covered in detail in Chapter 4, "Protocols."

At Least Two Computers   It seems obvious, but if there are not at least two computers, there is no need for a network. A single computer doesn't need a network to access the information on its own hard drive. Getting information from computer A to computer B without using the sneakernet is what drove the development of networks.

A Resource That Can Be Shared You already know from our earlier discussion that resources are anything that needs to be shared. This can include physical entities such as printers and scanners, or it can be files and folders located on another computer, as shown in Figure 1.3. If it can be shared and moved from one computer to another, it can be considered a resource.

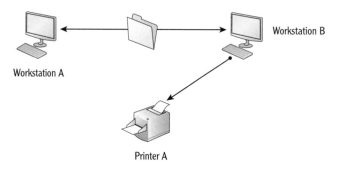

Workstation B

Workstation A

Printer A

FIGURE 1.3 Sharing resources

A Transmission Medium Some form of communications medium is also required. The most common form is a cable, but wireless communications are becoming increasingly widespread because of certain advantages to this approach. Both methods are shown in Figure 1.4.

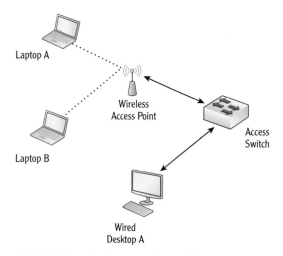

Laptop A

Wireless
Access Point

Access
Switch

Laptop B

Wired
Desktop A

FIGURE 1.4 Transmission mediums

MEDIUM? DO I NEED A OUIJA BOARD?

A communications *medium* is any process that can be used by two computers to transfer data. It can be bounded (via a cable) or boundless (wireless).

A Communications Agreement One of the main stumbling blocks present when computers were first being networked was a language problem. As you know, two people who need to converse cannot do so unless they speak a common language. Likewise, computers have to be speaking the same language in order to have a communications agreement. Networking languages are called *protocols*. In Figure 1.5, workstation 2 is able to communicate with workstation 3 because they are both using TCP/IP, but cannot communicate with workstation 1 because it is using IPX/SPX, a different networking protocol.

◄

Protocols are discussed in Chapter 4.

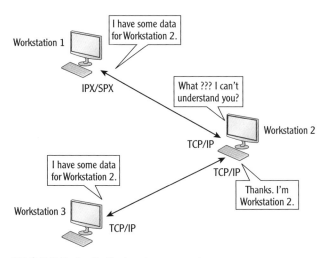

FIGURE 1.5 Protocol agreement

Before the standardization of network protocols, brought about by the explosion of the Internet and the introduction of reference models such as the OSI and the DoD models, computers from different vendors could not be networked together because they used proprietary and dissimilar network protocols.

In addition to the minimum requirements for a network, additional components are usually present in varying combinations. *Repeaters* are devices designed to regenerate or strengthen transmission signals to avoid attenuation

◄

The OSI and DoD network models are covered in Chapter 2, "The OSI Model."

or weakening of the signal, which leads to data corruption. *Hubs* are junction boxes with no intelligence that are used to connect devices together on the same physical network. Switches can act as hubs but provide vastly improved performance and offer additional functions not available in hubs. Routers, as discussed earlier, are used to connect networks and allow computers located on different networks to communicate. Cisco routers and switches are intelligent because of the Cisco Internetwork Operating System (IOS), which is included in and is used to manage the functions of these products. The Cisco IOS is discussed in Chapter 12, "Managing the Cisco IOS." Routers, switches, and hubs are covered in detail in Chapter 10.

PROPRIETARY VS. STANDARD

The term *proprietary*, used often in the IT world, refers to any process or way of doing something that works only on a single vendor's equipment. The opposite of this is a *standard*, which is any way of carrying out a function that the industry has agreed upon. An everyday example of a standard is the ubiquitous wall socket. A standard was developed so that consumers could be assured that any electrical device would match this standard outlet type.

   As the next few chapters unfold, you will gain new perspectives about these requirements as you learn more about the details of each. Now let's look at some characteristics of various types of networks.

Classifying Networks by Function

Networks can be classified according to a number of different characteristics. They can differ based on location, and they can differ in the security relationship that the computers have with another. These are not the only ways networks can differ, but they are commonly used distinctions. In this section, the distance factor is examined in a discussion of LANs and WANs. After examining LANs and WANs, you will take a closer look at defining networks by security relationships in the "Defining Network Architectures" section.

Understanding LANs

If you survey networking books, you will find that the distinction between a local area network (LAN) and a wide area network (WAN) differs from one text to the next. In some treatments of this subject, the difference lies in physical location, while in others the distinction is discussed in terms of the speed of the connection. Because this text is designed to prepare you to manage Cisco routers and switches, a Cisco perspective is appropriate.

Cisco defines a *LAN* as a high-speed data network covering a small geographical area. For the purposes of this discussion, a LAN is a single physical location, which could be a part of a building, an entire building, or a complex of buildings.

In the vast majority of cases, the network will use a networking technology called Ethernet. Other technologies do exist (such as one called Token Ring), but Ethernet has become the de facto standard technology that is used for connecting LANs.

◄

Ethernet is discussed in more detail in Chapter 2 and Chapter 5, "Physical and Logical Topologies."

STANDARDS

As stated earlier in this chapter, a standard is an agreed upon way of doing things. In the networking world, there are two types: official and de facto. An *official standard* is one that all parties agree to and is usually adopted by a body formed to create standards, such as the International Organization for Standardization (ISO). A *de facto standard*, on the other hand, is one that becomes the standard simply by being the method that all parties gradually choose to use over a period of time, without a formal adoption process.

Ethernet networks are typically built, owned, and managed by an organization. It is impractical for the organization to connect offices in two cities with Ethernet cabling (for many reasons that will be discussed later, one of which is a limit on cable length of about 100 ft.).

In a LAN, all of the computers are connected with a high-speed connection. *High speed* is a relative term, but in this case, it indicates at least 10 Mbps. In most cases today, the connection will be either 100 Mbps or 1,000 Mbps. The location may contain multiple buildings; it could even be an entire complex, but if the buildings are connected with a high-speed connection, they would still collectively be considered a single LAN.

◄

Cables are discussed in Chapter 9.

Understanding WANs

A *wide area network (WAN)* is a collection of LANs connected to one another with a WAN technology or with the Internet, allowing it to function as one large network. In the previous section, the impracticality of a company strung together by private Ethernet lines from one office to another was mentioned. Above and beyond the cable length issue, there would be issues of where to place the cables and how to maintain them.

The solutions that are available are as follows:

► Leasing a WAN connection from a telecommunications company

► Using the Internet

When a WAN connection is leased from a telecommunications provider, the company offloads all maintenance and simply uses the existing network that the telecommunication provider built. The advantage to this approach is that your connection is dedicated, meaning there is no other traffic on it. WAN technologies do not use Ethernet. There are a variety of WAN connection types, such as Frame Relay, Integrated Services Digital Network (ISDN), and Point-to-Point Protocol (PPP), and each has advantages and disadvantages.

Another available option is to use the Internet. When this approach is taken, the company creates a logical connection called a *virtual private network (VPN)* between the offices by using the Internet as the physical medium. It is called *private* because the information that crosses the Internet from one office to another is typically encrypted so that if it is intercepted, it cannot be read.

Regardless of the underlying details, a WAN is used to connect LANs. The relationship between the two network types is illustrated in Figure 1.6. The figure depicts three LANs in different cities using the wide area connection to form a WAN.

WAN technologies are beyond the scope of this book. For more information, simply search for WAN methods on the Internet.

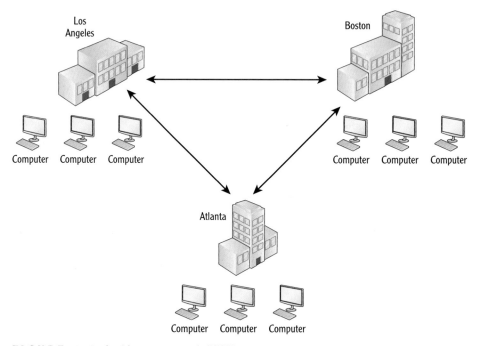

FIGURE 1.6 A wide area network (WAN)

Defining Network Architectures

The *architecture* (or structure) of a network can be discussed from both a physical and a logical viewpoint. For example, in the previous section you looked at how distance can be used to differentiate networks into architectures called LANs and WANs. The architecture of a network can also describe the rules and processes used on the network. The security relationships that exist among the computers on the network can define different architectures. In this section, the difference between peer-to-peer and client-server architectures is explored.

Understanding Peer-to-Peer Networks

Peer-to-peer networks were the first type of networks to appear. This type of network is often referred to as a *workgroup*. In a peer-to-peer network, each computer is in charge of its own security, and the computers have no security relationship with one another. This does *not* mean that the users on the computers cannot share resources; otherwise, it wouldn't be a network!

There are certain shortcomings to this paradigm. In a workgroup, a user can access resources on another computer only if that user has an account on the computer where the resource resides. Moreover, depending on how the sharing is set up, she may also have to identify herself and provide a password to access the resource.

The ramifications of this can be illustrated with an example. Suppose you have four computers in an office that are used by four different users. If your goal is to allow all users to access resources located on all four computers, you would have to create an account for each person on all four computers. That means you would be creating 16 accounts in all (4 computers × 4 people). That's a lot of work! (I guess it's a form of job security!)

Figure 1.7 illustrates this situation. Each computer is named after its user, and as you can see, all users must have an account on all computers. Also note each user can be given different levels of access. Note that the passwords that a user has been assigned on any two computers have no relationship to each other. A user can have the same password on all computers, or a different password on each computer, with no effect on functionality because they are not related to each other in any way in a peer-to-peer network.

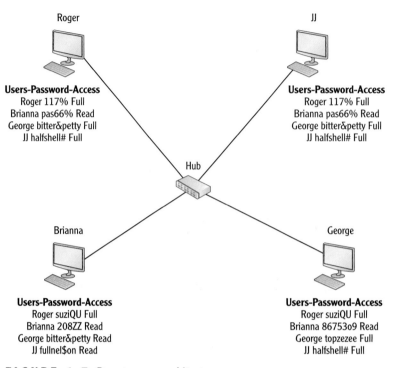

FIGURE 1.7 Peer-to-peer architecture

Another challenge with workgroups is that after the number of computers gets beyond 10, two problems occur. First, because of the nature of the communication process that occurs in a workgroup, traffic overwhelms the physical infrastructure, and the network gets very slow. This occurs because in order to locate each other, the computers must broadcast for one another. A broadcast is akin to a person calling out in a crowded room, "Who is Joe?" Then, when Joe answers, you send him the data. In Figure 1.8, workstation 10 is seeking to connect to a computer named Bannarama, so a broadcast is sent out to every computer. Then Bannarama answers with its IP address.

Moreover, unlike humans, the computers can remember who is who for only a minute or so, and then they must broadcast again.

The second problem that occurs when more than 10 computers are present in a peer-to-peer network has to do with the design of client operating systems. Most client operating systems (meaning any operating system that is not a server operating system) can host only 10 concurrent connections from other computers at a time. So if a popular file is located on a computer in a workgroup, and 10 computers are already connected, the 11th computer won't be able to access the resource until a computer disconnects!

An *IP address* is a number in a specific format that is used to identify a computer. This topic is covered in detail in Chapter 7, "Classful IP Addressing."

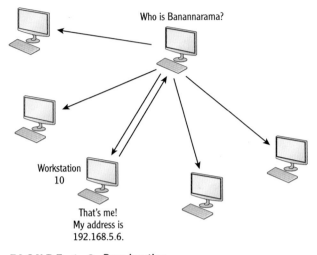

Who is Banannarama?

Workstation
10

That's me!
My address is
192.168.5.6.

FIGURE 1.8 Broadcasting

Workgroups still have their place and their advantages. One is low cost when compared with a client-server network. Obviously, no servers (which cost more than client computers) need to be purchased. Workgroups are also quite simple to set up when compared with client-server networks. Home networks are usually peer-to-peer, and many small office and home office (SOHO) networks function well as workgroups.

However, in medium to large networks, the management of security becomes an administrative nightmare. As discussed earlier, each user must have an account on every computer that he will use or access over the network. Also, peer-to-peer networks are not scalable. When a network can be grown (with respect to the number of computers) without causing additional network traffic or additional administrative effort, it is said to be scalable.

In summary, the advantages of a peer-to-peer network are as follows:

▶ Low cost

▶ Easy to set up

▶ No server required

The disadvantages of a peer-to-peer network are as follows:

▶ No centralized control of security

▶ Administrative burden of maintaining accounts on all computers

▶ Not scalable

Understanding Client-Server Networks

The most obvious difference between a client-server network and a peer-to-peer network is the presence of at least one server. This brings up an issue that needs to be addressed before you encounter it. There are two explanations of a *client-server network* that are commonly used. Both are applicable, so let's cover both.

First, a client-server network can be explained in terms of resource access. When viewed from this perspective, it means that the shared data is centralized on a device called a file server.

WHAT'S THE DIFFERENCE BETWEEN A CLIENT AND A SERVER, ANYWAY?

Which computer is the client and which is the server is simply a matter of perspective. If the computer is seeking to access a resource on another computer, it is acting as a *client*. If it possesses a resource that another computer accesses, it is acting as a *server*. Consequently, computers in a peer-to-peer network will be acting as either at various times, depending on whether they are accessing a resource or allowing access to a resource.

A directory server or domain controller maintains the location of all resources in the network (including the computers themselves) and the locations of each. The computers in the network use this server to find things. Instead of broadcasting to find resources, the computers check with the directory server, which results in a great reduction of traffic!

▶

A *file server* is a computer that contains resources (files) that users in the network need. A server's operating system is designed differently than one that will be used on client computers. It is *not* bound by a limit to the number of connections. Hundreds of computers can connect. The advantage is that the security surrounding the resources can be centralized on that server.

Using our example from Figure 1.7, if there was a file server in that network, we would not have to create an account for every user on all computers. We would have to do that only one time, on the server where the resources are located.

The other explanation of a client-server network takes this a step further. These networks are sometimes called *domain-based networks*. In this case, the server is a special type of server called a *directory server* or *domain controller*.

The domain controller creates a group security association between the computers that are members of what is commonly called a *domain* (or a *realm* in Unix). After a user is made a member of the domain, the user will have two types of user accounts: a local account on her computer, as she had in the peer-to-peer network, and a domain account. The domain account will be created on the domain controller where it will be stored.

This domain account will allow the user to log into the domain from any computer that is a member of the domain. This simplifies the account creation process in the same way illustrated in the explanation of using a file server. The accounts are created one time on the domain controller, and then the account will work on any computer in the domain.

The domain controller, rather than the individual computers, is responsible for validating the credentials of users. Whenever a user logs into the domain from a member computer, the login request is sent to the domain controller, which verifies the name and password and then sends the user an access token. An *access token* is a file that lists the resources that the user is allowed to access in the network, regardless of where the resource is located.

The benefit of this security paradigm is a feature called *single sign-on*. After logging into the domain, a user will not be prompted for a password again, even when accessing resources. It doesn't even matter which computer the resource is on!

On other hand, there are disadvantages to implementing a client-server network. The hardware and software required to deploy servers is significantly more expensive than client software found in a peer-to-peer network. Configuring and maintaining these servers also requires a much higher degree of skill.

Moreover, when a single domain controller is in use, a single point of failure has been introduced to the operation of the network. If something happens to the domain controller, such as a hardware failure, all access to resources can be interrupted. For these reasons, most networks deploy multiple domain controllers to eliminate this single point of failure, further adding to the cost of deploying a client-server network.

In summary, these are the advantages of a client-server network:

- ▶ Centralized administration
- ▶ Single sign-on
- ▶ Reduced broadcast traffic
- ▶ Scalability

Disadvantages of a client-server network are as follows:

- ▶ Higher cost for server software and hardware
- ▶ More challenging technically to implement
- ▶ Single point of failure with a single domain controller or single file server

◀

Scalability **means that the network can grow without the congestion problems that arise when a peer-to-peer network grows larger.**

Figure 1.9 compares the peer-to-peer and client-server networks.

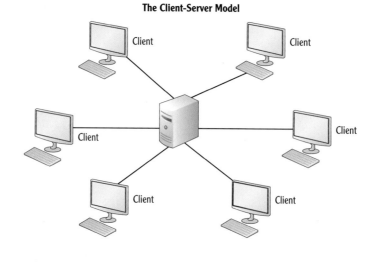

The Client-Server Model

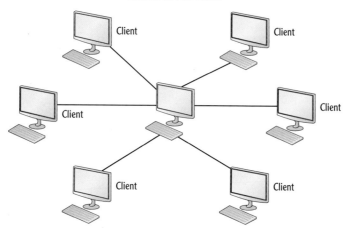

The Peer-to-Peer Model

FIGURE 1.9 The client-server model (top) and the peer-to-peer model (bottom)

THE ESSENTIALS AND BEYOND

Networks allow computers to communicate and share resources. At their simplest, the requirements are two computers connected by communications media sharing a resource. The advantages of networks are resource sharing, lower software and peripheral costs in the enterprise, workplace flexibility, improved communications and security, and centralized administration.

A LAN is a network of computers connected with a high-speed connection and located in one physical location. A WAN is a group of geographically distributed LANs joined by a WAN connection. A LAN can be either a peer-to-peer network or a client-server network. Resource access and security are distributed in a peer-to-peer network, while both are centralized in a client-server network.

ADDITIONAL EXERCISES

You are a consultant specializing in network design. Consider the following scenarios and propose a design using the principles discussed in this chapter (LAN, WAN, peer-to-peer, client-server). Be prepared to discuss and defend your answer.

▶ An auto parts chain with 75 locations in five states

▶ A doctor's office with three computers

▶ A call center in which the users work in three shifts using a single set of computers

REVIEW QUESTIONS

1. Which of the following is *not* an advantage of networking computers?

   A. Resource sharing   C. Potential for increased productivity

   B. Reduced security for data   D. Improved communications

2. A _____ server is one that forms a security association between network members and helps to locate resources.

   A. File   C. Security controller

   B. Directory services   D. Network browser

3. What is the minimum number of computers required to form a network?

   A. One   C. Three

   B. Two   D. Four

4. True or False: Telecommuting is when a user works from another physical location.

(Continues)

THE ESSENTIALS AND BEYOND (Continued)

5. What is a protocol?

    A. A type of transmission medium   **C.** A communications agreement

    B. A security agreement   **D.** A suggested best practice

6. _____ refers to any process or way of doing something that works only on a single vendor's equipment.

    A. Proprietary   **C.** De facto

    B. Standard   **D.** Registered

7. Which statement is true with regard to a LAN?

    A. Distributed across a large   **C.** Leased from a
            geographical area   telecommunications company

    B. High speed   **D.** Requires a server

8. True or False: A de facto standard is one that all parties agree to and is usually adopted by a body formed to create standards.

9. A peer-to-peer network is also sometimes called a _____ .

    A. Realm   **C.** Workgroup

    B. Domain   **D.** Organizational unit

10. Which of the following are shortcomings of a peer-to-peer network?

    A. Difficult to implement   **C.** High cost

    B. Requires server   **D.** Network congestion

CHAPTER 2

The OSI Model

When the benefits of networking computers first became apparent, one of the challenges of doing so was a lack of standardization among the makers of hardware and software. Most networking solutions of the time were proprietary in nature, making it difficult to mix computer solutions from different companies. To put it in the vernacular of the time, everyone was "doing their own thing." While that was a popular slogan and approach to life at the time, it was not a good situation for networking.

In this chapter, two reference models developed to address this situation are discussed. The model that the International Organization for Standardization (ISO) created is the primary focus of the chapter. Another reference model, the Department of Defense (DoD), or the Transmission Control Protocol/Internet Protocol (TCP/IP), model (which is covered fully in Chapter 3, "TCP/IP"), is briefly discussed as a point of comparison. Keep in mind that these are only models, and some parts of the models evolved differently in the real world than originally envisioned. However, they did serve the purpose of establishing common ground that resulted in the interoperability that gives us the robust networks that we have today. Specifically, this chapter covers the following topics:

▶ **Using reference models**

▶ **Introducing the layers of the OSI model**

▶ **Describing the OSI encapsulation process**

Using Reference Models

In the early days of networking, various manufacturers were using incompatible networking protocols and systems for identifying and locating computers on a network. The idea of locking customers into a system by making the system proprietary seemed like a good idea in the beginning. But it soon became apparent to the industry that if everyone got on the same page, everyone could sell more hardware and software.

What the industry needed was a vendor-neutral organization to bring order out of the chaos. The *International Organization for Standardization (ISO)* became that organization.

THE ISO

The International Organization for Standardization (ISO) creates all sorts of standards, and they are not limited to computers and networking. The ISO has developed more than 18,500 international standards on a variety of subjects, and some 1,100 new ISO standards are published every year.

This group created a reference model called the *Open Systems Interconnection (OSI) model* to act as a common blueprint for all vendors to work from, with the goal of promoting interoperability among vendors.

The ISO went about this job by creating standards. Standards are entirely voluntary in nature. They are not laws. No vendors are required to abide by them. In some cases, some vendors chose not to follow the standard until it became apparent that the standard had been widely adopted. Most vendors saw the creation of standards as a benefit and came onboard. In fact, many of the people working on the committees that created these standards came from these companies.

It's only natural that some vendors, particularly large ones, had more influence on decisions that were made than others. The ideal approach would have been to examine all proposals and select the best one on an impartial technical basis, but in reality, some industry voices were louder than others. Cisco was and remains a large player in how networking is done.

Regardless of each player's size and influence, all parties appreciated the benefits of reference models. In this section, you'll look at some of those benefits and then explore another model before diving into the OSI model itself in the next section.

Understanding the Benefits of Reference

Reference models provide a common blueprint from which software and hardware developers can work. The benefits of using reference models such as the OSI model and the TCP/IP, or DoD, model (discussed in the next section) are as follows:

▶ It encourages standardization by defining what functions are performed at particular layers of the model.

▶ It breaks the communication process into parts, taking a modular approach that allows each layer to perform its particular function without regard to the other layers. This ultimately aids in component development at each layer by providing an assurance that the layer can be made to communicate with the layers above and below it.

▶ It prevents changes in one layer from causing a need for changes in other layers, speeding development.

▶ It allows various types of software and hardware to communicate through a standardized communication process from layer to layer.

▶ It encourages vendors to build on each other's developments through use of a common framework.

During the following discussion of reference models, keep in mind that the *layers*, as they are called, represent logical functions that are a part of a communication process between two entities, usually computers. The goal of breaking a complicated communication process into parts, or modules(which is why this process is described as *modular*), is to avoid the need to completely reinvent the entire communication process when a new development takes place. By standardizing the interface between two layers (*interface* just means the way they exchange information), a change can be made on one layer without requiring a change at any other layer. As long as the standard interface between the two layers remains unchanged, the process continues to work smoothly.

Exploring Reference Model Examples

Although the OSI model is where we will spend the bulk of our focus, it is not the only reference model. The Department of Defense (DoD) created a four-layer model in the early 1970s based on the protocol that eventually became the protocol of the Internet and later the de facto standard for LAN protocols, called the TCP/IP or Internet model.

The TCP/IP model uses four layers, and the OSI model uses seven, but they explain the same process of packet creation or encapsulation. All of the same functions take place in each model; in the TCP/IP model, they are just organized logically into fewer layers. As you will see, some of the TCP/IP layers correspond to, or map to, multiple layers of the OSI model.

Figure 2.1 illustrates how the OSI and the TCP/IP models are related to one another. Refer to this figure as the layers of the OSI model are explained and keep in mind that the process of encapsulation is the same in both models; only the number and names of the layers are different.

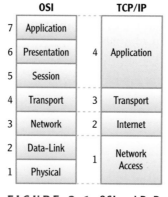

FIGURE 2.1 OSI and DoD models

THE IMPORTANCE OF BOTH MODELS

Most reference model mappings, whether they concern protocols or devices, will be in terms of the OSI model. However, with respect to the study of the TCP/IP protocol suite, it is important that you understand the TCP/IP model, which is covered in detail in the next chapter.

Introducing the Layers of the OSI Model

There are seven layers in the OSI model; each layer plays a role in creating a package of data along with critical information describing the data. This package will be sent from one device to another device, where it will be taken apart and read. This process is called *encapsulation* and *de-encapsulation* and will be explained more fully in the last section of this chapter.

First, the role of each layer must be understood to grasp the encapsulation process. Let's explore each layer and its job in the process. Notice in Figure 2.1 that the functions discussed in the three top layers of the OSI model are condensed into the Application layer of the TCP/IP model, and the functions of the two bottom layers of the OSI are combined in the Network Access layer of the TCP/IP model.

The layers are numbered from the perspective of package reception rather than package creation. This means that the Physical layer is layer 1, and the numbers progress to layer 7, the Application layer. In this discussion, we are approaching the model from the perspective of package creation, so we will begin with discussing layer 7, the Application layer, and work our way up to layer 1, the Physical layer.

A WORD ABOUT LAYER NUMBERING

In this book and most treatments of network modeling, the TCP/IP model is used to discuss the TCP/IP protocol suite and its operation. However, in most Cisco documentation, the layer numbers of the OSI model are used for purposes of describing device and protocol mappings. For example, a switch is said to be a layer 2 device, and a router a layer 3 device, rather than layers 1 and 2, respectively, as they would be if using TCP/IP layer numbers. You should learn both OSI and TCP/IP layer names and numbers.

Understanding the Application Layer

The *Application layer* (layer 7) is where the encapsulation process begins. This is where users interface with the model by working through the service or application they are using. The information on this layer is specific to the service or application that is requesting information to be transferred to another device. An example protocol that operates at this layer is Hypertext Transfer Protocol (HTTP). This is used to transfer web pages across the network. The application data that exists on this layer in that case would be a Hypertext Markup Language (HTML) document, and we would refer to it generically as data. The encapsulated application data could also be a Portable Document Format (PDF) or Microsoft Word document. It could be the text of an email or a Microsoft Excel spreadsheet as well. Other examples of protocols that operate at this layer are Domain Name System (DNS) queries, File Transfer Protocol (FTP) transfers, and Simple Mail Transfer Protocol (SMTP) email transfers.

Understanding the Presentation Layer

The *Presentation layer*, referred to as layer 6, is responsible for the manner in which the data from the Application layer on the source device is represented (or presented) to the Application layer on the destination device. If any translation between formats is required, the Presentation layer will take care of it. A good example of this occurs when data is encrypted; this layer ensures that the data that is presented to the destination application can be read and understood.

ENCRYPTION

Encryption scrambles the data so that it cannot be read if intercepted. When encryption is performed, only the destination device has the ability to unscramble, or decrypt, the data. This operation is represented in Figure 2.2.

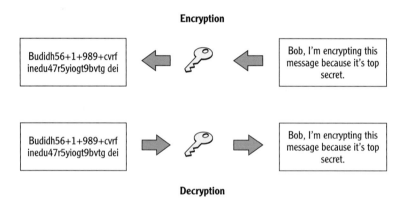

FIGURE 2.2 Encryption/decryption

Another example is compression. The compression process eliminates redundant information so that the data takes up less space. When the data arrives at the destination, the redundant data is added back in. This process is illustrated in Figure 2.3.

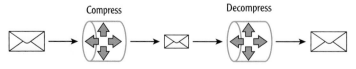

FIGURE 2.3 Compression

If data arrives compressed, the Presentation layer ensures that it is uncompressed before it goes to the Application layer. The reverse of both of these processes is also true. If the data is arriving from the Application layer and needs to be encrypted or compressed, the Presentation layer will take care of that.

ENCRYPTION—WHERE SHOULD IT BE DONE?

Although encryption can be done at the Presentation layer as described earlier, it can also be done at the Data-Link layer (discussed later). Where the encryption takes place affects the amount of information encrypted. If the process is done at the Presentation layer, only the data is encrypted. If done at the Data-Link layer, the entire package is encrypted. In some cases, it is desirable to "hide" some of the information about the data that is contained on the other layer. If that were the case, the encryption should be done on the Presentation layer.

The Presentation layer accomplishes its job by adding information to the package that will be used on the receiving end to make any format translations necessary. This information will go "in front" of the data from the Application layer, and the resulting package will be handed down to the Session layer. When the Session layer receives this package, it will consider the entire package to be data without concerning itself with specific information added by either upper layer.

Understanding the Session Layer

The *Session layer*, referred to as layer 5, is responsible for coordinating the exchanges of information between the layer 7 applications or services that are in use. In the earlier example of the web page, the Session layer would be managing the session between the browser on the source computer and the browser on the destination computer.

The Session layer starts, maintains, and ends the session between the applications. It is important to be clear that this does *not* mean managing the session between the computers. That occurs at a different level. This session is built and closed *after* the physical session between the computers has taken place. To accomplish this goal, the Session layer adds information relevant to managing the session "in front" of the information it received from the Presentation layer. As all the layers do, it considers all the information from above as data and does not concern itself with the specific information added at layers 7 and 6.

◄

When discussing the front and back of this package of information, the *front* is the information that the destination device will receive first, and the *back* is what will be received last.

THE APPLICATION LAYER IN THE TCP/IP MODEL

At this point, I should point out that all of the activities that have taken place thus far as processes in the OSI model take place on the single Application layer of the TCP/IP model, as shown in Figure 2.1.

Understanding the Transport Layer

Whereas the Session layer manages the session between the application on the source computer and the application on the destination computer, the Transport layer is responsible for identifying the application to the destination computer. It does this by using what are called *port numbers*. The port numbers have been standardized so there is no confusion.

In the web page example, the Transport layer would use the port number assigned to the HTTP protocol, which is port 80. Figure 2.4 illustrates how a server acting as a Telnet, FTP, and web (HTTP) server would use the port number assigned to Telnet, FTP, and the web service (ports 23, 21, and 80, respectively) to communicate with different computers requesting different services.

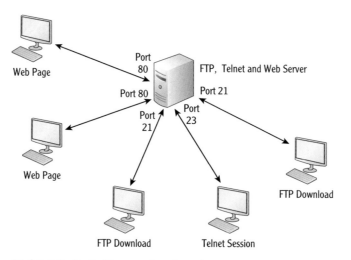

FIGURE 2.4 The use of port numbers

PORT NUMBERS

The kind of ports being discussed here are not physical ports but software ports. Computers are capable of using up to 65,535 ports. Port numbers 1 through 1,023 are called *well-known ports*, as they have been standardized. Port numbers 1,024 through 49,151 are available to be registered by software makers to use as identifiers between network endpoints of their applications. These must be registered with the Internet Assigned Numbers Authority (IANA). The numbers 49,152 through 65,535 are called *dynamic ports* and are used at random by the computers. Chapter 3 covers how those are used.

The OSI model as originally conceived was not tied to any particular set of Transport layer communication methods. Each networking protocol could have its own set of transmission processes operating at various levels of the model, including the Transport layer. Because TCP/IP became the standard for the Internet and subsequently for LANs as well, we will focus our attention on the protocols in the TCP/IP suite. But other networking protocol suites such as Internetwork Packet Exchange/Sequenced Packet Exchange (IPX/SPX, Novell's propriety networking protocol) also have their own Transport layer mechanisms. This is a mere historical footnote, however, because all operating systems (including Novell) now use TCP/IP.

There are two protocols in the TCP/IP suite that operate on the Transport layer: TCP and User Datagram Protocol (UDP). As a result, port numbers come in two types, depending on the Transport layer protocol that is in use. The protocol that is used for a particular transmission depends on the type of delivery that is required. This is not something that is a choice available to you as a user. The choice is made for you based on the type of transmission.

There are three types of transmissions in a network: unicast, broadcast, and multicast. The characteristics of each are listed here and are illustrated in Figure 2.5:

Unicast   When a single source host is sending information to a single destination host, it is called a unicast. This is also known as one-to-one.

Broadcast   When a single host is sending information to all other hosts on the network, it is called a broadcast. This is also known as one-to-many.

Multicast   When a single host is sending a transmission to some, but not all, of the hosts on the network, it is called a multicast. This is also known as one-to-some.

Unicast transmission – One host sends and the other receives.

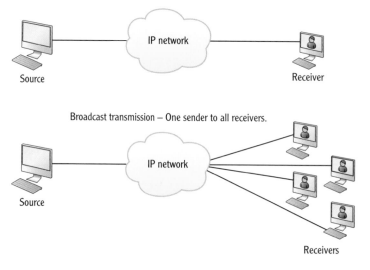

Broadcast transmission – One sender to all receivers.

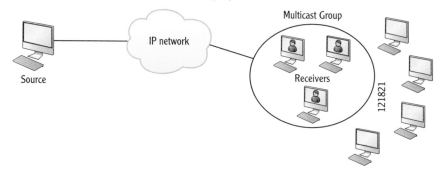

Multicast transmission – One sender to a group of receivers.

FIGURE 2.5 Transmission types

When a transmission is either broadcast or multicast (which means in either case, multiple destination hosts are involved), the protocol used is UDP.

When the transmission is a unicast (one-to-one), the protocol used is TCP. The characteristics of these two protocols are quite different. Those differences are discussed in Chapter 3. But for now, understand that the Transport layer identifies the Transport layer protocol and the port number, as shown in Figure 2.6.

The characteristics of TCP and UDP are covered completely in Chapter 3.

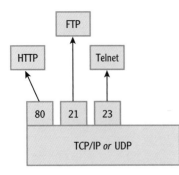

FIGURE 2.6 TCP and UDP
port numbers

To accomplish its goal of identifying the Transport layer protocol and the port number, the Transport layer adds the port number and type "in front" of the information it receives from the Session layer. For example, it would add *TCP 23* to indicate Telnet, because Telnet uses the TCP protocol and port 23. As all the layers do, it considers all the information from above as data and does not concern itself with the specific information added at layers 5, 6, and 7.

Understanding the Network Layer

The *Network layer* is responsible for identifying the destination device by its logical identification. That logical identification, when we are discussing TCP/IP, is called an IP address.

An *IP address* is a number that uniquely differentiates a host from all other devices on the network. It is based on a numbering system that makes it possible for computers (and routers) to identify whether the destination device is on the local network or on a remote network.

◄

IP addresses are discussed in Chapter 6, "Numbering Systems," Chapter 7, "Classful IP Addressing," and Chapter 8, "Classless IP Addressing."

LOCAL VS. REMOTE

If the source and destination hosts are on the same network, the destination device is considered to be on the local network. If the two computers are on different networks, the destination device is considered to be on a remote network. What constitutes local and remote from an IP addressing standpoint is covered in Chapters 7 and 8.

The protocol in the TCP/IP suite that identifies the IP address of the destination and adds this information to the package is called the *Internet Protocol (IP)*.

To accomplish its goal, the Network layer adds the IP address "in front" of the information it receives from the Transport layer. As all the layers do, it considers all the information from above as data and does not concern itself with the specific information added at layers 4, 5, 6, and 7.

The process used by IP to identify the IP address can vary and is covered in Chapter 4, "Protocols."

Understanding the Data-Link Layer

The *Data-Link layer* is responsible for converting the logical identifier (in the case of TCP/IP, an IP address) to a physical identifier. The specific type of Data-Link identifier depends on the Data-Link protocol in use. For Ethernet, this identifier is called a *Media Access Control (MAC) address*. It is applied to the network adaptor by the manufacturer during production, as shown in Figure 2.7.

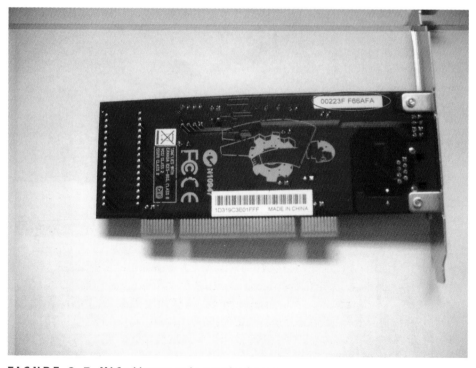

FIGURE 2.7 MAC addresses and network adaptors

ETHERNET AND 802.3

Ethernet is a widely used networking technology that operates at both the Physical and the Data-Link layers of the OSI model. Ethernet is probably the technology you will most likely come in contact with because it is used in almost all LANs. 802.3 is the standard that specifies how Ethernet works so that all implementations of Ethernet are the same and therefore compatible. 802.3 and other members of the 802.*xx* family of standardized technologies are discussed more completely in Chapter 4.

WAN protocols such as Frame Relay and their characteristics such as DLCIs are beyond the scope of this book.

◄

MAC addresses are not the only type of layer 2 (Data-Link layer) addresses. An example of a WAN protocol, Frame Relay, uses layer 2 addresses called Data-Link Connection Identifiers (DLCIs) to identify endpoints in a Frame Relay network. Although they look quite different from MAC addresses, they serve the same purpose.

Just as the Network layer identifies the IP address and labels the package with it, the Data-Link layer must do the same for the MAC address. At this point in the process, the IP address is known, and the MAC address is not. Using another protocol in the TCP/IP suite, Address Resolution Protocol (ARP), the MAC address will be learned and placed in the package.

To accomplish its goal, the Data-Link layer adds the MAC address "in front" of the information it receives from the Network layer. As all the layers do, it considers all the information from above as data and does not concern itself with the specific information added at layers 3, 4, 5, 6, and 7. At this point, all information added to the front of the package by layers 3–7 will collectively be referred to as *upper-layer data*. And the Data-Link layer will place a header on the package called the *Data-Link header*.

Unlike the other layers, however, the Data-Link layer will also add something to the end of the package called a trailer. The *trailer* contains some information that is mathematically related to the data (remember, *data* refers to all the information from layers 3–7) in such a way that it can be used by the destination device to perform a cyclic redundancy check (CRC). This check verifies that the data that left the source computer did not change *at all* during the transmission. If the data does not pass this check, the destination device will discard it because it usually indicates that the data has either been corrupted (damaged) in transit or has been intercepted and altered. The main parts of the resulting package are shown in Figure 2.8.

◄

The process that is used to "learn" the MAC address is discussed in Chapter 3. The format of MAC addresses is discussed in Chapter 6 and Chapter 11, "LAN Operations."

◄

When discussing the front and back of this package of information, the *front* is the information that the destination device will receive first, and the *back* is what will be received last.

Data-Link Layer Header	Upper-Layer Data	Data-Link Layer Trailer

FIGURE 2.8 Header, data, and trailer

Understanding the Physical Layer

At the *Physical layer*, the entire package including header, trailer, and data will be converted into bits for transmission. All information that traverses the network is in this form, meaning it is all a series of ones and zeros that can be reconverted on the other end and read. The physical medium must be capable of representing these ones and zeros in some form or fashion.

The manner in which these bits are represented depends on the physical medium in use. If it is a wired network, the bits will be represented with the presence or absence of an electrical charge. If it is a wireless medium, the bits will be represented with radio waves that are altered or modulated so that the ones can be differentiated from the zeros. Finally, if the cable is fiber-optic, light patterns generated by a small laser (on and off) will be used to indicate ones and zeros.

Describing the OSI Encapsulation Process

Now let's put it all together with an example and see how all of the pieces fit together. Imagine that you are on your company website and you have clicked a link on the page. By doing so, you have just made a request of the web server to send you a document (most web pages exist as documents with an .html extension). This document will be sent to your computer, which will use the proper application (your Internet browser) to display the document so you can view it.

So that we have some real information to use in the example, details about the two computers (your laptop and the web server) are shown in Table 2.1. Refer to it as we take the information and identify where it goes in the process and how it is used. To simplify the process, we are going to assume that the web server is not located on the Internet, but is located on the same network as your computer. This is not unusual, as many organizations use web servers on the local network to provide information to employees.

TABLE 2.1   Computer details for sample

Computer	IP Address	MAC Address	Port Number
Web server	192.168.5.1	5-5-5-5-5-5	TCP 80
Laptop	192.168.5.2	6-6-6-6-6-6	TCP 80

MAC ADDRESSES

Please note that the format of the MAC addresses in Table 2.1 is not correct, but has been simplified for this example. The correct format of MAC addresses and the meaning of each section in a MAC address are covered in detail in Chapters 6 and 11.

Identifying the Process on the Source Device

Using the information shown in Table 2.1, the web server will create the package containing the web page by using the following steps:

▶ Layer 7 obtains the data in the form of the HTML document.

▶ Layer 6 adds information about the formatting.

▶ Layer 5 adds information required to create a session between the web server and the web browser on the laptop.

▶ Layer 4 adds the transport protocol and the source and destination port numbers, in this case TCP (it's a unicast) and port 80 (HTTP).

▶ Layer 3 adds the source and destination IP addresses, in this case a source of 192.168.5.1 and a destination of 192.168.5.2.

▶ Layer 2 learns the destination MAC address and adds the source and destination MAC addresses, in this case, a source of 5-5-5-5-5-5 and destination of 6-6-6-6-6-6.

▶ Layer 1 converts the entire package into bits and sends it across the network to the laptop.

Identifying the Process on the Destination Device

Referring to Table 2.1, the laptop will receive this package and will handle it in the following way:

▶ Layer 1 receives the bits in electrical format, converts them to be read by layer 2, and hands them to layer 2.

▶ Layer 2 examines the destination MAC address to see whether it is addressed to it, sees the MAC address of 6-6-6-6-6 (its own), drops that part of the transmission, and hands the remaining data to layer 3.

▶ Layer 3 examines the destination IP address to ensure that it is its own (192.168.5.2), drops that part, and hands the rest of the package to layer 4.

▶ Layer 4 examines the destination port number (port 80), alerts the browser that HTTP data is coming in, drops that part, and hands the rest of the package to layer 5.

▶ Layer 5 uses the information that was placed on this layer by the web server to create the session between the web server and the web browser and then hands the rest of the information to layer 6.

▶ Layer 6 performs any format translation that may be required and hands the remaining data (the HTML document) to layer 7.

▶ The layer 7 application (the web browser) receives the HTML document and opens the document in the browser window.

Although this example used the transfer of a web document, the process is the same for *any* transmission between two computers, regardless of the type of data or the protocol in use. Now that you have a good basic understanding of the process, in Chapter 3, you'll explore this process in terms of the TCP model, which some would say is a more realistic representation of the real world because the TCP/IP protocol is used on the Internet and on the vast majority of LANs.

THE ESSENTIALS AND BEYOND

The Open Systems Interconnection (OSI) model was created by the International Organization for Standardization (ISO) to bring some order and thus interoperability to the networking devices that manufacturers were creating. It broke the communication process into seven layers, each describing a step in the process of data encapsulation.

The benefits of reference models, including the OSI model, is that they encourage standardization and interoperability, help enhance development on specific layers without requiring a change to other layers, and encourage hardware and software developers to build on one another's accomplishments through their modular approach.

ADDITIONAL EXERCISES

In the following list, identify the OSI layer where the information would be located:

▶ UDP 52

▶ 188.69.44.3

▶ PDF document

▶ 5-5-5-5-5-5

▶ TCP 80

▶ 10.6.9.7

▶ Bit pattern

REVIEW QUESTIONS

1. Which of the following is *not* an advantage of networking reference models?

    A. They encourage standardization by defining what functions are performed at particular layers of the model.

    B. They ensure that networks perform better.

    C. They prevent changes in one layer from causing a need for changes in other layers, speeding development.

    D. They encourage vendors to build on each other's developments through use of a common framework.

2. Which organization created a four-layer reference model in the early 1970s?

    A. OSI

    B. ISO

    C. DoD

    D. IEEE

(Continues)

THE ESSENTIALS AND BEYOND *(Continued)*

3. Which layers of the OSI model map to the Application layer of the DoD, or TCP/IP, model?

    A. Physical

    B. Application

    C. Presentation

    D. Session

4. Which layers of the OSI model map to the Network Access layer of the DoD, or TCP/IP, model?

    A. Application

    B. Session

    C. Data-Link

    D. Physical

5. Which layer of the OSI model is responsible for coordinating the exchanges of information between the layer 7 applications or services that are in use?

    A. Application

    B. Session

    C. Data-Link

    D. Physical

6. What is the information that is used on layer 3 of the OSI model?

    A. A bit pattern

    B. MAC addresses

    C. IP addresses

    D. Port numbers

7. What two pieces of information are communicated in the following: TCP 23?

    A. Port number and transfer speed

    B. Transport protocol and encryption type

    C. Port number and transport protocol

    D. Transfer speed and encryption type

8. What are the port numbers from 1 to 1,023 called?

    A. Well-known

    B. Dynamic

    C. Registered

    D. Static

9. Which type of transmission is referred to as one-to-one?

    A. Multicast

    B. Anycast

    C. Unicast

    D. Broadcast

10. What transport protocol is used for broadcasts?

    A. TCP

    B. RDP

    C. UDP

    D. ARP

CHAPTER 3

TCP/IP

In 1969, the U.S. Department of Defense, acting through its Advanced Research Projects Agency (ARPA, now called DARPA) and in partnership with U.S. universities and the corporate research community, created a four-node network called the ARPANET. This baby step toward what is today known as the Internet used the Network Control Protocol (NCP). In 1974, when NCP proved incapable of handing the increasing amount of traffic, the design for a new set, or suite, of networking protocols was presented called *Transmission Control Protocol/Internet Protocol (TCP/IP)*.

Over the next five years, the protocol went through four version updates. In 1979, version 4, which we have used until just recently and are still using in combination with version 6, was presented and adopted. By 1983 it was mandated that all machines that connected to the ARPANET use this protocol. When this mandate was handed down, it set in motion the adoption of TCP/IP as the protocol of the coming Internet and of any LANs that wanted to connect (without using any protocol conversion) to the Internet.

Because of TCP/IP's key role in all networking, it is important that you have a good understanding of this protocol, its parts, and its operations. This chapter is dedicated to TCP/IP. Specifically, this chapter covers the following topics:

- ▶ **Understanding the TCP/IP model**
- ▶ **Describing the TCP/IP encapsulation process**
- ▶ **Describing the functions at the Transport layer**
- ▶ **Describing the functions at the Internet layer**
- ▶ **Describing the functions of ARP**

Understanding the TCP/IP Model

In Chapter 2, "The OSI Model," the OSI model and the TCP/IP model were compared side by side. But that chapter only briefly noted the TCP/IP model and focused most of our attention on the OSI model. It is important that equal, if not greater, attention is allotted to the TCP/IP model because it describes the encapsulation process from the perspective of the protocol that is the most widely used networking protocol and the one with which you will probably work the most in your career.

TCP/IP is not the only networking protocol ever used. Other networking protocols were created by networking software and operating system companies to support networking between their products. Some of these protocols worked quite well, as long as all of the computers and devices were capable of using the protocol. The problem was that companies such as Microsoft, Novell, and Apple had all gone in different directions and created their own networking protocols. There was no common language.

PROPRIETARY LAN PROTOCOLS

Some early examples of proprietary LAN protocols and the companies that developed them are as follows:

- ▶ NetBEUI (Microsoft)
- ▶ IPX/SPX (Novell)
- ▶ AppleTalk (Apple)

A reference model mapping is used to link a protocol or device with the model layers that contain the information that the protocol or device acts upon.

▶

A translation mechanism did exist, but when TCP/IP became a requirement to connect to the Internet, it seemed pointless to resist switching to this standard. One by one, all of the aforementioned companies and smaller companies as well made TCP/IP the native networking protocol of their products. It is now the common language of networking worldwide.

This section covers the four layers of the TCP/IP model and how they correspond to the seven layers of the OSI model.

Beyond this chapter, you will find that reference model mappings, whether they concern protocols or devices, will be in terms of the TCP/IP model. However, with respect to the study of the TCP/IP protocol suite, it is important that you understand the OSI model as well.

A WORD ABOUT LAYER NUMBERING

In this book and most treatments of network modeling, the TCP/IP model is used to discuss the TCP/IP protocol suite and its operation. However, in most Cisco documentation, the layer numbers of the OSI model are used for purposes of describing device and protocol mappings. For example, a switch is said to be a layer 2 device and a router a layer 3 device rather than layers 1 and 2, respectively, as they would be if using TCP/IP layer numbers. You should learn both the OSI and TCP/IP layer names and numbering schemes.

Exploring the Four Layers

As you learned in Chapter 2, the TCI/IP model contains four layers: the Application layer, the Transport layer, the Internet layer, and the Network Access layer. Considering the importance of this model, a brief review of the layers and a discussion of the function of each is in order. Later in this chapter, a section is devoted to the detailed operation of the Transport and Internet layers, where the TCP/IP suite functions.

Layers use protocols. A protocol is an agreement on how something is done. In networking, a *protocol* defines how the information that is transmitted from one computer to another is structured. Some protocols are special function protocols, and some are networking protocols. The function of a protocol is largely determined by the layer of the TCP/IP model at which it operates.

Networking protocols provide transport services to the special purpose protocols. They also define the rules of communication between devices. In this respect, networking protocols are like languages. The devices must share at least one common language. TCP/IP is a networking protocol and is composed of a set of subprotocols that form what is called the *TCP/IP suite*.

The protocols in the TCP/IP suite are as follows:

▶ Transport Control Protocol (TCP)

▶ User Datagram Protocol (UDP)

▶ Internet Protocol (IP)

▶ Address Resolution Protocol (ARP)

▶ Internet Control Message Protocol (ICMP)

▶ Internet Group Management Protocol (IGMP)

These protocols are discussed further in the sections of this chapter that discuss their relevance with the layers.

As you can see in Figure 3.1, besides the six protocols of the TCP/IP suite, other protocols and services can also be mapped to this model. Although not shown in this figure, devices can also be mapped to the model. More details about the figure follow later in this section, so use it as a guide throughout the discussion of the processes of encapsulation and de-encapsulation.

Encapsulation is discussed in the section "Describing the TCP/IP Encapsulation Process" later in this chapter.

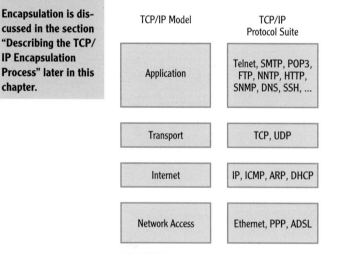

FIGURE 3.1 TCP/IP model

The four layers of the TCP/IP model are as follows:

The Application Layer The Application layer is the user applications' interface to the networking process that is facilitated by TCP/IP. When a user attempts to access anything, the computer has to decide whether the object is located locally on the hard drive or is somewhere out on the network. If the computer determines that the network is required, the Application layer begins the process of creating the package (or series of packages, in most cases) that will be used to request the object or information from the remote device, or alternately to transfer requested information to another device. As you will learn later in this chapter, the name used to describe this package will change as it is transferred from one layer to another.

The information that is contained in the package that will be handed down to the Transport layer includes the data itself (for example, a web page or a document) and all other information required to establish the session between the source and destination service or application and to manage the format or presentation of the data. In doing this, the Transport layer on the source device uses port numbers to identify protocols and services. These port numbers are used to communicate this information to the Transport layer on the destination device. When routers make decisions about the handling of packets based on port numbers, it is said that they are operating at the Transport layer because the routers are using information that is placed in the packet at that layer.

The Transport Layer   The parts of the TCP/IP suite dedicated to using the information provided by the port numbers are located at the Transport layer. UDP and TCP are the two subprotocols of TCP/IP that operate on this layer. As you learned in Chapter 2, the protocol selected at this layer will be a function of the transmission type (unicast, multicast, or broadcast) and the port number specified between the Application layer and the Transport layer. The two protocols are discussed in detail in the section "Describing the Functions at the Transport Layer" later in this chapter. The protocol and port number required are added to the package, and the package is handed down to the Internet layer.

The Internet Layer   At the Internet layer, the logical addresses of the source and destination devices are determined and placed on the package. This information, in the form of IP addresses, is used by the devices on the network that can operate at the Internet layer in the process of routing the package to its final destination. As you may have surmised by now, this is why routers are Internet layer devices. They use information placed in the package at the Internet layer (IP addresses) to make routing decisions. In the section "Describing the Functions at the Internet Layer," you will learn more about this process. In the section "Describing the Functions of ARP," you will see how ARP uses IP addresses to identify the MAC address that will be required at the Network Access layer, There are two more protocols operating at the Internet layer: ICMP and IGMP, which are covered in detail in Chapter 4, "Protocols."

The Network Access Layer   At the Network Access layer, the source and destination physical addresses are put on the front of the package in a part called the *header*. Information used to perform a frame check sequence on the message is placed at the back of the package in a section called the *trailer*.

Packets are discussed in the section "Understanding Data and PDUs" later in this chapter.

Although one of the protocols in the TCP/IP suite that operates at the following layer is called *IP*, the layer itself is called the *Internet layer*.

Trailers and frame check sequences are discussed later in this chapter, in the section "Describing the Contents of Frames."

Finally, the package is converted to ones and zeros in the format required by the physical medium in use. If the computer is connected with a cable, the format will be electrical impulses. If the computer is connected to a wireless network, the format will be radio waves. If the computer has a fiber-optic connection, the format will be light waves. This final operation is performed by the network adaptor in the computer, which is why you must have an Ethernet (wired), wireless, or fiber-optic network adaptor, respectively, in a computer to operate on those network types, so that the bit patterns (the ones and zeros) can be sent in the required format.

Comparing the OSI and TCP/IP Models

As you learned in Chapter 2, the OSI model and the TCP/IP model can be placed side by side for comparison, as shown in Figure 3.2. You also learned that both models describe the process of encapsulation, which is the building of an information package that can be transmitted across a network, and then de-encapsulation, which is the process of taking the package apart and processing the information on the destination device.

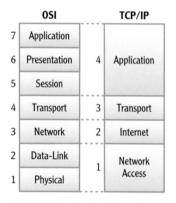

FIGURE 3.2 OSI and TCP/IP models

You already know the following about these two models from Chapter 2:

▶ There are seven layers in the OSI model and four in the TCP/IP model.

▶ The top three layers of the OSI model (Application, Presentation and Session) map to the Application layer of the TCP/IP model.

▶ The bottom two layers of the OSI model (Data-Link and Physical) map to the Network Access layer of the TCP/IP model.

The OSI model was developed before the networking protocol TCP/IP was developed. Therefore, OSI was a general model that could be only predictive in nature and not necessarily reflective of how internetworking eventually evolved. As the old saying goes, "The battle plan goes out the window when the first bullet is fired."

The TCP/IP model, on the other hand, was developed after TCP/IP was developed, and therefore is not so much a prediction of how things could be, but a description of how things are. That's why in most cases descriptions of networking processes are discussed in terms of the four layers of the TCP/IP model rather than the OSI model. Particularly with Cisco routers and switches, most operations will be framed in terms of the TCP/IP model.

Some of the detailed differences in how certain operations are performed in the TCP/IP model as compared to how it was envisioned they would be done in the OSI model are as follows:

▶ In the OSI model, it was envisioned that the Session layer would handle the establishment and management of the communication session between the application or service being used. In TCP/IP, those functions are performed by the TCP/IP protocol itself at a different layer, the Transport layer.

▶ Data conversion into generic formats understood by both sides of the communication is performed at the Presentation layer of the OSI model. These functions take place in the Application layer of the TCP/IP model.

▶ The Application layer in the OSI model is responsible for providing an interface to the user application as an entry point to the networking process. Both models perform this function at the Application layer but in different ways. The difference between these processes is beyond the scope of this book, but the method used in the TCP/IP model is more direct as there fewer layers in the process.

▶ The identification of a protocol or service occurs at the Transport layer in both models. However, in the TCP/IP model, this layer is also where the connection services (UDP or TCP) are provided.

▶ The connection services noted in the preceding list item occur on the Network layer of the OSI model, which maps to the Internet layer of the TCP/IP model. On the Internet layer of the TCP/IP model, the IP protocol of the TCP/IP suite operates and is a connectionless service.

◀

Chapter 2 outlines the OSI model as a potential framework for how the network transmission process would occur. In this chapter, using the TCP/IP model, the process is depicted as it occurs using TCP/IP.

◀

TCP and UDP are explained in the section "Describing the Functions at the Transport Layer" later in this chapter.

► When TCP/IP was developed, it was decided that the division of the bottom layer into Data-Link and Physical layers was unnecessary. Thus their functions are combined in the Network Access layer of the TCP/IP model.

► The OSI model envisioned the host devices as deaf, dumb, and blind bystanders to the networking process, not participants (thus the term *dumb terminal*). In the TCP/IP model, the hosts participate and take part in functions such as end-to-end verification, routing, and network control. They act as intelligent role players in the transfer of information.

Thankfully, the specific differences as illustrated in the preceding list are less important than knowing the details of how network operations are handled in the TCP/IP model.

Describing the TCP/IP Encapsulation Process

The generic term *data package* is often used to describe the data container of information sent from one computer to another. Another term for this that is thrown around somewhat imprecisely in networking circles is *packet.* However, in the Cisco world, using the term *packet* in such a manner is technically incorrect.

As a data package is being built and pieces are being handed down from one layer to the next, this unit of information has a different name at each step. As you will see in the following sections, it is called a packet at only one specific point in the process. The following sections cover the package building process called *encapsulation.*

Understanding Data and PDUs

In Chapter 2, you learned that the information passed from an upper layer down to a lower layer is seen as a single piece of data to the lower layer. For example, when the Internet layer hands the information from the upper layers down to the Network Access layer, the Network Access layer is not aware of which part came from which layer. It sees that entire unit as one piece of data. This monolithic (from the perspective of the lower layer) chunk of data is called a *protocol data unit (PDU)*.

When the information is handed down from layer to layer, the name of the PDU changes, as shown in Figure 3.3. Let's take a closer look at what is contained in each type of PDU.

Describing the Contents of Data

In the "Exploring the Four Layers" section, you learned that the Application layer adds any required information concerning the presentation and formatting of the data to the header and hands it down to the Transport layer. When this PDU is delivered to the Transport layer, it is simply called *data*.

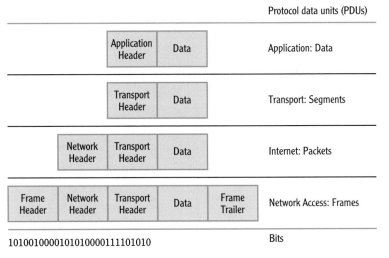

FIGURE 3.3 Protocol data units

Describing the Contents of Segments

The Transport layer adds port number information to the data that was handed down from the Application layer. Earlier in this chapter, you learned that this information consists of the Transport protocol (either TCP or UDP) and the port number of the requested service or application. As you can see in Figure 3.3, this is added in the form of a Transport header, meaning it is in front of the data so that it will be read by the destination device before the actual data is read. This allows the destination device to "know what is coming," so to speak, or what is being requested. After this information has been added, the ensuing PDU is called a *segment.*

Describing the Contents of Packets

This segment PDU is handed down from the Transport layer to the Internet layer. The Internet layer adds the required logical address information to the segment. As you learned in the section "Exploring the Four Layers," this information consists of the IP addresses of the source and destination devices. In Chapter 4, you will learn how the source device "learns" the IP address of the destination device.

After this information has been added to the segment in the form of a Network header, the PDU is now called a *packet.* So now you can see that referring to the entire unit as a packet (although it is done all the time in casual conversation) is actually quite imprecise. It is called a packet only at this point in the process. The packet is now handed to the Network Access layer.

Describing the Contents of Frames

The Network Access layer receives the packet and adds physical address information in the form of a *frame header,* also commonly called a *Data-Link header.* This information is the physical address, or Media Access Control (MAC) address, of the source and destination devices. In the section "Illustrating the ARP Broadcast," you will learn how the source device uses the IP address placed in the PDU by the Internet layer to determine the MAC address of the destination device. In the section "Describing the Logic of MAC-to-IP-Address Conversion," you will learn what role these two types of addresses play in the routing process. An even more detailed discussion follows in Chapter 11, "LAN Operations."

The Network Access layer then does something the other layers did not. It also adds what is called a *frame trailer* (or *Data-Link trailer*). This section contains information that can be used to check the integrity of the data, called a *frame check sequence (FCS).* This verification will be performed by the next device to receive this frame (which, as you will see in Chapter 11, could be a switch, a router, or the destination device) and by all other devices in the path to the destination device. This check is done so that no energy is expended at any point handling or reading data that is corrupted. Now the frame is ready to be sent out on the media.

INTEGRITY AND THE FCS

When the data in a frame is said to have *integrity*, it means that the data has not changed even 1 bit (remember it's all ones and zeros, or bits). Such a change can occur through data corruption or data manipulation by hackers. The FCS process examines the data before it leaves and places a number in the end of the frame (trailer) that can be used to verify this integrity at each step in the routing process. If the FCS calculation doesn't succeed, the data is dropped.

Understanding the Conversion to Bits

At this point, the construction is complete, and the frame is ready for delivery. The network adaptor converts the information into a series of ones and zeros that can be read by any device receiving this frame. At the beginning of the frame is a series of ones and zeros that are designed to allow the receiving device to lock on to or synch up with the signal. This information is not part of the information added by the upper layers and is used solely for the purpose of synching up. Once the receiving device has synched up with the frame, it will start reading the data, starting with the frame header and proceeding to the network header and so on.

When the destination device receives the frame, the entire process is carried out in reverse. Each layer reads the information placed in the frame by the corresponding layer on the source device until the data arrives at the port of the correct service or application ready to be read. The encapsulation process and the de-encapsulation process are shown in Figure 3.4.

Although they are not the only protocols in the TCP/IP suite, the main players in the vast majority of data transfers are TCP, UDP, IP, and ARP. These four protocols operate on the Transport and Internet layers. In the next sections, you will examine some of the main processes that occur in these two layers and the parts these protocols play in those processes.

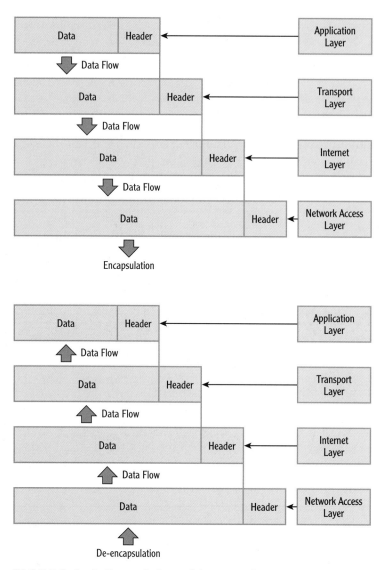

FIGURE 3.4 Encapsulation and de-encapsulation

Describing the Functions at the Transport Layer

The two protocols in the TCP/IP suite that operate at the Transport layer are TCP and UDP. Both utilize port numbers to label segments with the services or applications required at the destination before handing the segment down to the Internet layer. These labels placed in the Transport header by the source device are read when the segment is at the Transport layer of the destination device. However, the services that these two protocols provide to the frame after it leaves the computer are quite different. In this section, you'll examine their characteristics.

Understanding TCP

Several terms can be used to describe the operation of TCP. First, you'll look at each description and how each relates to TCP. Then in the following section, "Understanding UDP," you'll examine the effect that these features and functions have on the types and volume of information TCP places in the Transport header.

Connection-Oriented   TCP is described as connection-oriented because the source and destination device create a state of connection that will be verified by both ends before any data transfer takes place. There is even a predictable script to this dance called the *TCP three-way handshake*. Unless these three steps are completed successfully, no data transfer will take place.

Earlier, in the section "Comparing the OSI and TCP/IP Models," specific differences between the two models are discussed. If you think that something sounds a little strange as you read through the following sections, it might help to flip back to that section. You might be thinking of functionality that is more specific to the OSI model instead of the TCP/IP model.

THE TCP THREE-WAY HANDSHAKE

The TCP three-way handshake contains the following steps and is covered in detail in Chapter 4. In the figure, the abbreviation SYN stands for synchronization request, SYN/ACK for acknowledgment of receipt of the request and ACK means acknowledgment of synchronization and the establishment of the connection.

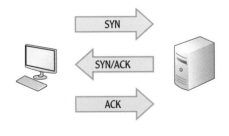

Guaranteed Delivery   TCP delivery is said to be guaranteed because the receiving device must acknowledge the receipt of each frame. If this acknowledgment has not been received, the source device will send the frame again.

Stateful   TCP is also said to be stateful because each data transfer must be accomplished from a "state" of connection. If for some reason this state is lost, it must be reestablished again by using the three-way handshake before the data transfer can resume. Many times, slow network transfers can be traced to frequent losses or "resets" of the connection due to transitory network problems.

Along with acknowledgments, TCP also provides many other features that you will look at in detail in Chapter 4, such as sequencing, flow control, and windowing. As a result of these features, TCP is said to be very reliable and self-adjusting to conditions on the network. This is why it is utilized for unicast (one-to-one) transfers. The downside is that this comes at a cost.

The Transport header that TCP places in front of the segment (called a *TCP header*) is much larger than the header placed in the segment by UDP. All of the additional services (using the three-way handshake to establish the connection, the guarantee of delivery, and the maintaining of state) require more-detailed information to be passed back and forth between the source and destination device, and that information takes space. This extra information and the space it requires is called *overhead*.

The TCP header is shown in the next section.

Understanding UDP

Describing UDP could almost be accomplished by reversing everything I have said about TCP. Let's look at each characteristic of UDP and then assess the resulting effect on the Transport layer header that UDP attaches to the segment handed down from the Application layer.

Non-Connection-Oriented   UDP is non-connection-oriented because no connection is established before data transfer begins. As a result, UDP frames exit the computer much faster with no "wait time" for a connection. On the other hand, many of the services that TCP provides that require a state of connection (such as acknowledgments and sequencing) are not available to a UDP frame.

Nonguaranteed Delivery   UDP delivery is said to be nonguaranteed because the receiving device is not required to acknowledge the receipt of each frame. In most cases, this situation is not as bad as it may seem. Many of the upper-layer protocols that use UDP as their Transport protocol have their own built-in methods of acknowledgment. Therefore, acknowledgment would be redundant at this layer.

Stateless   UDP is also said to be stateless because each data transfer need not be accomplished from a "state" of connection. When a device sends a UDP frame, it does so with a sort of blind trust that the frame will get where it's going!

The Transport header that UDP places in front of the segment (called a *UDP header*) is much smaller than the header placed in the segment by TCP. This space savings results in UDP having low overhead. In Figure 3.5, the two headers are side by side for comparison. Don't be concerned at this point with the names of the fields, but note that the TCP header is 20 bytes in size, and the UDP header is only 8 bytes. The part marked *data* (if any) is the data portion handed down from the Application layer. Chapter 6, "Numbering Systems," covers bytes and bits, and Chapter 4 provides more detail about the header contents.

CHECKSUMS AND FRAME CHECK SEQUENCES

Frame check sequences (FCSs) are also referred to as *checksums*. As you can see in the TCP, UDP, and IP headers in Figure 3.5, the field is actually called *16-bit UDP checksum*. Cisco proprietary protocols use a field called *frame check sequence*, and FCS is often used in Cisco documentation, so I have used that term in this text.

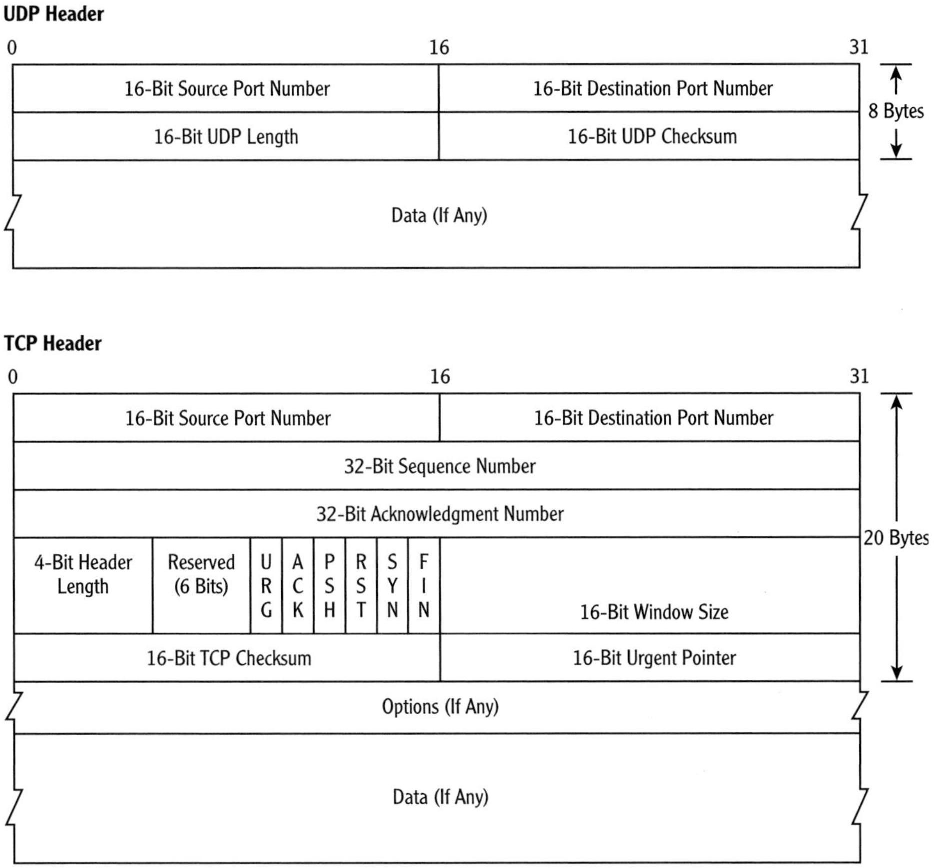

UDP Header

TCP Header

FIGURE 3.5 TCP and UDP headers

Describing the Functions at the Internet Layer

While the protocols operating at the Transport layer are concerned with ensuring that the proper applications or services on the source and destination devices can locate one another, the protocols on the Internet layer are responsible for getting the packet labeled with source and destination IP addresses. Information provided on this layer is used for routing purposes. This Internet layer information is what routers are interested in as they make routing decisions.

As you will see later in the section "Describing the Logic of MAC-to-IP-Address Conversion," while the information placed in the frame header (MAC address) may change many times during the transit from source to destination, the information in the IP header will stay the same the entire way. In this section, IP addressing, routing, and packet forwarding are all briefly discussed. IP addressing is covered in detail in Chapter 7, "Classful IP Addressing," and Chapter 8, "Classless IP Addressing." Routing and packet forwarding are explained in Chapter 11.

THE IP HEADER

Although the layer at which the IP protocol operates is called the *Internet layer*, the part of the header that IP places on the packet is generally referred to as the *IP header*.

Defining Logical Addressing

Logical addresses are those that can be managed, changed, or assigned by a human. IP addresses are an example of logical addresses, but not the only one. As an example, Chapter 2 briefly mentioned a proprietary networking protocol called IPX/SPX. This Novell protocol had its own system of logical addresses that were called network numbers and node numbers. Because we are discussing only TCP/IP, the logical addresses covered here are IP addresses.

IP addresses in their simplest form allow each computer or device on a network to be uniquely identified from any other device. In Chapters 7 and 8, you will learn that this numbering system can be used to group computers into what are called subnets. *Subnets* are subdivisions of the larger network. Computers in the same subnet share a common section of the IP address, similar to how family members might share the same last name. When a computer wants to send data to another device that is in a different subnet, routing must take place.

Performing Routing

When the source device places the source and destination IP addresses in the IP header, that information will not change as the packet is routed across the networks. Each router will examine what the destination address is, perform its part of the routing process, and leave this unchanged. When the response goes back from the destination to the source device, this fact remains the same. The IP addresses will not be altered at any point.

Routers maintain routing tables that can be used to indicate in which direction to send a packet, based on the section of the IP address that is referred to in the previous section using the analogy of the family last name. This section is called the *network portion* or in some cases the *subnet portion* of the address, depending on how the network is logically organized by the administrators. The process of passing a packet from one router to another is called *packet forwarding*.

Accomplishing Packet Forwarding

Even though it is physically the same block of information, when a router deals with the transfer of data, it is said to be forwarding a packet, while switches are said to be forwarding frames. This is because routers read and act upon the information that was placed in the PDU called a packet (IP addresses). Switches read and act upon information placed in the PDU called a frame (MAC addresses). Routers and switches are discussed in greater detail in Chapter 10, "Network Devices."

After the Internet layer has done its job of labeling the packet with the IP addresses, the physical addresses must be placed in the frame. That is the job of the Address Resolution Protocol, or ARP, covered in the next section.

Describing the Functions of ARP

When data is being transferred from one network or subnet to another, routing takes place and Internet layer information is utilized (IP addresses) by the routers to perform this function. However, when data is sent within a network or subnet, routing is not required. In that case, operations happen at the frame level. In this section of the chapter, you'll look at how the Address Resolution Protocol, or ARP, does its job of identifying and placing the source and desti-nation MAC address in the frame and why the MAC addresses (unlike the IP addresses) may change many times as the data travels across the network.

Illustrating the ARP Broadcast

After the Internet layer places the source and destination IP addresses in the packet, and before the frame is delivered to the Network Access layer, where it will become a frame and have a frame header and trailer attached, the source and des-tination MAC addresses must be known so they can be placed in the frame header.

The numbering system used in MAC addresses and the details of how they are permanently applied to a network adaptor are covered in some detail in Chapter 6. But just so you can take a quick look at one, Figure 3.6 shows the MAC address of a wireless network's adaptor card. This particular one is in the form of a PC card that plugs into a PC card slot on a laptop that enables you to add wireless func-tionality. The MAC address has been circled.

FIGURE 3.6 MAC address

Learning the source MAC address does not require any network activity. It is the MAC address that is assigned to the network adaptor in the source machine. However, determining the destination MAC address does require the help of ARP. ARP operates at the Internet layer, but the fruit of its labor (the MAC address) is attached at the Network Access layer. Therefore, the MAC address is a part of the frame header and not the packet header. ARP broadcasts on the local network (remember, a broadcast goes to every computer). The essence of its message is, "If this is your IP address, send me your MAC address." All of the computers receive the message, but only the computer that possesses the destination IP address responds. Then the MAC address is placed in the frame. When the source and destination computer are in the same subnet, the process is as simple as Figure 3.7. When they are not, the process is a bit more complicated, and I cover that in the last section of this chapter.

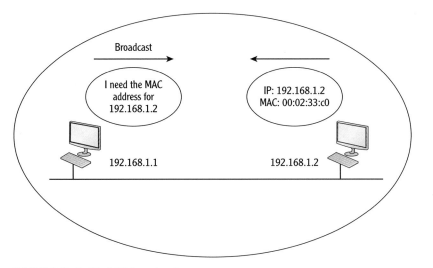

FIGURE 3.7 ARP broadcast

ARP—INTERNET LAYER OR NETWORK ACCESS LAYER?

ARP has classically been placed on the Internet layer, but it does part of its work on the Network Access layer, when it performs the ARP broadcast and supplies the MAC address for the Network Access layer frame.

Describing the Logic of MAC-to-IP-Address Conversion

In any network with computers that are located in different subnets and that need to reach other, the computers are configured with three values by the administrator. Those values are as follows:

>   **IP address**—This uniquely identifies the computer.
>
>   **Subnet mask**—This value identifies the subnet in which the computer is located.
>
>   **Default gateway**—This is the IP address of the nearest router in the network.

▶

The IP address, subnet mask, and default gateway values are discussed in detail in Chapters 7 and 8.

After the source computer determines the destination IP address, it will determine whether that destination computer is in the same network or subnet as itself. This process, called *anding*, is covered in Chapter 7. For now, realize that this process allows the computer to determine this network information.

If it is determined that the two computers are in the same network, the process proceeds as shown in Figure 3.7. However, if that is not the case, ARP will broadcast for the MAC address of the router or the default gateway, not the MAC address of the destination computer. It is important to realize that the IP address of the destination computer will still go into the packet, but the destination MAC address placed in the frame will be that of the router. ARP will determine the MAC address of the router in the same fashion as it would if it were determining the IP address of a computer—that is, with a local broadcast.

When the frame is sent out, it will go to the router. When the router receives the frame, it will perform a lookup in its routing table and determine in which direction to send the packet based on the IP address of the destination computer. However, if the destination computer is not located on one of the local interfaces of the router and the router needs to send this packet to another router, it will place the MAC address of the next router in the frame and leave the destination IP address unchanged. If this packet needs to go across many routers, the MAC address will keep changing. The MAC address will always be the MAC address of the next router until the packet arrives at the local subnet where the destination computer is located. *Only then* will the MAC address of the destination computer be placed in the frame.

As a simple illustration of this process, let's assign some IP addresses and MAC addresses to two computers and three routers and see what happens to the addresses as they go across the network. The network is arranged as shown in Figure 3.8. To understand this process, you need to know that the three routers will each have two sets of addresses, one for each interface in use. Interfaces on a router are network connections. For example, RTR2 has one interface that connects to RTR1 and another that connects to RTR3. The interfaces are also labeled in the diagram. Do not worry about understanding the IP addresses or the MAC addresses at this point. Just try to follow the logic of how the MAC addresses change and the IP addresses do not.

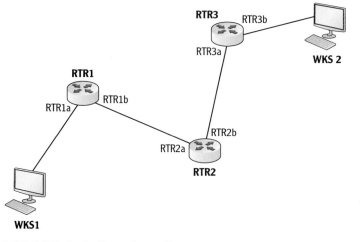

FIGURE 3.8 Frame forwarding

The IP addresses and the MAC addresses of each device are shown in Table 3.1.

TABLE 3.1   Device IP addresses and MAC addresses

Device	IP Address	MAC Address
WKS1	192.168.5.5	a-a-a-a-a-a
RTR1a	192.168.5.6	b-b-b-b-b-b
RTR1b	172.16.5.5	c-c-c-c-c-c
RTR2a	172.16.5.6	d-d-d-d-d-d
RTR2b	10.6.9.5	e-e-e-e-e-e
RTR3a	10.6.9.6	f-f-f-f-f-f
RTR3b	27.3.5.9	g-g-g-g-g-g
WKS2	27.3.5.10	h-h-h-h-h-h

There will be four handoffs to get this packet from WKS1 to WKS2. Table 3.2 shows the destination IP addresses and destination MAC addresses used at each handoff.

TABLE 3.2 Handoff destination addresses

Handoff	Packet (IP) Destination Address	Frame (MAC) Destination Address
WKS1 to RTR1a	27.3.5.10	b-b-b-b-b-b
RTR1b to RTR2a	27.3.5.10	d-d-d-d-d-d
RTR2b to RTR3a	27.3.5.10	f-f-f-f-f-f
RTR3b to WKS2	27.3.5.10	h-h-h-h-h-h

As you can see, the destination IP address in the packet does not change, but the MAC address in the frame changes at each handoff.

THE ESSENTIALS AND BEYOND

TCP/IP is the most important networking protocol you will study, and as such its operations are important to understand. Like the OSI model, it is used to describe the process of encapsulation. There are four layers in the TCP/IP model as opposed to seven in the OSI model. Those four layers are the Application, Transport, Internet, and Network Access layers.

At each layer of the model, the PDU is referred to differently. It begins at the Application layer as data and then changes to a segment, a packet, a frame, and finally to a series of bits to be transmitted.

The TCP/IP suite operates at the Transport and Internet layers. At the Transport layer, TCP and UDP operate and connect services and applications by using port numbers. At the Internet layer, IP and ARP provide IP and MAC addressing.

Working together, this suite of protocols handles all transfer of data across a network, both within a LAN and between LANs.

ADDITIONAL EXERCISES

Using Figure 3.8 (shown earlier) and Table 3.3, fill out Table 3.4 with the destination IP address and destination MAC address that would be in the packet and frame, respectively, at each handoff if a packet were sent from WKS1 to WKS2.

(Continues)

The IP addresses and the MAC addresses of each device are shown in Table 3.3.

TABLE 3.3   Device IP addresses and MAC addresses

Device	IP Address	MAC Address
WKS1	16.8.8.8	v–v–v–v–v–v
RTR1a	16.8.8.15	a–a–a–a–a–a
RTR1b	77.6.8.12	d–d–d–d–d–d
RTR2a	77.6.8.46	q–q–q–q–q–q
RTR2b	54.97.66.4	w–w–w–w–w–w
RTR3a	54.97.66.46	s–s–s–s–s–s
RTR3b	196.64.3.3	n–n–n–n–n–n
WKS2	196.64.3.74	e–e–e–e–e–e

TABLE 3.4   Handoff destination addresses

Handoff	Packet (IP) Destination Address	Frame (MAC) Destination Address
WKS1 to RTR1a		
RTR1b to RTR2a		
RTR2b to RTR3a		
RTR3b to WKS2		

REVIEW QUESTIONS

1. In what year was it mandated that all computers connected to the ARPANET use TCP/IP?

   A. 1979   C. 1983

   B. 1969   D. 1974

(Continues)

THE ESSENTIALS AND BEYOND *(Continued)*

2. Which of the following is a layer in the OSI models *not* found in the TCP/IP model?

    A. Application   **C.** Network Access

    B. Presentation   **D.** Internet

3. Which layer in the TCP/IP model uses port numbers?

    A. Network Access   **C.** Transport

    B. Application   **D.** Internet

4. The Internet layer is where the _____ is placed.

    A. Port number   **C.** MAC address

    B. IP address   **D.** Data

5. How many protocols are in the TCP/IP suite?

    A. Five   **C.** Seven

    B. Four   **D.** Six

6. Which of the following is *not* a difference between the OSI and TCP/IP models?

    A. In the OSI model, it was envisioned that the Session layer would handle the establishment and management of the communication session between the devices. In TCP/IP, that function is performed by the TCP/IP protocol itself at a different layer, the Internet layer.

    B. Data conversion into generic formats understood by both sides of the communication is performed at the Presentation layer of the OSI model. These functions take place in the Application layer of the TCP/IP model.

    C. When TCP/IP was developed, it was decided that the division of the bottom layer into Data-Link and Physical layers was unnecessary and thus all functions are combined in the Network Access layer of the TCP/IP model.

    D. The OSI model envisioned the host devices as deaf, dumb, and blind bystanders to the networking process, not participants (thus the term dumb terminal). In the TCP/IP model, the hosts participate and take part in functions such as end-to-end verification, routing, and network control. They act as intelligent role players in the transfer of information.

    (Continues)

THE ESSENTIALS AND BEYOND   (Continued)

7. What is the PDU called at the Transport layer?

   A. Data   C. Frame

   B. Segment   D. Packet

8. At what layer is the PDU called a frame?

   A. Network Access   C. Transport

   B. Application   D. Internet

9. Which of the following describes UDP?

   A. Connection-oriented   C. Stateless

   B. Guaranteed   D. Used for unicasts

10. Which protocol is responsible for identifying the destination MAC address?

   A. TCP   C. UDP

   B. RDP   D. ARP

CHAPTER 4

Protocols

A protocol *is an* agreement on how something is done. There are many types of protocols. There are business protocols that define how business is properly carried out and social protocols that define what type of behavior is acceptable. *Networking protocols* define the rules of communication between devices.

It is possible for computers to be enabled for more than one networking protocol at a time, but to interact with another computer, both devices must share at least one networking protocol. In this respect, protocols are like languages. If both devices don't speak a common language, they can't communicate.

In this chapter, protocols at every layer of the TCP/IP model are discussed. Some of these are networking protocols and some are special function protocols, such as SMTP, which transfers emails. As you have learned, routing is the process of determining the best route to a packet's destination. This best route can be configured manually on the router (called *static routing*), or the router can be configured to use a routing protocol, which dynamically learns the routes. There is also a routed protocol, which is a networking protocol such as TCP/IP, that can be routed, but it does not perform the routing. Routing and routed protocols are compared and contrasted in this chapter as well. Specifically, this chapter covers the following topics:

- ▶ **Understanding the function of protocols**

- ▶ **Exploring Application layer protocols**

- ▶ **Exploring Transport layer protocols**

- ▶ **Exploring Internet layer protocols**

- ▶ **Exploring Network Access layer protocols**

Understanding the Function of Protocols

The function of a protocol is largely determined by the layer of the TCP/IP model at which it operates. The layer on which it operates is dependent on the type of information that it uses in the process of carrying out its job. For example, if a protocol uses Transport layer information (port numbers) to perform its job, it will be a Transport layer protocol. If it uses MAC addresses, it will be a Network Access layer protocol.

However, there is another way to classify networking protocols such as TCP/IP. There are routed protocols and routing protocols. In this section, routing and routed protocols are discussed.

Defining Routed Protocols

A *routed protocol* is a networking protocol that is capable of being routed. This means that the protocol was designed for transferring information to networks other than the network in which the source device resides. That requires its design to include some method of identifying devices and groups of devices that can be used in the routing process.

Routing services are provided to routed protocols in one of two ways. In static routing, routes are manually configured on the routers at the command line. In dynamic routing, routers on the network are configured to use a routing protocol to determine routes.

Not all networking protocols are capable of being routed. Therefore, they are not routed protocols, even though they are networking protocols. An example is NetBEUI, an early Microsoft protocol. It was designed as a protocol for small workgroups of computers that were located on the same physical segment. It uses no numbering system of any kind, and the computers are identified by names that each machine broadcasts out to the other machines when required. The protocol can't be routed because there is no information for the router to use to determine where it came from and where it needs to go.

Other protocols such as TCP/IP, IPX/SPX, and AppleTalk were designed with routing in mind. Each has a numbering system that can be used by routers to determine the source and destination and the path required to get the packet from point A to point B.

Defining Routing Protocols

A *routing protocol* obtains and uses the information required to route the packets of the routed protocol. For example, in an IP network, the routing protocol will use routing tables that are constructed in terms of IP addressing information to determine how to get the IP packets to their destination. Cisco routers are capable of routing IP, IPX, and AppleTalk even though they use different numbering systems. In today's networks, it is hard to find IPX and AppleTalk being routed, however.

Routing protocols were developed as an alternative to manually creating the routing tables in the routers from the command-line interface of the router. Configuring routes from the command line is called *static routing*. There are several reasons why routing protocols are preferable to static routing. First, routing protocols have the capability to react to changes in the network, such as a malfunction of a link in the network. Second, they can choose the best route to a destination when multiple routes to the same destination exist. Finally, they have the capability to learn the routes and populate the routing tables without manual programming by the administrator. The rest of this chapter is devoted to routed protocols.

◄

Chapter 15, "Configuring Static Routing," and Chapter 16, "Configuring Dynamic Routing," cover in detail the characteristics and the configuration of both static routing and routing protocols.

Exploring Application Layer Protocols

Protocols that operate at the Application layer are dedicated to a very specific function. For example, DNS, which gets its name from the hierarchical system that its uses called the Domain Name System, does nothing but handle requests from computers that are trying to match an IP address with a computer name (which is discussed in detail later in this section).

Application layer protocols have a dependent relationship with the protocols that operate at the lower levels of the TCP/IP model. There is no mechanism built into these protocols to locate the source and destination and get the application data where it needs to go. The Application layer protocol depends on TCP, UDP, IP, and ARP to take care of that function. In this section, you'll learn about the purpose and operation of some of the most common Application layer protocols.

Describing FTP

File Transfer Protocol (FTP) is a connection-oriented protocol dedicated to moving files from one computer to another. It operates on a client-server model, which means that the FTP client application is used to request the data, and the FTP server will respond and send the data. It can be executed from the command line with FTP commands, but many FTP applications now do not require any typing of commands.

FTP uses TCP port 21 for the client to connect to the server and then uses port 20 for the file transfer. If used in what is called *passive mode,* the transfer will occur using a random port number chosen by the client. This is an example of an upper-layer protocol (FTP) using the services of the lower-layer protocol (TCP).

CROSS-LAYER COMMUNICATION

When the Transport layer receives the data from the Application layer, it reads the header placed on the data by that layer to determine the port number that needs to be placed on the segment.

In this case, because a TCP port is in use, all rules of engagement that go along with TCP are in effect. This means that the TCP handshake must complete successfully, all packets must be acknowledged, and if the session is interrupted, it will need to be rebuilt with the handshake to resume data transfer. The handshake is covered in more detail later in this chapter, in the section "Reviewing TCP."

Authentication can be used when connecting to the FTP server. However, it is important to note that the authentication packets that go back and forth between the client and the server are sent in clear text. This means that if the packets were to be captured with a protocol analyzer, or *sniffer,* the username and password could be read.

For this reason, in many cases FTP uses anonymous authentication, which means that users are allowed to connect without a name and a password. In either case, the lack of a secure connection makes FTP ill-suited for secure transfers. Other secure alternatives to FTP do exist, such as SSH File Transfer protocol. Despite the relative lack of security, FTP is still the most widely used file transfer protocol for two reasons. In the vast majority of cases, the information is not sensitive or valuable enough for a hacker to go to the trouble of capturing and decoding the packets and obtaining a username and password. Moreover, it is a mature and well-known standard that benefits from all of the features of TCP (acknowledgments, sequencing, and so on).

SSH

For more information on Secure Shell FTP, see the following website: http://en.wikipedia.org/wiki/SSH_File_Transfer_Protocol.

Describing TFTP

Trivial File Transfer Protocol (TFTP) is the connectionless version of FTP. TFTP has a very limited set of capabilities and provides no authentication. It is designed to be lightweight and fast, and so it uses UDP as its transport protocol. UDP packets are very small, and UDP transfer is fast and perfectly suited for TFTP. The port number is UDP 69 to begin the connection, but the client and server may change to random ports for the transfer afterward.

TFTP is rarely used as a substitute for FTP. However, because of its low memory requirements and simplicity, it is often used to connect to a server and to download router operating systems and configuration files to a Cisco router. Because TFTP uses UDP, it is connectionless and does not incur the overhead of TCP, nor does it enjoy any of the benefits of TCP such as acknowledgments and sequencing.

TFTP

In Chapter 12, "Managing the Cisco IOS," you will learn how to use TFTP to transfer a router operating system (called the Cisco IOS) from a TFTP server to a router. It is also possible to have a router boot its IOS from a TFTP server rather than from its usual local location on the router. You will learn more about that in Chapter 12 as well. In both cases, TFTP is the protocol in use.

Describing SMTP

Although it is not the only protocol involved in the sending and receiving of email, *Simple Mail Transfer Protocol (SMTP)* is the Internet standard used when email is transferred from one server to another. The use of this standard is what allows a Microsoft Exchange email server to send mail to a Novell GroupWise email server and receive email from an IBM Lotus Notes email server. All of these servers (and other brands as well) use SMTP to transfer email.

SMTP is a store-and-forward protocol that has also been used in other situations that can benefit from its capability to attempt a connection, fail, store the information, and try again later. For example, SMTP is an alternative to TCP/IP when transferring Microsoft Active Directory replication traffic between Active Directory sites. When a connection is unreliable, SMTP's store-and-forward nature is beneficial.

EMAIL PROTOCOL

The following image shows how SMTP and client protocols are used together to make email transfers.

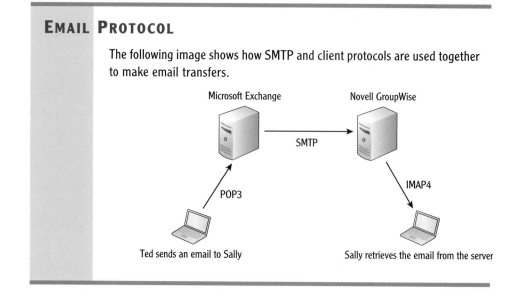

Microsoft Exchange   Novell GroupWise

SMTP

POP3   IMAP4

Ted sends an email to Sally   Sally retrieves the email from the server

It is a text-based and command-driven protocol that can be executed from a command line, although email servers will execute these commands automatically when required. It also is client-server in nature, with the SMTP client making requests of the SMTP server. These requests are called *transactions*. The SMTP server can also respond to email clients by using protocols such as Post Office Protocol (POP3) or Internet Message Access protocol (IMAP4). (The 3 and 4 simply stand for versions of the POP and IMAP protocols, respectively.) These protocols are required because SMTP only delivers email. It cannot request email. SMTP uses TCP port 25 so it is connection oriented and thus benefits from all of the features and overhead of TCP.

OVERHEAD

TCP and UDP both have packet headers. The header on the TCP packet is almost three times the size of the UDP header. The TCP packet header is larger because more space is required to hold all the information that TCP uses to perform acknowledgments, sequencing, and other functions. The amount of space used in the header is often referred to as *overhead*. This is why TCP is said to have more overhead than UDP.

Describing DNS

If DNS did not exist, we could not connect to websites on the Internet or other computers on a LAN without knowing the IP address of the computer hosting the website or the IP address of the computer on the LAN. DNS takes care of this for us—and because most of us don't even know our own computer's IP address, this is an incredible benefit. DNS performs resolution of an IP address to a computer name or website name. It operates in a hierarchical arrangement known as the *DNS namespace*.

The DNS namespace refers to the naming system used in DNS. To prevent DNS servers on the Internet from being overwhelmed with the number of names to resolve, the servers are organized into a hierarchy. Each level of the hierarchy contains part of the information required to locate a website or company domain. By storing and delivering the name-to-IP-address information in this fashion, the servers have a much more manageable amount of data with which to work. There are three levels to this hierarchy:

▶ Root level

▶ Top level

▶ Domain level

When you see the DNS name for a website, different parts of the name are derived from different levels of the hierarchy. Consider the following name:
abc.com.

The dot (period) at the far right (which is not required and is usually left off in the real world) represents the root level. The com part is from the top level, and the abc is from the domain level. The period between abc and com is required and important to include for proper interpretation of the name by the DNS servers. When a computer needs to know the IP address for abc.com, it will begin a search at the root level. The root-level servers have information about *only* top-level servers (.com, .mil, .net, and so forth). The root-level server will direct the query to a top-level server (.com in this case). The .com server will know all records that end in .com, including abc.com. The server will return the IP address to the computer, and then the computer can make an IP-address-to-IP-address connection with that web server.

DNS servers on the Internet are managed by a collection of universities, private corporations, and the Internet Corporation for Assigned Names and Numbers (ICANN). Individual companies also operate their own DNS servers, which then rely on the Internet DNS servers to locate computers outside of the company.

The complete details of DNS are beyond the scope of this book, but let's take a look at how a DNS server operating on a LAN does its job.

Each computer is configured with the address of the DNS server. This IP address can be either configured statically or provided automatically from a DHCP server.

Dynamic Host Configuration Protocol (DHCP) is discussed in detail in Chapter 7, "Classful IP Addressing."

This is a server that provides IP addressing configuration information to computers automatically, saving the administrative effort and human error inherent in performing this configuration statically on each device. One of the items that the DHCP server can issue to the computers is the IP address of the DNS server.

DNS is another client-server protocol. A series of messages pass back and forth between the DNS client and the DNS server, resulting in the DNS server providing the IP address of the computer whose name the DNS client requested. These requests, called *queries*, and responses, called *resolutions*, use UDP port 53. Because of its low overhead, UDP is fast and works well for these transfers. This is an example of the Transport protocol (UDP) leaving the reliability up to the upper-layer protocol (DNS). If a DNS client does not receive a reply in a certain amount of time, the client will make additional attempts.

Multiple DNS servers often exist in a network to provide fault tolerance. When this is done, the DNS servers must keep their records synchronized. These sets of records are called *zones*, and the synchronization is done with a process called *zone transfers*. For this operation, DNS does not use UDP; it uses TCP port 53. This process is displayed in Figure 4.1.

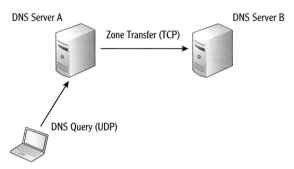

FIGURE 4.1 DNS use of TCP and UDP

Describing SNMP

Simple Network Management Protocol (SNMP) is an Application layer protocol used to manage and monitor devices on a network from a central location. These devices can include any device type for which information is contained in a management information base (MIB). MIBs describe the structure of the management data of a device subsystem; they use a hierarchical namespace containing object identifiers.

These devices can include computers, routers, switches, wireless access points, and more. The system operates with three components:

▶ The managed device—the actual computer or other hardware

▶ An agent—software that runs on managed devices

▶ A network management system (NMS)—software that runs on the manager device

SNMP uses UDP to transfer messages back and forth between the management system and the agents running on the managed devices. Inside the UDP packets (called *datagrams*) are commands from the management system to the agent. These commands can be used either to get information from the device about its state (*SNMP GetRequest*) or to make a change in the device's configuration (*SetRequest*). If a GetRequest command has been sent, the device will respond with an *SNMP response*. If there is an item of information of particular interest to an administrator about the device, that administrator can set what is called a *trap* on the device. A trap is designed to send a message (*SNMP trap*) to the management system if a certain event occurs. These communications are illustrated in Figure 4.2.

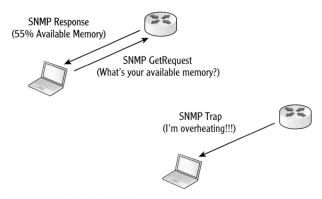

FIGURE 4.2 SNMP messages

SNMP also uses more than one port in its operations. The SNMP agent receives requests on UDP port 161. The management system may send requests from any available source port to port 161 in the agent. The agent response will be sent back to the source port on the manager. The management system receives notifications (traps) on port 162. The agent may generate notifications from any available port.

Exploring Transport Layer Protocols

The Transport layer is responsible for identifying the Application layer protocol to the destination computer. It does this by using what are called port numbers. You also learned that there are two transport protocols: UDP and TCP. UDP is used for broadcast and multicast transmissions, and TCP is used for unicast transmissions. TCP and UDP use these port numbers to identify services, protocols and applications that operate on the Application layer.

In this section, you'll look at more details of UDP and TCP, paying particular attention to the additional features of TCP that allow it to add reliability and help maximize network performance.

Reviewing TCP

As you learned in Chapter 3, "TCP/IP," TCP creates a state of connection that is verified on both ends of the communication before data transfer takes place. The fact that the receiving device must acknowledge the receipt of each frame also guarantees delivery of information. Beyond these basic concepts, TCP has a number of features that make it more complex than UDP but also more reliable. The features of TCP are as follows:

Sequencing   Data transmission in most cases requires many packets. When packets are being routed across the network, there is no assurance that the packets will arrive at the destination in the same order that they were sent. This is due to multiple paths to the destination, changing network conditions, and other factors. As packets are sent, TCP places a sequential number on each packet. This allows the destination device to place the packets in the proper order after all of the packets that are a part of the transmission arrive. These numbers are also a part of the acknowledgment system explained in the next section.

Acknowledgments   Earlier you learned that TCP provides reliability in that the destination device acknowledges each packet it has received so that any missed packets can be retransmitted. It does not do this by sending an acknowledgment (ACK) packet back for each packet received. That would create tremendous traffic. The solution is much more elegant than that. The computers arrive at an agreement concerning how many bytes of data can be sent before the cumulative data must be acknowledged (this is called *windowing*, covered in the next section). By signaling the number that it needs to receive next, the destination computer is also signaling what it has received and, in effect, what it has missed. This process is displayed with no errors in Figure 4.3 and with errors in Figure 4.4.

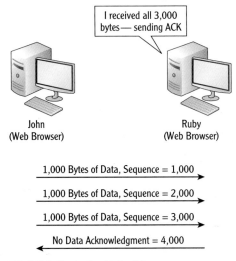

FIGURE 4.3 ACK with no errors

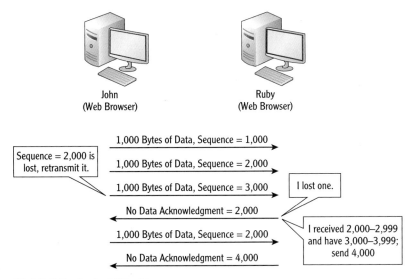

FIGURE 4.4 ACK with errors

Windowing and Flow Control   In the preceding paragraph on acknowledgments, you learned that the source and destination computers agree on the amount of data to send before an acknowledgment is required. This amount is not static. It can change, which is a good thing. If network conditions allow, larger sets of data can be sent between acknowledgments without errors. If, on the other hand, errors start to occur, the amount can be decreased (in poor network conditions, larger amounts of data sent between acknowledgments tend to increase the possibility of errors). The process of monitoring the network conditions and window size with a goal of reducing the number of acknowledgments required is called *flow control.*

This automatic adjustment process is accomplished with the TCP *sliding window*—a window of transmitted data between ACKs. This process is managed with a field in the TCP header called the Window field. If a series of sets of data are successfully sent with no errors, the window size might be increased. If, on the other hand, errors are starting to occur, the window's size might be decreased. The value in the Window field is the amount of buffer space available for incoming data on the destination device. The sending device monitors this value as each ACK is received.

The TCP Three-Way Handshake   As you learned in Chapter 3, TCP is a stateful protocol—a state of connection is established before any transmission takes place. This is accomplished with a predictable process called the TCP three-way handshake. At different points in the process, the two computers are in various states. The entire process is illustrated in Figure 4.5.

The steps are as follows:

> **SYN**   This is sent from the computer requesting a connection or synchronization. After the sending computer sends SYN, the computer is said to be in the SYN_SENT state.
>
> **SYN ACK**   Before the receiving computer receives the SYN packet, it is said to be in a LISTENING state. After the receiving computer receives the SYN packet, it will transition to the SYN_RCVD state and will transmit a packet called the SYN ACK, the purpose of which is to let the sending computer know that the SYN packet was received.
>
> **ACK**   When the sender receives the SYN ACK packet, it will transition to the ESTABLISHED state and transmit back an ACK packet. When the receiver gets this ACK packet, it will also transition to the ESTABLISHED state. At this point, a state of connection has been established.

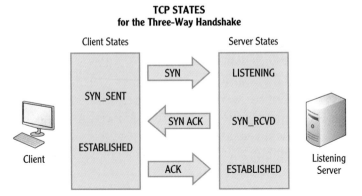

TCP STATES
for the Three-Way Handshake

FIGURE 4.5 TCP three-way handshake

If you look at the parts of a TCP header, you can see where the fields used for the aforementioned operations are located. As you can see in Figure 4.6, there are fields present for source port, destination port, sequence number, acknowledgment number, window, and other types of information.

Source Port (16)			Destination Port (16)	
Sequence Number (32)				
Acknowledgment Number (32)				
Data Offset	Reserved (6)	Flags (6)	Window (16)	
Checksum (16)			Urgent (16)	
Options and Padding				
Data (Varies)				

FIGURE 4.6 TCP header

The description of each field in the header is as follows:

Source port   This field identifies the source port.

Destination port   This field identifies the destination port.

Sequence number   This field is used in the sequencing process as discussed in the previous list item, "Sequencing."

Acknowledgment number   This field is used in the ACK process as discussed in the previous list item, "Acknowledgments."

Data offset   This field specifies the size of the header.

Reserved   This field is for future use and should be set to zero.

Flags   The 8-bit Flags field is used to relay control information between TCP peers. Among the eight flags are SYN, FIN, RESET, PUSH, URG, and ACK. SYN and ACK are used in the TCP handshake. For more information, see http://nmap.org/book/tcpip-ref.html.

Window   This field indicates the size of the receive window as discussed in the previous list item, "Windowing and Flow Control."

Checksum   This value is used to verify the integrity of the information in the header to detect header corruption.

Urgent   This field is related to one of the use of the Urgent flag in the Flags field.

Options and Padding   This field is related to the Data Offset field and ensures that the length of the header is a multiple of 32 bits.

Data   This is the upper-layer data.

TCP OVERHEAD

As noted earlier in this chapter, the header on the TCP packet is almost three times the size of the UDP header. All the information that TCP uses to perform acknowledgments, sequencing, and other functions requires more space in the header. Consequently, UDP has less overhead than TCP.

Reviewing UDP

With regard to UDP, there's not a lot to add that hasn't already been said in Chapter 3. UDP has none of the features of TCP and none the overhead. As you can see in Figure 4.7, its header contains only fields for source port, destination port, length, checksum, and the data.

Source Port (16 bits)	Destination Port (16 bits)
Length (16 bits)	Checksum (16 bits)
Data . . .	

FIGURE 4.7 UDP header

The description of each field in the header is as follows:

Source port number   This field identifies the source port.

Destination port number   This field identifies the destination port.

Length   This field specifies the length in bytes of the entire datagram: header and data.

Checksum   This value is used to verify the integrity of the information in the header to detect header corruption.

Data   This is the upper-layer data.

Exploring Internet Layer Protocols

Two-thirds of the TCP/IP protocol suite operates on the Internet layer, so a lot of activity occurs here. This is the layer where routing occurs and where the resolution of IP addresses to MAC addresses occurs. There are also two protocols on this layer that we haven't really discussed yet: ICMP and IGMP. In this section, all of that is covered as well as the interactions of the protocols on the TCP/IP Internet layer "team."

Describing IP

Internet Protocol (IP) is a connectionless protocol that depends on TCP when connection-oriented operations are required. The IP header is attached to the segment containing everything that was added at the Application and Transport layers. This container is called an *IP datagram* or *packet*. It is capable of being routed because it is labeled with IP address information.

When the Application data with the TCP or UDP header attached is handed down to the Internet layer, IP will add its own header called the IP header. It is much like the other headers you have seen in that it contains fields in specific locations that contain values. In the TCP and UDP header, these fields contained information such as source port, destination port, sequence number, acknowledgment number, and window in TCP, and source and destination port number in UDP.

After IP has determined the destination IP address, usually through the DNS name resolution process, it places it along with the source IP address in the IP header.

The IP header, shown in Figure 4.8, includes exactly what you would expect: IP addresses.

◀

For more about DNS, see the section "Describing DNS" earlier in this chapter.

4-Bit	8-Bit	16-Bit	32-Bit
Version	Internet Header Length (IHL)	Type of Service (TOS)	Total Length (TL)
Identification		Flags	Fragment Offset (Offset)
Time To Live (TTL)	Protocol		Header Checksum
Source Address			
Destination Address			
Options		Padding	
Data			

FIGURE 4.8 IP header

The description of each field in the header is as follows:

Version   This identifies the version of IP. There are two current versions, 4 and 6. The version based on 32-bit IP addresses (the one we have been discussing) is version 4. Version 6 is a new version that uses a completely different numbering system. Version 6 is covered briefly in Chapter 8, "Classless IP Addressing."

Internet Header Length (IHL)   The Internet Header Length specifies the length of this IP header, which will include the use of a field seen later in the header called Options.

Type of Service (TOS)   The Type of Service is a field that can be used to mark the packet with a priority of sorts. It is not widely used because it has been replaced by a different method of accomplishing the same goal called *Differentiated Services Code Point (DSCP)*. This system uses the same 8 bits that were used for TOS but uses them differently and allows for more types of service and more-granular control of quality of service. You can find more information on DSCP at `http://en.wikipedia.org/wiki/Differentiated_services`.

Total Length (TL)   The Total Length is the length of the entire IP datagram, not just the header, measured in bytes.

Identification   This is used to identify pieces of a message that has been broken up into smaller pieces called *fragments*. This helps keep fragments from different messages organized at arrival.

Flags   These fields are used to mark a datagram to *not* be fragmented, or to indicate that it has been fragmented and there are more fragments to follow.

Fragment Offset (Offset)   This field is used to indicate where in the overall message this fragment should go.

Time to Live (TTL)   This is the Time to Live. This might be considered the lifetime of the datagram, which does have a limit to prevent a datagram that can find no destination from circling the networks forever. This is a number and not a time value. It indicates the number of routers or hops the datagram is allowed to go. When it has counted down to 0, the TTL is exceeded and the datagram is discarded.

Protocol   This indicates the protocol carried in the datagram (example: TCP, UDP, ICMP, and so forth). The protocols are identified by standardized numbers.

Header Checksum   This value is used to verify the integrity of the information in the header to detect header corruption.

Source Address   This the source IP address.

Destination Address   This is the destination IP address.

Options   This field is used for special options beyond the scope of this discussion. You can find out more about options at `http://simplestcodings` `.com/2010/10/08/tcp-header-format/`.

Padding   This field is used to ensure that the length of the header is a multiple of 32 bits.

Data   This is everything that was added by the upper layer.

Describing ARP

Address Resolution Protocol (ARP) is responsible for resolving the IP address to the MAC address of the destination. As you learned in Chapter 3, that is not necessarily the MAC address of the ultimate destination. As a quick review, if the source and destination are in the same local network or IP subnet, the MAC address will be the MAC address of the destination device and no routers become involved.

However, if that is not the case, ARP will learn the MAC address of the local router, a setting on the device called the *default gateway*. When the router receives the packet, it will use the destination IP address, which will still be the IP address of the ultimate destination, and route the packet to the correct subnet. If the packet is routed through multiple routers, the MAC address will continue to change, but the destination IP address will remain that of the destination device and will not be resolved to the MAC address of the ultimate destination until it has reached the local subnet where the device resides.

Subnets are discussed in Chapter 8.

▶

To review the ARP
resolution process,
see Chapter 3.

As you also learned in Chapter 3, ARP uses an ARP broadcast to learn the MAC, regardless of whether it is resolving the destination MAC address or the router MAC address.

When this broadcast occurs, the Transport layer protocol that will be used is UDP, because it is a broadcast.

Describing ICMP

Internet Control Message Protocol (ICMP) is used by devices to send messages to one another to convey error conditions that may occur. It is not used to transfer data. These errors are reported back to the original source IP address. Earlier, in the section "Describing IP," you learned that IP operating without TCP is connectionless. Because ICMP is transported in an IP datagram with no Transport protocol involved, it is connectionless.

As a network technician, your use of these error messages will be through the use of command-line utilities, such as ping and traceroute. By typing these commands and the destination IP address, you can obtain valuable trouble-shooting information when connectivity problems exist between devices.

ICMP packets contain error codes that will be displayed on the screen when these commands are issued that relate information about the error condition that exists. Let's examine both of these commands and discuss some of the more common error codes and what they mean. When the ping command is issued and is successful, meaning the destination is reachable, the destination will respond with what is called a reply. The initiating ping is called an *echo request*, and the response is called an *echo reply*. The default number of times the destination will respond is four. In Figure 4.9, a successful execution of the command is displayed.

```
Microsoft Windows [Version 6.1.7601]
Copyright (c) 2009 Microsoft Corporation.  All rights reserved.

C:\Users\tmcmillan>ping 192.168.21.3

Pinging 192.168.21.3 with 32 bytes of data:
Reply from 192.168.21.3: bytes=32 time<1ms TTL=128
Reply from 192.168.21.3: bytes=32 time<1ms TTL=128
Reply from 192.168.21.3: bytes=32 time<1ms TTL=128
Reply from 192.168.21.3: bytes=32 time<1ms TTL=128

Ping statistics for 192.168.21.3:
    Packets: Sent = 4, Received = 4, Lost = 0 (0% loss),
Approximate round trip times in milli-seconds:
    Minimum = 0ms, Maximum = 0ms, Average = 0ms

C:\Users\tmcmillan>
```

FIGURE 4.9 Echo request and reply

When the destination cannot be reached, an error code will be displayed. The most common of these are as follows:

Destination Unreachable   This indicates that the IP datagram could not be forwarded. This also includes an error code (number) that indicates more detail—for example, that there is no routing table entry, or the destination is reachable but did not respond to ARP.

Request Timed Out   This indicates that the TTL of the datagram was exceeded. This means you did not even get a response from a router. This can occur if the router is configured to *not* respond to ICMP, which is not uncommon. This is the situation in Figure 4.10.

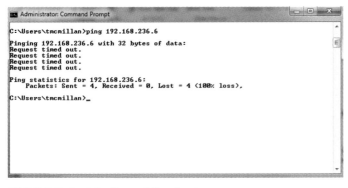

FIGURE 4.10 **Request timed out**

PING

In Chapter 7, you will learn how to use the ping command to determine the exact nature of a problem.

Another useful command that uses ICMP is traceroute or tracert. On a Cisco router or switch, the command is traceroute. On a Windows computer, the command is tracert.

Whereas ping determines whether you can establish connectivity, traceroute helps you determine exactly where in the network that connectivity broke down. It does this by utilizing the TTL field in the IP datagram (see the section entitled "Describing IP"). It sends a series of ICMP datagrams, and with each successive transmission, it adds one to the TTL. This causes each router in the path to respond. When no response is received from a router, the problem has been located.

In the following example, the output of the traceroute command executed from a router, the command succeeded, and it took four hops to get there. There were responses from three routers and one from the destination device. The output also indicates how long each response took.

```
router#traceroute 150.1.4.2
Type escape sequence to abort.
Tracing the route to 150.1.4.2
1 150.1.1.2 4 msec 0 msec 4 msec
2 150.1.2.2 4 msec 4 msec 0 msec
3 150.1.3.2 0 msec 0 msec 4 msec
4 150.1.4.2 4 msec * 0 msec
```

In Figure 4.11, the Windows version, tracert, has been executed to locate the path to a website. You can see that in step 10, it timed out, indicating a problem at that Internet router. It could be that the router is configured not to respond to ICMP.

```
C:\Users\tmcmillan>tracert www.nascar.com
Unable to resolve target system name www.nascar.com.

C:\Users\tmcmillan>tracert www.msn.com

Tracing route to us.co1.cb3.glbdns.microsoft.com [65.55.17.25]
over a maximum of 30 hops:

  1     9 ms    <1 ms    <1 ms   10.88.2.6
  2     1 ms    <1 ms    <1 ms   208-47-7-130.dia.static.qwest.net [208.47.7.130]
  3     6 ms     6 ms     6 ms   frp-edge-04.inet.qwest.net [205.168.14.213]
  4     7 ms     6 ms     6 ms   frp-core-02.inet.qwest.net [205.171.22.49]
  5    22 ms    22 ms    22 ms   chx-edge-03.inet.qwest.net [67.14.38.1]
  6    22 ms    22 ms    22 ms   63-234-10-14.dia.static.qwest.net [63.234.10.14]
  7    23 ms    22 ms    22 ms   xe-0-0-1-0.ch1-16c-1a.ntwk.msn.net [207.46.43.82
]
  8    76 ms    76 ms    94 ms   ge-4-1-0-0.co1-64c-1b.ntwk.msn.net [207.46.40.96
]
  9    77 ms    77 ms    97 ms   xe-0-1-0-0.co1-96c-1b.ntwk.msn.net [207.46.33.18
3]
 10     *         *         *    Request timed out.
 11     *
```

FIGURE 4.11 Tracert

Describing IGMP

The final Internet layer protocol in the TCP/IP suite is *Internet Group Management Protocol (IGMP)*. This protocol is used for multicasting. The protocol operates between routers and hosts that belong to what are called multicast groups. *Multicast groups* of devices maintain their unicast IP addresses for normal transmissions, but they also share a common multicast address as a group.

Multicast IP addresses are a special range of IP addresses that are dedicated to this purpose and cannot be given to individual devices. When a multicast group is assigned a multicast address, any multicast traffic for the group will be sent to this IP address. The routers on the network will be aware of the devices that are members of the group, as the devices register with the routers. The routers will then send any traffic sent to the multicast address to the individual group members.

Multicast addresses are discussed further in Chapters 7 and 8.

The benefit of multicasting is that it reduces traffic in the network. With unicasting, the server sends a separate message to each separate device. This results in a lot of messages being sent over the network. On the other hand, with multicasting, the server sends one single transmission across the network to the router. That reduces the load on the network. The router then sends transmissions to the group members to finish the communication. The two methods are illustrated in Figure 4.12.

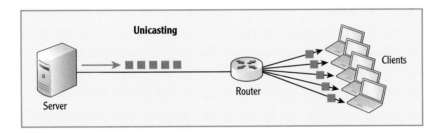

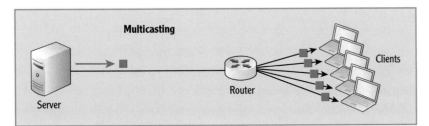

FIGURE 4.12 Multicasting

Exploring Network Access Layer Protocols

Protocols of the Network Access layer can be categorized as either LAN protocols or WAN protocols. These protocols use some sort of information to identify the individual hosts in a LAN and to identify the endpoints in a WAN. MAC addresses are an example of this, but not the only example. In this section, both types of Network Access layer protocols are covered.

Because the Network Access layer of the TCP/IP model includes the functionality of the Data-Link layer of the OSI model, protocols at this layer are often referred to as Data-Link layer protocols.

Defining Network Access Layer Protocols on the LAN

A number of technologies have been used to connect computers on a LAN through the years. At the Network Access layer, we generally refer to these elements as *technologies* because there is both a protocol and a physical implementation. For example, when Ethernet is used, specific types of cabling and network cards must be used. These technologies operate at the Network Access layer of the TCP/IP model. (From an OSI model perspective, these technologies operate at the Data-Link and Physical layers.)

Back in 1980, many proprietary methods had been developed to enable computers to communicate on a network. The Institute of Electrical and Electronics Engineers (IEEE), a nonprofit professional association created in 1963, set out to create standards for the emerging field of networking. Organizing into working groups, some of the more promising and popular networking methods were standardized.

A set of standards was created over a period of some years in a process that is still ongoing today. It included a numbering system for the standards that was derived from the fact that it was February 1980, or the second month of '80, leading to all of the standard numbers starting with 802. In this section, some of the major standards—including the most popular today, Ethernet—are discussed in terms of the IEEE standards. Each standard is identified by a number following a period—for example, Ethernet is 802.3.

802.1 and 802.2   These two standards formed the foundation for the rest. 802.1 described LAN operations such as bridging, which is the process used at the Network Access layer to transfer information, and 802.2 created a new layer just above the MAC layer called the Logical Link Control (LLC) layer. The LLC layer made multiplexing possible (running multiple LAN protocols on the network) and added some additional functions that may or may not be utilized by a particular networking technology. Ethernet, for example, makes no use of 802.2.

802.3   802.3 described the operations of Ethernet. It included many amendments or additions as time went by. Amendments specify a particular implementation, option, or update to a standard and are identified with letters added to the end of a standard number. For example, 802.3a is Ethernet operating at 10 Mbps over thin coaxial cable. Physical connections for networks using Ethernet can be deployed using a wide range of copper cabling and fiber-optic cabling. When Ethernet operates over wireless connections, it must be encapsulated in a different Network Access layer technology such as 802.11. Ethernet can operate in either a bus or star topology.

Network topologies are covered in Chapter 5, "Physical and Logical Topologies."

▶

802.5   This is an IBM protocol that is no longer in use but worth mentioning because of the unique way that it operates. It uses a star topology physically but a ring topology logically. It also uses unique methods to control access to the network by the devices. These methods are called *contention methods*.

802.11   One the more recent standards, 802.11 standardizes wireless LAN transmission using radio waves. When used in conjunction with Ethernet, it encapsulates the Ethernet frame in its own special Network Access layer frame type. It also uses a unique contention method because of the characteristics of radio transmission.

◀

Contention methods are discussed in both Chapter 5 and Chapter 11, "LAN Operations."

Defining Network Access Layer Protocols on the WAN

Wide area networks (WANs) usually connect locations or LANs. When we use the term *wide area network*, we usually are *not* speaking of the Internet, although certainly offices can be connected through Internet connections. Connections using WAN protocols such as Frame Relay and PPP use networks that are physically separate from the network that we use for the Internet.

These network connections are private in the sense that corporations and individuals pay a fee to a telecommunications company to use the network. The telecommunications company builds, operates, and maintains the network, turning a profit by charging for access to the network, somewhat like a private toll road. These are called *leased lines*.

When the data from the LAN needs to traverse these leased lines, the Network Access layer Ethernet header on the frame must be removed, and a type of Network Access layer header specific to the WAN protocol in use must be placed on the packet. When the frame arrives in the other location, the Network Access layer WAN header is removed, and a Network Access layer Ethernet header is placed on the packet so it can then be transported on the local LAN to its final destination. The WAN protocol acts somewhat like a ferry boat that carries cars across a river, only in this case it is carrying Ethernet packets across the WAN link.

Just as Ethernet uses MAC addresses at the Network Access layer, WAN protocols have addresses as well. For example, Frame Relay connections are identified by a Network Access layer identifier called a Data-Link Connection Identifier (DLCI). This number is used to specify the location in the Frame Relay network.

Another example is Point-to-Point Protocol (PPP). This is used on both analog and digital phone lines between locations. On a digital line called an Integrated Services Digital Network (ISDN), the identifier is called a Service Profile Identifier (SPID). This number, issued to the location used to identify it, usually incorporates the phone number of the line.

WAN technologies are beyond the scope of this book but are worth briefly discussing as a point of comparison to the LAN concepts covered earlier and to place LAN networking into context with WAN networking.

THE ESSENTIALS AND BEYOND

Protocols are the communication languages of networking. Some perform specific functions, while others are networking protocols. Networking protocols can be categorized as either routed or routing. A routed protocol is one that is designed in such a way that it can be routed between remote networks, while a routing protocol is responsible for performing the routing function.

Protocols operate at all four layers of the TCP/IP model. The layer at which a protocol operates is determined by the information it uses to do its job. At the Network Access layer, protocols can be classified as either LAN protocols or WAN protocols. These two types of protocols will create and attach different types of Network Access layer headers on the packets they transport. WAN protocols carry LAN packets across the WAN connection to be delivered to remote LANs.

ADDITIONAL EXERCISES

1. Using the following list, write the layer of the TCP/IP model at which each protocol operates.

ICMP _____

PPP _____

DNS _____

TFTP _____

ARP_____

Ethernet _____

IP _____

SMTP _____

UDP_____

FTP _____

TCP _____

IGMP_____

Frame Relay _____

(Continues)

THE ESSENTIALS AND BEYOND *(Continued)*

2. In this exercise, you will work with a partner using two computers that are connected to the same network and can already communicate.

A. Click Start ≻ All Programs ≻ Accessories ≻ Command Prompt. When the command prompt box opens you will first determine the IP address of the computer you are using. Type the following command:

Ipconfig

The computer will display an IP address, subnet mask and default gateway. Write down your IP address.

B. At the command prompt type the following command and insert your partner's IP address:

ping *ip address* (for example **ping 192.168.5.5**)

Press Enter.

C. Make note of what you see and describe what the message is telling you.

REVIEW QUESTIONS

1. What determines the layer at which a protocol operates?

A. The specific information it uses in its processes	**C.** The type of upper-layer data it processes
B. The amount of information it requires in its processes	**D.** The underlying network technology

2. Which if the following is *not* a routed protocol?

A. IPX/SPX	**C.** TCP/IP
B. NetBEUI	**D.** AppleTalk

3. Which of the following is an Application layer protocol?

A. TCP	**C.** DNS
B. ICMP	**D.** IP

4. Which of the following is a connection-oriented protocol used to transport files across the network?

A. SMTP	**C.** IP
B. FTP	**D.** TFTP

(Continues)

THE ESSENTIALS AND BEYOND *(Continued)*

5. What port number does TFTP use to begin the connection?

   A. TCP 23   **C.** UDP 69

   B. UDP 21   **D.** TCP 80

6. Which protocol is used to transfer a router operating system (called the Cisco IOS) from a server to a router?

   A. FTP   **C.** TFTP

   B. SNMP   **D.** SMTP

7. Which of the following is *not* a component of SNMP?

   A. Agent   **C.** Managed device

   B. Network management system   **D.** Queries

8. Which protocol is responsible for sequencing the packets?

   A. IP   **C.** UDP

   B. TCP   **D.** ARP

9. Which of the following is *not* a part of the TCP handshake?

   A. SYN   **C.** ACK

   B. FIN   **D.** SYN-ACK

10. In which header type is the protocol number found?

   A. TCP   **C.** IP

   B. UDP   **D.** ICMP

CHAPTER 5

Physical and Logical Topologies

A *network* topology *describes* the physical connections and logical communication pathways between objects in a network. The term is used to describe a variety of networking concepts. Topologies are used to describe connections between computers (or *hosts*) in a network, between routers in a network, or even between wide area network connections.

Topologies come in two varieties, physical and logical. A physical topology describes the way in which the devices are connected together. For example, they could be connected end-to-end in a straight line or connected in a circle (or ring). The logical topology describes how the devices communicate or the shape of the communication path. In many cases, the physical and logical topology are the same—but not always, as you will see in this chapter.

Specifically, this chapter covers the following topics:

▶ **Designing the physical topology**

▶ **Designing the logical topology**

Designing the Physical Topology

The *physical topology* defines the physical connections between the devices and the shape that these connections form. In most cases, it is easy to see this shape. In other cases, such as the way in which a star is usually implemented in an enterprise, it is not quite as obvious.

This section covers all of the common physical topologies, giving special attention to their respective advantages and disadvantages. Many of the topologies, such as bus, ring, star, mesh, and hybrid, are most commonly applied to LAN design. Point-to-point and point-to-multipoint topologies are more commonly applied in WAN design. They describe the manner in which routers that host WAN connections are designed.

Implementing a Bus Topology

The *bus topology* was one of the earliest physical topologies to be implemented. In this topology, the devices are connected one to another in a straight line, as shown in Figure 5.1.

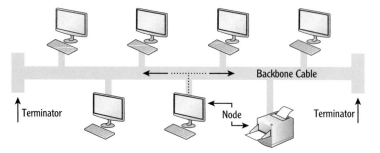

▶

A *node* is simply a device on the network, such as a computer, printer, or server.

FIGURE 5.1 Bus topology

In this topology, each end of the *bus* (a term used to describe the cable from end to end), or *backbone cable*, must have a special connector called a *terminator* installed. The terminator prevents signals that reach the end of the cable from being reflected or propagated back in the opposite direction. It accomplishes this by absorbing the electrical energy of the signal.

When a computer transmits on a bus network, the transmission is sent in both directions from where the computer is positioned on the bus. The transmission locates the destination computers by IP or MAC address. Each device on the bus examines the signal, but all except the computer to which the packet is addressed will ignore it.

CABLING IN A BUS TOPOLOGY

In a bus topology, coaxial cable is used and comes in two types that exhibit different characteristics:

Thicknet is thicker, less flexible, and more expensive but can be up to 500 meters long without attenuation. (For more on attenuation, see the special topic "Attenuation and Cable Length" later in this section.)

Thinnet is smaller gauge, more flexible, and less expensive but can be up to only 185 meters long without attenuation.

Advantages of the Bus Topology

▶ Easy to implement

▶ Requires less cable than some of the other topologies

▶ Inexpensive

▶ Easy to design

Disadvantages of the Bus Topology

▶ If the cable is broken at any point, the entire network is down.

▶ Terminators are required at both ends.

▶ If the network shuts down, locating the break is difficult.

▶ There are limits on cable length and number of nodes.

▶ Performance degradation occurs under traffic load.

▶ Introducing or connecting new devices takes the network down.

ATTENUATION AND CABLE LENGTH

Every type of cable (the common cable types are discussed in Chapter 9, "Cabling") has a maximum cable length before the cable suffers from *attenuation*, or weakening of the signal. When an electrical signal travels down a cable, it meets resistance in the cable that can be measured in ohms. This resistance weakens, or attenuates, the signal. If the signal becomes too weak, reading it correctly when it arrives at the destination will be impossible. The result is usually corrupted or garbled data. For this reason, cable length characteristics must be taken into consideration.

Implementing a Ring Topology

A *ring topology* is just what you would expect from the sound of the name. The devices are connected one to another as they are in a bus topology, except that the cable loops around and forms a closed circle, as shown in Figure 5.2.

When a computer transmits on a ring network, the transmission is usually sent in only one direction from where the computer is positioned on the bus.

As you will see later in this chapter, an FDDI ring is an exception to the rule about transmissions on a ring travelling in one direction.

◀

The transmission locates the destination computer by IP or MAC address. Each device on the ring examines the signal, but all except the computer to which the packet is addressed will ignore it.

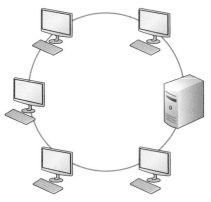

FIGURE 5.2 Ring topology

Advantages of the Ring Topology

► Performs better than a bus under load

► Prevents collisions

► Can be larger than a bus because each device serves as a repeater for the signal

Disadvantages of the Ring Topology

► If the cable is broken at any point, the entire network is down.

► If the network shuts down, locating the break is difficult.

► Introducing or connecting new devices takes the network down.

Implementing a Star Topology

Although you may not recognize it because of its implementation, the *star topology* is the most common topology used in networks today. All of the devices are connected to a central device and communicate through the central device. This device may be either a hub or a switch. This arrangement is shown in Figure 5.3.

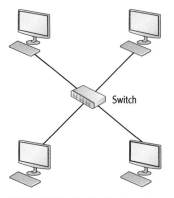

FIGURE 5.3 Star topology

In the star topology, when a device transmits, the transmission goes to the hub or switch. What occurs next depends on whether a hub or switch is being used. If a hub is present, the transmission will be sent to all devices, and all but the destination device will ignore it. If a switch is present, the switch will send the transmission only to the connection where the destination device is located.

Advantages of the Star Topology

▶ It has better performance than bus or ring, especially if a switch is used.

▶ If a cable goes bad, only the device connected to it is affected.

▶ It can support a larger number of computers than the bus.

▶ It's easy to troubleshoot.

▶ No network disruption occurs when adding or removing devices.

Disadvantages of the Star Topology

▶ Single point of failure at the hub or switch

▶ Performance dependent on central device

▶ Size limited by physical connections on the hub or switch

The reason that most people don't recognize this topology in use is that usually the central device is not sitting in the middle of the other devices, as pictured in Figure 5.3. The central device is usually out of sight in another room, and the cables go through the wall to connect to it, as shown in Figure 5.4. The computers connect to wall outlets; the cables run through the walls and then connect to the switch in the switch closet.

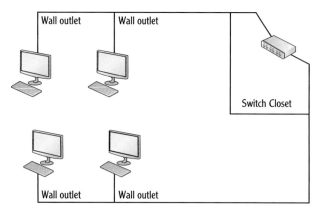

FIGURE 5.4 Star implementation

Implementing a Mesh Topology

In a *mesh topology*, each computer has an individual connection to every other computer, as shown in Figure 5.5. This topology is difficult and expensive to implement but offers the most fault tolerance of any of the designs discussed thus far.

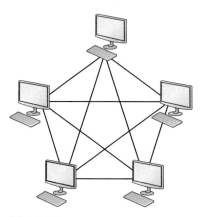

FIGURE 5.5 Mesh topology

The mesh topology requires that each computer have the hardware to support multiple network connections. In the example in Figure 5.5, that would mean four network cards for each computer. This topology requires cable to run between each computer as well. The advantage this provides is that if any connection fails, only the two computers using that connection are affected *and* they can still use one of the other pathways to communicate.

Advantages of the Mesh Topology

> ▶ Best fault tolerance

> ▶ Easy to troubleshoot

> ▶ No network disruption when adding or removing devices

Disadvantages of the Mesh Topology

> ▶ Expensive to implement

> ▶ High maintenance cost

> ▶ Limitation on number of devices in each mesh

Implementing a Hybrid Topology

A *hybrid topology* is one in which two or more of the aforementioned topologies are used in combination. One of these combinations is shown in Figure 5.6. In this example, a bus network backbone is connected to a ring network and a star network. Usually the different topologies are connected to a central computer that hosts a connection to each other topology.

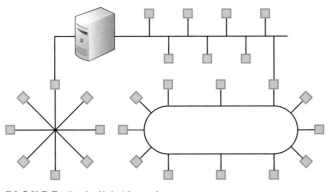

FIGURE 5.6 Hybrid topology

Advantages of the Hybrid Topology

▶ Very flexible

▶ Reliable

Disadvantages of the Hybrid Topology

▶ Expensive to implement

▶ Can be difficult to add nodes

Implementing a Point-to-Point Topology

A *point-to-point topology* is one in which two devices are connected to one another directly, with no other devices on the connection. This does *not* mean that a device can host only a single point-to-point connection. It simply means that each point-to-point connection the device hosts is dedicated to the communication between itself and the one other device. An example is shown in Figure 5.7.

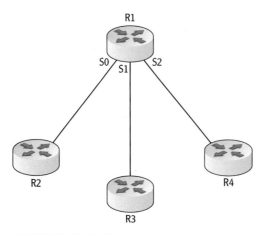

FIGURE 5.7 Point-to-point using multiple interfaces

In Figure 5.7, the router R1 is hosting three individual point-to-point connections. Each one of the links carries traffic only between the two devices on either end of the connection. On these point-to-point links, there will *never* be any traffic other than what is sent between the two routers on either end. Router R1 in Figure 5.7 is using three physical interfaces (S0, S1, and S2) for this point-to-point topology.

ROUTER INTERFACE NUMBERING

Router interfaces are simply network connections such as network adaptor cards on a computer. Routers have multiple interfaces, and these interfaces can be of several types. Some examples are Ethernet, serial, and fiber. When a router has multiple interfaces of a certain type—for example, three Ethernet interfaces—they will be numbered starting at 0. The three interfaces of router R1 in Figure 5.7 are serial, so the numbering would be S0, S1, and S2.

Instead of the three physical interfaces that the router is using in Figure 5.7, it could be using a single interface. To understand how this can work, you need to understand a few concepts of WAN technology. First, this type of WAN topology is implemented when using a telecommunications network, as discussed in Chapter 4, "Protocols." Therefore, physically speaking, after the frames (this is the Network Access layer, so remember, they are called *frames*) enter the telecommunications network, they can be routed to each multiple destination by its identifier (either SPID for ISDN or DLCI for Frame Relay).

In Figure 5.8, Router R1 is using only a single physical interface Serial 1 (S1), but it has been logically subdivided into S1.1, S1.2, and S1.3. Then different DLCIs were assigned for routing in the telecommunications network. The routers R2, R3, and R4 also have been assigned DLCIs. The DLCIs are the Network Access layer addresses.

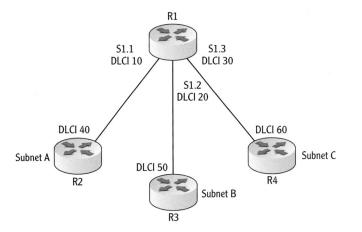

FIGURE 5.8 Point-to-point using one interface

Even though at first glance this may appear to be like the point-to-multipoint topology that is covered in the next section, it is actually different because each link is its own subnet.

Subnets and subnetting are covered in Chapter 8, "Classless IP Addressing."

Implementing a Point-to-Multipoint Topology

A *point-to-multipoint topology* is one in which a single physical connection on one router is connected to more than one device on the other end, as shown in Figure 5.9. This requires that the physical interface be divided logically into multiple subinterfaces on the router, just as is done in a point-to-point topology that connects to multiple endpoints. This may appear on the surface to be the same as the topology illustrated in Figure 5.8, but there is a big difference. In Figure 5.9, the same setup is used as in Figure 5.8, but all three connections are in the same subnet. That means that all three connections are part of the same network or subnet.

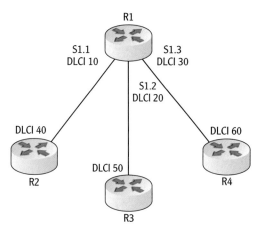

All connections in the same subnet

FIGURE 5.9 Point-to-multipoint

WAN Technology

A detailed discussion of WAN technology is beyond the scope of this book. To learn more on this topic, see the Cisco *Internetworking Technology Handbook* at http://docwiki.cisco.com/wiki/Internetworking_Technology_Handbook.

Designing the Logical Topology

The *logical topology* defines the communication process between the devices and the shape that these communication flows form. This section covers some noteworthy logical topologies. With the exception of the star topology, you will rarely, if ever, encounter these in the real world. As a point of comparison to the star and from a historical perspective, they are still worth exploring. Included in this section is a special topology that is physically one topology and logically another!

MORE TOPOLOGIES

The most common logical topologies are covered in this section. For more information on both logical and physical topologies, see http://en.wikipedia.org/wiki/Network_topology.

Understanding the Token Ring Topology

Token Ring was a networking technology created by IBM in 1985. It operates at the Network Access layer of the TCP/IP model. It is physically a star topology, with the devices all connected to a central device called a Media Access Unit (MAU). It also used special IBM connectors and cables.

Logically, however, the network was a ring topology. When signals entered the MAU, they followed a pathway that led out to each device and then in again to the MAU and back out to the next device. Also the contention mechanism used was quite different from that of Ethernet. It was called *token passing*. A special packet called a *token* was passed around the ring, and a device could transmit only if the token came around and was not being used. This prevented collisions.

Token Ring was never widely accepted for several reasons. Although it operated at 16 MB at a time when 10 MB was considered good, it was soon surpassed by Ethernet in speed. Moreover, it required using all IBM connectors, cables, and MAUs. For this reason, Token Ring networks are no longer in use.

In Figure 5.10, the physical and logical topology of Token Ring is illustrated. As you can see, although the devices are connected to a central device, the communication pathway forms a ring.

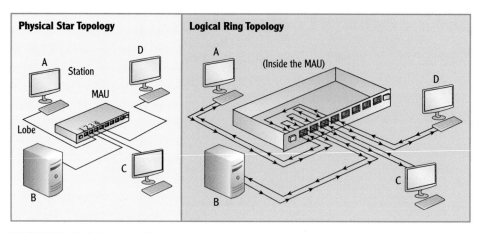

FIGURE 5.10 Token Ring

Understanding the FDDI Ring Topology

A *Fiber Distributed Data Interface (FDDI)* ring operated as both a physical and logical ring. It used token passing but not the token passing used in Token Ring (802.5). It used a different type (802.4) in which use of the token is time-based. The FDDI topology could use either copper or fiber-optic cabling.

It also used a double ring for fault tolerance. The rings operated in opposite directions, as shown in Figure 5.11. This network was often used as a backbone in an enterprise to which other networks connected.

FDDI is also considered a legacy technology as it has been replaced with more-economical and saleable alternatives. It also suffers from distance limitations and is expensive to implement. In most applications where FDDI was once used, either Gigabit Ethernet or Fiber Channel is now in use.

▶

Cabling is covered in detail in Chapter 9.

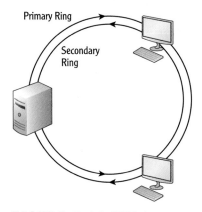

FIGURE 5.11 FDDI ring

Understanding the Star Topology

The *star topology* is the same physically and logically, but it is so prevalent in today's LANs that it is worth spending some additional time discussing how it works. As you learned in the section "Implementing a Star Topology," all devices are connected to a central device that is implemented as either a hub or a switch. You also learned that the operations of the central device are quite different depending on whether a hub or a switch is present.

If a hub is in use, every transmission that comes into the device is sent out every port except the port on which it arrived. You will learn more about hardware in Chapter 10, but for now the important thing to keep in mind is that hubs have no "intelligence." They are simply junction boxes. So these devices simply forward the frames everywhere.

As you will learn in Chapter 10, switches do have intelligence. After they have learned the MAC addresses of the devices connected to each port, they will forward frames only to the destination devices and not to all ports.

This is significant because of the contention method used in Ethernet networks. A *contention method* defines the way in which access to the wire is arbitrated. A good analogy is the various ways in which access to a road can be managed. A traffic light is one approach to maintaining order at the intersection of two roads. Another approach is four-way stop signs. Even a roundabout could be used. They all do the same thing in different ways.

Earlier in this section, you learned about a contention method called *token passing*. In this method, a packet called a *token* passes around the network, and a device can send *only* if the token arrives empty. This eliminates collisions. Collisions occur when two devices send an electrical signal at the same time and the signals collide on the wire. This destroys both signals, requiring both devices to retransmit. When this occurs frequently, the data transfer rate of the network plummets.

In an Ethernet star topology, collisions are not eliminated; they are managed. One factor that greatly affects the frequency of collisions is the device in the middle of the star. If it is a hub, there will be many more collisions than if it is a switch. Because a switch sends frames only to the port where the destination device is connected, this greatly reduces the mathematical possibility that collisions will occur.

The contention method used in Ethernet is called *Carrier Sense Multiple Access/Collision Detection (CSMA/CD)*. It has mechanisms that help minimize but not eliminate collisions. Its operation is as follows:

1. When a device needs to transmit, it checks the wire. If a transmission is already underway, the device can tell. This is called *carrier sense*.

2. If the wire is clear, the device will transmit. Even as it is transmitting, it is performing carrier sense.

3. If another host is sending simultaneously, there will be a collision. The collision is detected by both devices through carrier sense.

4. Both devices will issue a jam signal to all the other devices, which indicates to them to *not* transmit.

5. Then both devices will increment a retransmission counter. This is a cumulative total of the number of times this frame has been transmitted and a collision has occurred. There is a maximum number at which the device aborts the transmission of the frame.

6. Both devices will calculate a random amount of time and will wait that amount of time before transmitting again. This calculation is called a *random back-off*.

7. In most cases, because both devices choose random amounts of time to wait, another collision will not occur.

Star Topologies

Ethernet is certainly the most famous star topology, but it is not the only one. Any networking technology that uses a hub and spoke design with a central connection point or hub is a star. That means that an 802.11 wireless network that uses an access point is also a star. In WAN topologies, the topology that is usually called a hub and spoke is also a star.

The Essentials and Beyond

A network topology describes the physical connections and logical communication pathways between objects in a network. Topologies come in two varieties, physical and logical. A physical topology describes the way in which the devices are connected together. The logical topology describes how they communicate or the shape of the communication path.

A local area network can be laid in a bus, ring, star, mesh, or hybrid topology. In many cases the physical and logical topology are the same, but in some cases they are not. A token ring topology is a physical star but is logically a ring topology. This topology is also unique in that it uses a token-passing contention method.

(Continues)

THE ESSENTIALS AND BEYOND *(Continued)*

Wide area networks are typically implemented in either a point-to-point topology or point-to-multipoint topology. When these networks are implemented, they are usually connecting routers in remote locations that are using a leased telecommunications network.

The most common topology found in LANs is the star topology using Ethernet as the Network Access layer protocol. This protocol uses a contention mechanism called Carrier Sense Multiple Access/Collision Detection (CSMA/CD).

ADDITIONAL EXERCISES

You work for a network design firm that offers consulting services to small and mid-size businesses. For each of the following clients, choose the topology that comes closest to meeting the requirements set forth by each client.

1. **Ajax Cleaning Service** requirements:
   - ▶ Use of as little cable as possible
   - ▶ Inexpensive
   - ▶ Easy to implement

2. **Acme Employment Agency** requirements:
   - ▶ Support for large number of computers
   - ▶ Easy to troubleshoot
   - ▶ No network disruption when adding or removing devices

3. **Smith and Smith Law Firm** requirements:
   - ▶ Maximum fault tolerance
   - ▶ Money is no object
   - ▶ Easy to troubleshoot

REVIEW QUESTIONS

1. Which of the following is *not* a LAN topology?

   A. Star   **C.** Point-to-multipoint

   B. Bus   **D.** Mesh

2. True or False: The physical and logical topology is always the same.

(Continues)

THE ESSENTIALS AND BEYOND *(Continued)*

3. Each end of the _____ topology must have a special connector called a terminator installed.

    A. Star   **C.** Hybrid

    B. Bus   **D.** Mesh

4. Which of the following is *not* a disadvantage of the ring topology?

    A. If the cable is broken at any   **C.** Introducing or connecting new
          point, the entire network is down.   devices takes the network down.

    B. If the network shuts down,   **D.** Terminators are required at
          locating the break is difficult.   either end.

5. Which topology uses either switches or hubs?

    A. Star   **C.** Hybrid

    B. Bus   **D.** Mesh

6. Which topology provides the best fault tolerance?

    A. Star   **C.** Hybrid

    B. Bus   **D.** Mesh

7. What type of type of topology requires the use of subinterfaces on the router?

    A. Point-to-point   **C.** Point-to-multipoint

    B. Bus   **D.** Mesh

8. What is the central device in a Token Ring network called?

    A. Switch   **C.** MAU

    B. Hub   **D.** Router

9. Which topology has built-in fault tolerance?

    A. Token Ring   **C.** FDDI ring

    B. Bus   **D.** Mesh

10. Which topology uses the CSMA/CD contention method?

    A. Star   **C.** Hybrid

    B. Bus   **D.** Mesh

CHAPTER 6

Numbering Systems

You don't have to be a mathematics major to have success networking with Cisco routers and switches, but you do need to understand two numbering systems that are very important when working with computers and networking. These numbering systems are no more complicated than the decimal numbering system. However, unlike the decimal system that we all learned in the second or third grade and is second nature to us, most people are unfamiliar with these alternate systems.

In this chapter, you will learn how these numbering systems (which are sometimes also referred to as *notation*) work and, perhaps more important, why they matter when working with computers. Specifically, this chapter covers the following topics:

▶ **Exploring binary numbering**

▶ **Exploring hexadecimal numbering**

▶ **Applying conversions**

Exploring Binary Numbering

The *binary numbering system* is capable of every function that the decimal system is. There are some who say that the only reason we use the decimal system, which is based on the number 10, is because we have 10 fingers and toes. Regardless, it is true that the only difference between the binary and decimal system is the number on which each is based.

The decimal system is based on the number 10, and the binary system is based on the number 2. This means that there are 10 and 2 values, respectively, in each system. Those values for the decimal system are 0–9 (with the digit 0 counting as one of the numbers), and for the binary system the values are 0–1. This section explains the binary numbering system. You will see the many properties it shares with the decimal system and how it differs from decimal system.

Understanding the Base-2 Numbering System

The binary numbering system is called a *base-2 numbering system* because it has two possible values: 0 and 1. This means that because there are only two characters, or values, available in this system, the largest possible single value is 1, not 9 as in the decimal system. To illustrate the effect this has, let's first review what we learned at a young age about the decimal system so you can see that binary works the same way but with a different base number.

In the decimal system, we have learned to accept that $9 + 1 = 10$. But 10 is *not* really one of the possible values of the decimal numbering system. Those values are 0, 1, 2, 3, 4, 5, 6, 7, 8, and 9. When you count incrementally, you progress from 0 to 9 as a single digit in one space. To indicate the value that comes after 9, you add an extra digit to the left of the existing space. The new value in the left space begins as 1, the value in the right space returns to 0, and you begin incrementing values upward in the right space again. Imagine the way a car odometer works. When the numbers in the tenths-of-a-mile column go to 8 and then 9, what happens next? The 9 goes back to 0, and the mile column to the left goes up by one. That is because each value in the mile column is worth 10 times what the tenth-of-a-mile column is worth.

For an example of the relationship of each position in a number using the decimal numbering system, consider the number 37,452. The 2 is in the 10^0 position, the 5 is in the 10^1 position, the 4 is in the 10^2 position, the 7 is in the 10^3 position, and the 3 is in the 10^4 position. So the base-10 values increment from right to left in the following order:

$$10^4 \quad 10^3 \quad 10^2 \quad 10^1 \quad 10^0$$

Just to review some math basics, any number to the zero power is 1, and any number to the power of 1 is itself. So in the base-10 numbering system, any digits in the far-right position are worth themselves (6 is worth 6, for example). Similarly, any digits in the next position to the left are worth 10^1, or themselves times 10 (6 is worth 60). As you move from right to left, the values of digits in those positions continue to go up by powers of 10 as shown here:

$$10^0 = 1$$

$$10^1 = 10 \times 1 = 10$$

$$10^2 = 10 \times 10 = 100$$

$$10^3 = 10 \times 10 \times 10 = 1,000$$

$$10^4 = 10 \times 10 \times 10 \times 10 = 10,000$$

$$10^5 = 10 \times 10 \times 10 \times 10 \times 10 = 100,000$$

$$10^6 = 10 \times 10 \times 10 \times 10 \times 10 \times 10 = 1,000,000$$

$$10^7 = 10 \times 10 \times 10 \times 10 \times 10 \times 10 \times 10 = 10,000,000$$

$$10^8 = 10 \times 10 \times 10 \times 10 \times 10 \times 10 \times 10 \times 10 = 100,000,000$$

Now, the base-10 numbering system is probably not new to you, but it's worth reviewing before we dive into binary because you will be surprised how similarly they work. In binary, because 1 is the largest value (like 9 in decimal), $1 + 1 = 10$. Yes, that is right; because 1 is the largest value in the system, after we count from 0 to 1, for the next number we must increment the next position to the left. This next position to the left is worth twice as much (not 10 times—remember, this is the base-2 system).

For an example of the relationship of each position in a number using the binary numbering system, consider the number 11,001. The 1 on the right end is in the 2^0 position, the 0 to its left is in the 2^1 position, the next 0 further left is in the 2^2 position, the next 1 is in the 2^3 position, and the leftmost 1 is in the 2^4 position. So the base-2 values increment from right to left in the following order:

$$2^4 \quad 2^3 \quad 2^2 \quad 2^1 \quad 2^0$$

Just as in decimal, any number to the zero power is 1, and any number to the power of 1 is itself. So in the base-2 numbering system, any digits in the far-right position are worth themselves (1 is worth 1). Similarly, any digits in the next position to the left are worth 2^1, or themselves times 2 (1 is worth 2). As you move from right to left, the values of digits in those positions continue to go up by powers of 2, as shown here:

$$2^0 = 1$$

$$2^1 = 2 \times 1 = 2$$

$$2^2 = 2 \times 2 = 4$$

$$2^3 = 2 \times 2 \times 2 = 8$$

$$2^4 = 2 \times 2 \times 2 \times 2 = 16$$

$$2^5 = 2 \times 2 \times 2 \times 2 \times 2 = 32$$

$$2^6 = 2 \times 2 \times 2 \times 2 \times 2 \times 2 = 64$$

$$2^7 = 2 \times 2 \times 2 \times 2 \times 2 \times 2 \times 2 = 128$$

$$2^8 = 2 \times 2 \times 2 \times 2 \times 2 \times 2 \times 2 \times 2 = 256$$

If this is confusing, here is another quick comparison of the two systems. When you count in the decimal numbering system, you start with 1 and count upward like this: 1, 2, 3, 4, 5, 6, 7, 8, 9, 10, 11, 12, 13, 14, 15, 16, and so on. When you count in the binary numbering system, you also start with 1, but when you count upward, the numbers look like this: 1; 10; 11; 100; 101; 110; 111; 1,000; 1,001; 1,010; 1,011; 1,100; 1,101; 1,110; 1,111; 10,000; and so on. If you compare the numbers, you can see that the value of 2 in the decimal system equals 10 in the binary system, and the value of 3 equals 11, the value of 4 equals 100, and so on, with the number 16 in the decimal system equaling 10,000 in the binary system. The two systems of counting work essentially the same way, just using different numbers.

So as you can see, the mechanics of how binary works is the same as with decimal, but the base is different. You need to be comfortable with converting binary numbers to decimal and vice versa. Later in this chapter, you'll learn how to make those two conversions.

Understanding the Relationship between Binary and Computers

At this point, you may be asking yourself why the binary numbering system is important and what it has to do with computers and networking. The fact is, it has *everything* to do with both! Almost everything that computers and network equipment do is done in binary. The very nature of digital electronics is binary.

The chips that reside on computers and other networking gear are packed with very tiny transistors and capacitors, which are the workhorses of computing. These transistors are switches. At least at this point in time, the switches that are used can hold only two states reliably. This means that information can be represented by using two possible states: off and on, or 0 and 1. This makes binary perfect for the job. It also works well because it can be used to represent information electrically in a cable by using the presence and absence of an electrical signal.

HOW DOES RAM STORE DATA?

Dynamic random-access memory (DRAM) stores each bit of data in a separate capacitor in an integrated circuit. The transistor is used to place a charge in the capacitor. The transistor is a switch that when on flows power to the capacitor, which is then charged. These two states, charged and uncharged, are the basis for data storage.

Now you may be wondering how information that includes letters, punctuation, and other special characters can be represented in binary. This is done by using specific 8-bit patterns for each character. A bit is a single value, or position, in a binary number. Eight of these bits make a byte. Special patterns of bytes are used to represent characters. Following are a couple of 8-bit binary numbers. If an agreement could be made for this particular pattern to be the letter A and another to be B and so on, we could use these patterns to store data.

A = 01000001

B = 01000010

That's exactly what has been done. There have been several sets of these pattern systems created. Because of the restrictions of using only 8 bits, which yield only 256 possibilities, the Unicode system was developed and has been widely adopted. It uses 2 bytes, or 16 bits, which means there are 65,536 possible patterns that can be assigned to letters, punctuation, and other special characters in multiple languages. It now has been expanded to 32 bits, and although certain parts of its number space (called *planes*) are unassigned or reserved, at this writing it consists of 109,000 characters.

Most of your time spent working with binary will be working with IP addressing. When we express IP addresses human to human or we enter IP address information on devices, we typically use what is called *dotted decimal notation*. An example of an IP address in dotted decimal notation is 192.168.6.1.

The computers and routers don't think in decimal terms. They communicate and represent these numbers in binary (as they do everything). We discuss binary-to-decimal conversion later in this chapter and the conversion of IP addresses to binary in the next chapter, but this particular IP address would be stored by a computer or router as the following:

11000000.10101000.00000110.00000001

In this example, each of the 8-bit patterns separated by a dot represents the decimal numbers in the dotted decimal format. Thankfully, we don't enter IP addresses in this format and we don't use this format to communicate about IP addresses with other people, but you do need to understand how to convert back and forth to understand the process of subnetting. We'll return to the conversion process at the end of the chapter and discuss IP addressing in Chapter 7 and subnetting in Chapter 8.

> Joe Becker from Xerox and Lee Collins and Mark Davis from Apple started working on the predecessor of Unicode in 1987. In 1993, the ISO standardized it.

◄

◄

> IP addressing is covered in Chapter 7, "Classful IP Addressing," and Chapter 8, "Classless IP Addressing."

Exploring Hexadecimal Numbering

Another numbering system that is used extensively in computers and networking is the *hexadecimal system* (or *hex*, for short). It is used to identify network cards (MAC addresses), and it is also used when very large numbers need to be represented by using fewer positions or columns than if we used decimal.

A good example of this is memory addresses. A memory address is a specific location in memory. It is used when something that has been placed into memory needs to be located, sort of like a street address. Individual memory addresses are very small, so there are a lot of them. Using hex instead of decimal allows these large numbers to be expressed with less space. In the next section, you will learn how the hex numbering system is capable of expressing such large numbers by using so few places.

Another area where hex is used is in the new version of Internet Protocol (IP), IPv6. As you will learn in Chapters 7 and 8, the current version, IPv4, yields a finite number of IP addresses (as does IPv6; it's just such a larger finite number that it's hard to grasp). The explosion of the Internet and the use of IP addresses for all sorts of devices never imagined before have caused the number yielded from IPv4 to become depleted.

IPv6 was developed to address that problem. It uses a different numbering system than IPv4 and incorporates hex into the scheme. IPv6 is beyond the scope of this book, but one of the reasons hex was used was for its ability to represent such large numbers easily.

An IPv4 address is 32 bits and can accommodate 4,294,967,296 IP addresses. An IPv6 address uses hexadecimal, is 128 bits long, and has a possible 340 undecillion IP addresses.

Understanding the Base-16 Numbering System

The hexadecimal system uses a base of 16. As you have already learned, the base number indicates how many possible values there are in the system. In this system, there are 16—and that causes a problem, because the decimal system, which we use to represent characters in binary and hexadecimal as well, goes up to only 9. To solve that problem, the numbers 10, 11, 12, 13, 14, and 15 use the letters a, b, c, d, e, and f. This means that the 16 values in the hexadecimal system are 0, 1, 2, 3, 4, 5, 6, 7, 8, 9, a, b, c, d, e, and f.

The following is the hex equivalent of 0–16 in decimal:

Decimal	Hex
0	0
1	1

Decimal	Hex
2	2
3	3
4	4
5	5
6	6
7	7
8	8
9	9
10	a
11	b
12	c
13	d
14	e
15	f
16	10

One of the advantages of the hexadecimal system is its ability to represent very large numbers by using significantly fewer positions or columns than in decimal. To understand why that is so, let's mentally go through the same process we did with decimal and binary. This will also show you that with the exception of the base number, hex works the same as those two systems.

In hex, because an f (which is worth 15) is the largest value (like a 9 in decimal), f + 1 = 10. Yes, that is right. Because f is the largest value in the system, after we count from 0 to f, for the next number we must increment the next position to the left. This next position to the left is worth 16 times as much (not 10 times; remember, this is the base-16 system).

For an example of the relationship of each position in a number using the hexadecimal numbering system, consider the number 3d97a. The *a* on the right end is in the 16^0 position, the 7 to its left is in the 16^1 position, the 9 is in the 16^2 position, the d is in the 16^3 position, and the 3 is in the 16^4 position. So the base 16 values increment from right to left in the following order:

$$16^4 \quad 16^3 \quad 16^2 \quad 16^1 \quad 16^0$$

Just as in decimal, any number to the zero power is 1, and any number to the power of 1 is itself. So in the base-16 numbering system, any digits in the far-right position are worth themselves (4 is worth 4, e is worth 14, and so on). Similarly, any digits in the next position to the left are worth 16^1, or themselves times 16 (1 is worth 16, 2 is worth 32, and so on). As you move from right to left, the values of digits in those positions continue to go up by powers of 16, as shown in the following list. (Of course, the numbers 16; 256; 4,096; and so on are all given in our familiar base-10 system. The main point here is simply that by using the hex system, you can fit more values into the same number of columns than you could with the decimal or binary systems.)

$$16^0 = 1$$

$$16^1 = 16 \times 1 = 16$$

$$16^2 = 16 \times 16 = 256$$

$$16^3 = 16 \times 16 \times 16 = 4,096$$

$$16^4 = 16 \times 16 \times 16 \times 16 = 65,536$$

$$16^5 = 16 \times 16 \times 16 \times 16 \times 16 = 1,048,576$$

$$16^6 = 16 \times 16 \times 16 \times 16 \times 16 \times 16 = 16,777,216$$

$$16^7 = 16 \times 16 \times 16 \times 16 \times 16 \times 16 \times 16 = 268,435,456$$

$$16^8 = 16 \times 16 \times 16 \times 16 \times 16 \times 16 \times 16 \times 16 = 4,294,967,296$$

So as you can see, the mechanics of how hex works is the same as with decimal, but the base is different. As an example of the type of large numbers that can be represented with few positions, or columns, the hex number ffffffff (using only eight places) is equal to 4,294,967,296 in decimal. (This is because each f is the 16th number. By placing f in all eight places, you are essentially demonstrating 16^8.)

You need to be comfortable with converting hexadecimal numbers to decimal and to binary. Later in this chapter, you'll learn how to make those conversions.

Identifying MAC Addresses

You already learned that Media Access Control (MAC) addresses, also called *physical addresses*, which reside on the Network Access layer of the TCP/IP model, are applied to network interface adaptors of various types. These permanent addresses, sometimes called *burned-in addresses (BIAs)*, are assigned to the adaptors by the manufacturer.

MAC addresses use the hexadecimal numbering system and follow standard formats that identify both the manufacturer and the individual device. There are two formats set forth by the IEEE, the most common of which is the MAC-48 format. A newer format, the EUI-64 format, is used with IPv6.

Some examples of items that have MAC addresses using the MAC-48 identifier are as follows:

- ▶ Wired Ethernet adaptors

- ▶ Wireless network adaptors

- ▶ Router interfaces

- ▶ Bluetooth devices

- ▶ Token Ring network adaptors

- ▶ FDDI network adaptors

The standard format for these addresses is six groups of two hex digits separated by a hyphen or a colon. It also is sometimes displayed in the three groups of four hex digits separated by a period. It's important to note that although we view and discuss these MAC addresses in their hexadecimal format, they are transmitted over the medium (cabling or wireless) in binary. Figure 6.1 shows an example of a MAC address as displayed by executing the `ipconfig/all` command on a computer at the command prompt. This command will display information about the network interfaces of the computer, including the MAC address.

```
C:\Users\tmcmillan>ipconfig/all

Ethernet adapter Local Area Connection:

   Connection-specific DNS Suffix  . : alpha.kaplaninc.com
   Description . . . . . . . . . . . : Broadcom NetXtreme 57xx Gigabit Controlle

   Physical Address. . . . . . . . . : 00-1A-A0-E1-95-AB
   DHCP Enabled. . . . . . . . . . . : Yes
   Autoconfiguration Enabled . . . . : Yes
   Link-local IPv6 Address . . . . . : fe80::ada3:8b73:a66e:6bc0%11(Preferred)
   IPv4 Address. . . . . . . . . . . : 10.88.2.177(Preferred)
   Subnet Mask . . . . . . . . . . . : 255.255.254.0
   Lease Obtained. . . . . . . . . . : Friday, April 08, 2011 7:05:01 PM
   Lease Expires . . . . . . . . . . : Friday, May 06, 2011 7:08:43 AM
   Default Gateway . . . . . . . . . : 10.88.2.6
   DHCP Server . . . . . . . . . . . : 10.88.10.55
```

FIGURE 6.1 MAC address output

Each part of this address communicates information. The address is divided into two sections, as shown in Figure 6.2. The left half of the address is called the *Organizationally Unique Identifier (OUI)*. The right half is called the *Universally Administered Address (UAA)*. Together they make a globally unique MAC address.

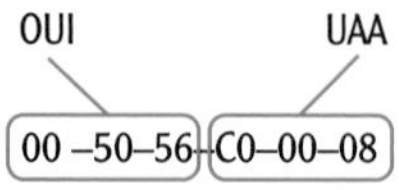

OUI   UAA

00 –50–56 C0–00–08

FIGURE 6.2 OUI and UAA

Depending on the manufacturer of the device, this MAC address may be represented in the following formats:

▶ 00-50-56-C0-00-08

▶ 00:50:56:C0:00:08

▶ 0050.56C0.0008

Applying Conversions

There are several types of numbering conversions that you need to be able to perform. It's not that you'll be doing this on a day-to-day basis, but you need to understand the concepts, especially as the decimal-to-binary conversions apply to IP subnetting.

Specifically, the conversions you are going to learn are as follows:

▶ Decimal-to-binary conversion

▶ Hex-to-decimal conversion

▶ Binary-to-hex conversion

Decimal-to-Binary Conversion

Converting a decimal number to binary, and vice versa, is an important concept for IP addressing. As you will learn in Chapter 8, subnetting that departs from classful subnetting is done on the binary level and requires an understanding of decimal-to-binary conversion. We are going to approach the conversion from that perspective. We'll start with the one most people seem to think is the easier of the two, binary to decimal, and then move on to decimal to binary.

We also are going to work with 8-bit binary numbers because IP addresses consist of four 8-bit sections, as you will see in the next chapter. An 8-bit binary number means we are using eight places, or bits. Consider the 8-bit binary number 10110111.

Earlier you learned that each position from right to left is worth an increasing power of two, as shown here:

$$2^7 \qquad 2^6 \qquad 2^5 \qquad 2^4 \qquad 2^3 \qquad 2^2 \qquad 2^1 \qquad 2^0$$

When you perform the calculations, a single bit in each position is worth the following values:

128	64	32	16	8	4	2	1

So if we line up the binary number with these bit positions, find their values, and total them, we will arrive at the decimal equivalent of the binary number. First line them up.

128	64	32	16	8	4	2	1
1	0	1	1	0	1	1	1

In every place where there is a 1, we add the value of that bit position, and everywhere there is a 0, we add 0. After totaling these values, we have the decimal equivalent:

$$128 + 0 + 32 + 16 + 0 + 4 + 2 + 1 = 183$$

So 10110111 is the equivalent of 183 in decimal.

To invert decimal to binary, a slightly different approach is required. Consider the decimal number 206. To convert this, we need to look at the bit position values, as shown here:

128	64	32	16	8	4	2	1

Working left to right, consider the value of each position. If that value does not exceed the value you are converting, place a 1 there and move on to the next position. If you cannot place a 1 there without exceeding the number you are converting, place a 0 there and move on to the next position.

So in this example, the first position is worth 128 and does *not* exceed the number we are trying to convert (206), so we would place a 1 there and move on to the next position. (So far we have 1.)

At the next position, if you can add the value of that position to the value you already have without exceeding the number you are converting, add a 1 and move on to the next position. If you cannot, put a 0 there and move on. In this example, if we add the value of the second position (64) to the first value (128), we would not exceed the number we are converting (128 + 64 = 192, which is less than 206). (Now we have 11.)

We continue this process and move to the next position. In this example, if we add the value of the third position (32) to the cumulative value we have so far (192), we would exceed the number we are converting (192 + 32 = 224, which is more than 206), so we place a 0 in the third position. (Now we have 110.)

In position 4, if we add the value of the fourth position (16) to the cumulative value we have so far (192), we would exceed the number we are converting (192 + 16 = 208, which is more than 206), so we place a 0 in the third position. (Now we have 1100.)

At position 5, if we add the value of the fifth position (8) to the cumulative value we have so far (192), we would *not* exceed the number we are converting (192 + 8 = 200, which is less than 206), so we place a 1 in the fifth position. (Now we have 11001.)

At position 6, if we add the value of the sixth position (4) to the cumulative value we have so far (200), we would *not* exceed the number we are converting (200 + 4 = 204, which is less than 206), so we place a 1 in the sixth position. (Now we have 110011.)

At position 7, if we add the value of the seventh position (2) to the cumulative value we have so far (204), we would *not* exceed the number we are converting (204 + 2 = 206, which not more than 206) so we place a 1 in the sixth position. (Now we have 1100111). Because we have arrived at the number we are converting, we can put 0s in all remaining positions to the right (in this case, only one position). We now have the binary equivalent (11001110).

If you feel unsure about the result, you can always check by adding the values of each bit position to double-check:

$$128 + 64 + 0 + 0 + 8 + 4 + 2 + 0 = 206$$

This is correct!

THERE'S GOT TO BE AN EASIER WAY!

Yes, there is an easier way to perform all the conversions in this section—by using the calculator that comes on your computer! You still *must* understand how to perform them manually (there will be no calculator available to you on any certification exams you may take). To use the calculator, choose Start ➣ Accessories ➣ Calculator. When the calculator appears on your screen, it will be in the default view. Click the View menu and select Programmer from the drop-down menu, and you will see the Programmer view shown in the following image. By setting the radio buttons that are circled to a specific numbering system, you can enter a number in that system and then change the radio button to a different system, and the calculator will make the conversion for you.

If you want to practice your conversion skills, you can try the Cisco Binary Game at `http://forums.cisco.com/CertCom/game/binary_game_page.htm`.

Hex-to-Decimal Conversion

To convert hexadecimal to decimal, the process is quite similar to the method used for the binary-to-decimal conversion. When you are a network technician, converting hex to decimal is not something you will do on a regular basis, but it is something you should understand. In some advanced routing protocols, hex is used in network addresses, and in IPv6 the hex numbering system is used. The only difference is the values of the bit positions. Consider the hexadecimal number 23ca5.

Earlier you learned that each position from right to left is worth an increasing power of 16, as shown here:

$$16^4 \qquad 16^3 \qquad 16^2 \qquad 16^1 \qquad 16^0$$

When you perform the calculations, a single bit in each position is worth the following values:

$$65,536 \qquad 4,096 \qquad 256 \qquad 16 \qquad 1$$

Now we place the hex number with its bit position as shown here:

65,536	4,096	256	16	1
2	3	c	a	5

We also have to keep in mind what the letters are worth in hex and convert them. In review:

$$a = 10$$
$$b = 11$$
$$c = 12$$
$$d = 13$$
$$e = 14$$
$$f = 15$$

Now we multiply each number by its bit position and then total the values as shown here:

$$(2 \times 65,536) + (3 \times 4,096) + (12 \times 256) + (10 \times 16) + (5 \times 1)$$

This equals the following:

$$131,072 + 12,288 + 3,072 + 160 + 5 = 146,597$$

So the hex number 23ca5 is equivalent to 146,597 in decimal.

Converting from decimal to hex takes a slightly different approach. Consider the decimal number 7,544. First we line up our hex values for each position and use the same method used for decimal to binary:

65,536 4,096 256 16 1

We also work from left to right, but in this case, we have to check each position for two conditions:

▶ Does the single position value exceed the number we are converting? If it does, place a 0 there and skip to the next position.

▶ If it doesn't, we need to insert a multiple of the hex value for that position. What is the largest value we can put there without exceeding the number we are converting?

So using the number 7,554, we look at the first position, which is worth 65,536, and we skip it because it exceeds the number we are converting. (There is no need to place a 0 there unless we have already generated at least one non-zero number.)

Moving to the next position, the number 4,096 is not larger than 7,554, so we can place a value there, but what value? If we place 1 there, we will be up to 4,096. If we place 2 there, we will exceed the number we are converting ($2 \times 4,096 = 8,192$, which is greater than 7,554), so we place a 1 there and move on (we are up to 1).

The next position is worth 256. If we add 256 to 4,096 we do not exceed 7,554 ($4,096 + 256 = 4,352$), so we can place a value here, but what value? Let's consider how many times 256 would go into the difference between the number we are converting and the cumulative total that we have so far. $7554 - 4,096 = 3,458$. Then, 3,458 divided by $256 = 13$. That means if we place a 13 there (13 is d in hex), we will hit the number we are converting exactly. We put zeros in all positions to the right, and that is the hex value.

1d00 is the hex equivalent of 7,554. To check this, we perform the hex-to-decimal conversion you learned earlier:

$$(1 \times 4,096) + (13 \times 256) + 0 + 0$$

$$4,096 + 3,458 = 7,554$$

This is correct!

Binary-to-Hex Conversion

This last conversion operation is one that you will rarely have to perform but is still handy to know. It can be used to verify your work when you have performed a hex-to-binary conversion. It takes a slightly different approach than the other operations. Consider the following 8-bit binary number:

11011011

Before we jump into this conversion, let's talk about bit values. You have already learned that 8 bits makes up a byte. If you divide a byte in half (4 bits), it's called a *nibble*. To convert binary into hex, we are going to divide the 8 bits into 2 nibbles and perform the conversion on each nibble and then put the two single values that result together to form the hexadecimal equivalent. If we do this to the preceding number, we will get the following:

1101   1011

We have 2 nibbles to convert, and we perform this conversion briefly to decimal and then to hex. For purposes of determining binary place values, we will consider them separately. In the first nibble on the left, convert 1101 to decimal:

$8 + 4 + 0 + 1 = 13$

Then we convert that to hex:

$13 = d$

That's the first value in the hex conversion. Now convert the second nibble:

$8 + 0 + 2 + 1 = 11$

$11 = b$

Put those two values together and you have the hex equivalent of 11011011:

db

To check this, we convert both values to decimal and compare them. First convert the binary, considering all 8 bits together for purposes of place value:

$11011011 = 128 + 64 + 0 + 16 + 8 + 0 + 2 + 1 = 219$

Then convert the hex value to decimal.

$db = (13 \times 16) + (11 \times 1) = 208 + 11 = 219$

Compare the two values.

$219 = 219$

The answer is correct!

THE ESSENTIALS AND BEYOND

Understanding the binary and hexadecimal numbering systems is important for understanding computers and networking. Both systems are used in the operations of computers and networking gear and in the communication systems they employ. The binary numbering system, which has only two values (0 and 1), underlies the operation of digital electronics. It is also important to understand binary when working with IP addressing and subnetting. Hexadecimal, a numbering system using a base of 16, is used in situations where large numbers need to be represented easily. Hexadecimal is used for memory locations, for Media Access Control (MAC) addresses, and in the representation of IPv6 IP addresses. MAC addresses are assigned to network adaptors and are used in network communications that occur at the Network Access layer. There are two parts to a MAC address: the Organizationally Unique Identifier (OUI) and the Universally Administered Address (UAA). Converting numbers from one system to another is a necessary skill, especially from binary to decimal and vice versa. This skill is utilized extensively when working with IP addressing.

ADDITIONAL EXERCISES

1. In this exercise, you will work with a partner. Each of you needs a computer. Both computers need to be connected to the same local area network.

   A. Open the command prompt by clicking Start ➣ Programs (or All Programs) ➣ Accessories ➣ Command Prompt.

   B. Type the command **ipconfig/all**. Locate the IP address and the physical or MAC address of your computer and write them down. An example is shown in Figure 6.3.

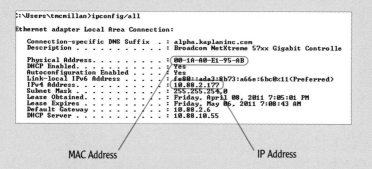

FIGURE 6.3 MAC and IP address

   C. Type the command **ping** followed by your partner's IP address. You should receive four replies.

(Continues)

THE ESSENTIALS AND BEYOND   *(Continued)*

D. Your computer just used an ARP broadcast to determine your partner's MAC address. It stored it in what is called the *ARP cache*, where it will reside for just a few minutes. The next command will allow you to see the contents of the ARP cache, which should include your partner's MAC address. Type the command **arp -a**. There may be multiple entries in the cache, but you should see you partner's IP address and MAC address listed.

E. Now type the command **arp -a** followed by your partner's IP address. You will see only your partner's entry and none of the others.

F. Compare your MAC address with that of your partner's and see if you can tell whether the network card came from the same manufacturer. Look at the OUI of the cards and see if they match. If they do, they are from the same company.

2. Convert the following decimal numbers to binary:

   A. 206
   B. 24
   C. 58
   D. 196
   E. 67

3. Convert the following binary numbers to decimal:

   A. 11000011
   B. 10101110
   C. 11111011
   D. 10101010
   E. 10111111

4. Convert the following hex numbers to decimal.

   A. a26
   B. 2b8
   C. 166
   D. cab
   E. 22a

(Continues)

REVIEW QUESTIONS

1. Which of the following is *not* an area where binary is used in networking technology?

   A. IP addressing

   B. Representation of data in transmission

   C. Data storage

   D. MAC addresses

2. What is the value of 2^0?

   A. 0

   B. 1

   C. 2

   D. There is no such thing as a zero power.

3. How does the Unicode system represent multiple language characters?

   A. 4-bit patterns

   B. 8-bit patterns

   C. 2-byte patterns

   D. 4-byte patterns

4. In which area is hexadecimal used?

   A. IP addresses

   B. Representation of data in transmission

   C. Data storage

   D. Memory addressing

5. What numbering system is used in IPv6?

   A. Binary

   B. Decimal

   C. Hex

   D. Octal

6. What is the best numbering system to use to represent very large numbers concisely?

   A. Binary

   B. Decimal

   C. Hex

   D. Octal

7. Which of the following is the abbreviation for another term for MAC address?

   A. OUI

   B. BIA

   C. PAA

   D. EUI

8. Which part of a MAC address identifies the manufacturer?

   A. OUI

   B. EUI

   C. BIA

   D. UAA

(Continues)

THE ESSENTIALS AND BEYOND *(Continued)*

9. Which part of a MAC address identifies the individual network card and not the manufacturer?

    A. OUI

    B. EUI

    C. BIA

    D. UAA

10. Which of the following is *not* an accepted representation of a MAC address?

    A. 00-50-56-C0-00-08

    B. 00/50/56/C0/00/08

    C. 00:50:56:C0:00:08

    D. 0050.56C0.0008

CHAPTER 7

Classful IP Addressing

Internet Protocol (IP) addresses are used to differentiate the computers on a LAN. They also include information that allows routers to route packets from a computer in one LAN to a computer in a different LAN. As you learned in Chapter 3, "TCP/IP," these activities occur on the Internet layer of the TCP/IP model.

For a Cisco network technician, an understanding of IP addressing and its configuration is essential. In this chapter, the basics of IP addressing, both for IPv4 and IPv6, are covered, laying the groundwork for more-advanced IP topics in Chapter 8, "Classless IP Addressing." Specifically, this chapter covers the following topics:

▶ **Describing the function of IP addresses**

▶ **Identifying IP address types**

▶ **Utilizing diagnostic tools**

▶ **Understanding DHCP**

▶ **Introducing IPv6**

Describing the Function of IP Addresses

The original version of TCP/IP was written in September 1981. In 1983, the DoD mandated that all of their computer systems would use the TCP/IP protocol suite for long-haul communications. This network eventually evolved into the Internet as we know it today, and TCP/IP is the protocol of the Internet. TCP/IP has become the networking protocol for LANs as well.

The Internet Protocol (IP) part of the TCP/IP suite handles the routing and addressing function at the Internet layer of the TCP/IP model. As you will learn later in this chapter, IP addresses, unlike MAC addresses, are logical and are managed by network technicians. Because IP addressing is designed and implemented by network technicians, it is important to understand its functions and factor these considerations into the design phase.

The two main functions of IP addressing are identification and segmentation. IP addresses serve to uniquely identify network devices, and the IP addressing system serves as a method of partitioning the network for purposes of security and/or performance. This section covers the two main functions of IP addressing.

Identification

IP addresses are used to differentiate one computer from another and act as a value that is used when attempting to locate a computer. Much as your home or office address is used for mailing purposes, these addresses are used as a destination value in the IP header of the packet sent to a computer.

As you learned in Chapter 3, MAC addresses can change many times en route from one computer to another, but the IP addresses in the IP header do not.

Both the source and destination IP addresses will remain the same. In Figure 7.1, you can see the Network Access layer header (labeled *Ethernet II*) and the Internet layer header (labeled *Internet Protocol*) of the packet.

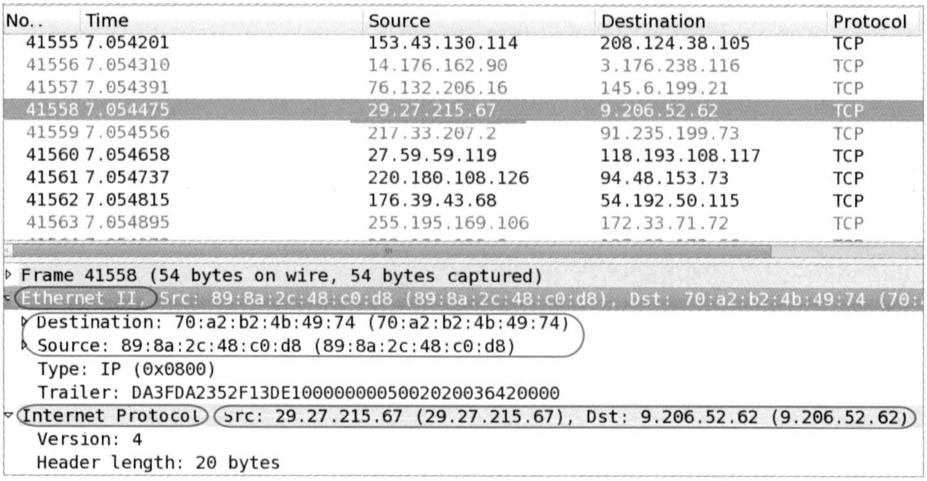

> **Media Access Control (MAC) addresses are Network Access layer addresses in hex that are permanently assigned to network cards and network device interfaces.**

No..	Time	Source	Destination	Protocol
41555	7.054201	153.43.130.114	208.124.38.105	TCP
41556	7.054310	14.176.162.90	3.176.238.116	TCP
41557	7.054391	76.132.206.16	145.6.199.21	TCP
41558	7.054475	29.27.215.67	9.206.52.62	TCP
41559	7.054556	217.33.207.2	91.235.199.73	TCP
41560	7.054658	27.59.59.119	118.193.108.117	TCP
41561	7.054737	220.180.108.126	94.48.153.73	TCP
41562	7.054815	176.39.43.68	54.192.50.115	TCP
41563	7.054895	255.195.169.106	172.33.71.72	TCP

```
▷ Frame 41558 (54 bytes on wire, 54 bytes captured)
▽ Ethernet II, Src: 89:8a:2c:48:c0:d8 (89:8a:2c:48:c0:d8), Dst: 70:a2:b2:4b:49:74 (70:
  ▷ Destination: 70:a2:b2:4b:49:74 (70:a2:b2:4b:49:74)
  ▷ Source: 89:8a:2c:48:c0:d8 (89:8a:2c:48:c0:d8)
    Type: IP (0x0800)
    Trailer: DA3FDA2352F13DE1000000005002020036420000
▽ Internet Protocol, Src: 29.27.215.67 (29.27.215.67), Dst: 9.206.52.62 (9.206.52.62)
    Version: 4
    Header length: 20 bytes
```

FIGURE 7.1 Ethernet and Internet Protocol headers

The information displayed in Figure 7.1 is a part of a packet capture from the network with a protocol analyzer, or *sniffer*. These devices capture copies of packets travelling on the network and use software to display the packets and their contents. This part of the capture is focused only on the Network Access and Internet headers, but the entire packet was captured. You can see the source and destination MAC addresses in hex, and in the IP section you can see the source and destination IP addresses. Each time the packet goes through a router, the

Network Access portion will be taken off and reconstructed using new destination and source MAC addresses. A new Network Access trailer will also be added. None of the other parts of the packet, including the IP header, will change.

Segmentation

Another function of IP addressing is to segment, or organize, computers into separate LANs. In the upcoming section "Identifying IP Address Types," you will learn how a portion of the IP address is used to do this. When computers are located in different LANs, they cannot communicate with one another without the assistance of a router. Even if they are physically connected to the same switch or even connected directly to each other, communication cannot occur if their IP addresses are in different networks.

Segmenting computers in LANs is done for the following reasons:

Better Performance   When a network segment becomes overloaded with computers, performance begins to suffer. You learned in Chapter 2, "The OSI Model," that devices use unicast transmissions to communicate one-to-one and broadcast transmissions to communicate to *all* other computers. Computers broadcast in any situation in which the destination IP address is unknown. When a computer broadcasts, every computer in its LAN must receive and process the packet. The set of computers defined by these broadcast recipients is called a *broadcast domain*. The larger the broadcast domain, the more broadcast traffic is created. This traffic competes with other traffic and congests the LAN.

As you will learn more about in Chapter 10, "Network Devices," routers do *not* forward broadcast traffic from one LAN to another. This keeps the broadcast traffic confined to each LAN. The result is smaller broadcast domains, resulting in better performance.

Security   When computers are in different LANs, access from one LAN to another can be controlled at the only path that exists between them—that is, at the router. This access is accomplished via access lists. These lists define what traffic is allowed between LANs and what traffic is not allowed. It can be broadly defined (as in *no* traffic is allowed), or it can be granular. For example, it may block traffic from one particular computer in LAN A from using HTTP with one particular computer in LAN B.

Network Expansion   Because the growth of any individual LAN will at some point result in declining performance, network growth will necessitate the creation of more LANs. The ability to create more LANs connected together with routers allows a network to scale, growing to any size without suffering performance degradation.

SCALING

Scaling means to increase size or capacity. For example, scaling a network means increasing the number of computers in the network. Scaling a server, on the other hand, means to increase its capacity, either by adding memory or more processors, which is called *scaling up*, or by adding servers in a *cluster* (a group of servers working together as one), which is called *scaling out*.

Problem Isolation   With smaller LANs segmented by routers, network problems are easier to isolate. Because much traffic is confined to the local LAN, the problems are likewise confined. Hardware problems with routers and switches also affect a smaller portion of the network when they occur.

In summary, network segmentation yields many benefits. In the next section, you will learn the parts of the IP address and the role that these parts play in accomplishing this segmentation.

Identifying IP Address Types

As you learned in Chapter 6, "Numbering Systems," IP addresses are 32 bits in length when expressed in binary. When humans work with IP addresses, however, it is usually done in what is called *dotted decimal format*. An IP address in this format looks like the following:

> 192.168.5.3

This format is called *dotted decimal* because the sections, or fields, are divided by dots, and the values are expressed in decimal instead of binary. Each of the four fields is called an *octet* because each section can be expressed in binary format by using 8 bits. So to convert 192.168.5.3 to its binary format, each decimal number would be converted to its equivalent in binary. Because each section is 8 bits in length, the result would be a string of 32 0s or 1s. The conversion of 192.168.5.3 is as follows:

> 11000000.10101000.00000101.00000011

There is more to understand about an IP address than its two formats, however. To understand how IP addresses are used to accomplish segmentation (or *subnetting*), you must understand the two parts of the IP address and their relationship to a second value that any device with an IP address will possess (which is the *subnet mask*). This section presents those concepts and introduces a set of IP addresses that have been specifically reserved for use on LANs.

Defining IP Address Classes

When IPv4 addressing was first designed, the IP addresses were organized into what are called *classes*. Five classes of addresses were defined, and the value of the first octet (the octet to the far left) determines the class in which an IP address resides. The standard defines this in binary terms. Three of the classes are intended for application to individual devices, one class is reserved for multicasting, and the fifth is labeled experimental.

When expressed in decimal format, the ranges of possible values for the first octet of the five classes are as follows:

> Class A—1 to 126
>
> Class B—128 to 191
>
> Class C—192 to 223
>
> Class D—224 to 239
>
> Class E—240 to 255

The standard defines these classes in terms of the first octet in binary. It defines the bits at the far-left side of the first octet, which are called the *most significant* or the *high-order* bits. All IP addresses in the same class will share the values of these defined bits. For example, every IP address in Class C will have the most significant bits in the first octet set to 11.

◄

The entire 127.0.0.0/8 network is missing from this list (reserved) because these addresses are used for diagnostics. This is discussed further later in this section.

HIGH-ORDER BITS

High-order bits, also referred to as the *most significant bits*, are the far-left bits in a bit pattern. They are termed most significant or high order because they are worth the most because of their position. For example, in the 8-bit pattern 11000000, the two leftmost bits are worth 128 and 64, respectively, which is higher than the value of any other bits in the pattern.

When expressed in this form, the five classes are as follows:

> Class A—0000
>
> Class B–1000
>
> Class C—1100
>
> Class D—1110
>
> Class E—1111

Because the first three classes (A, B, and C) are used for individual devices, that is where our focus will be. These three classes, from the first address to the last address in the class, are as follows:

> Class A—1.0.0.1–126.255.255.255
>
> Class B—128.0.0.1–192.255.255.255
>
> Class C—193.0.0.1–223.255.255.255

You may have noticed that some numbers are missing. The entire networks from 0.0.0.0–0.255.255.255 and 127.0.0.0–127.255.255.255 are not used. The first is called the *zero network* and is arbitrarily not used, and the second (127.0.0.0–127.255.255.255) is reserved for network diagnostics. Any of the IP addresses in the 127.0.0.0 network can be used to test a computer. If the address can be pinged successfully, the computer has the TCP/IP protocol installed and the network adaptor card is functioning.

The most famous of the IP addresses in the 127.0.0.0 network (127.0.0.1) is called the *local host*. It is also known as the *loopback address*, as it loops the signal back through the network card for an answer if you ping it. Although any of the IP addresses in the 127.0.0.0 networks will do this, 127.0.0.1 gets all the glory.

Identifying Network and Host Addresses

Each IP address has two parts, the *network* part and the *host* part. These two portions function in a manner similar to your street address and your house number. The network portion determines the LAN in which the computer is located, and the host portion identifies the computer in that LAN. The network portion begins at the far-left side of the IP address and continues uninterrupted until it meets the host portion. The host portion then continues to the far-right side of the IP address.

The point in the address at which the network portion ends and the host portion begins is determined by the class of the IP address. The computer uses a second value called the *subnet mask* to determine which portion is network and

> You will learn how to use the loopback address to troubleshoot in the section "Utilizing Diagnostic Tools" later in this chapter.

which portion is host. When the computer reads the subnet mask, each octet that is 255 is considered to be network, and each octet that is 0 is considered to be host. It then uses the octets that are set to the value of 255 to mask the network portion (which means it uses the mask to determine the network part). A computer cannot have an IP address without also having a subnet mask. The addressing is incomplete if both values are not present.

In *classful IP addressing*, the dividing line between the two is always done between octets. An example of an IP address from each class with the network part shaded red and host part shaded green is shown in Figure 7.2. Figure 7.2 also shows the subnet mask for each class. As you can see, the parts of the subnet mask that are 255s match the network portion of the address.

19.42.36.98   255.0.0.0
177.25.14.6   255.255.0.0
201.65.9.51   255.255.255.0

FIGURE 7.2 Subnet masks for each class

Classful IP addressing **is the IP addressing system used from 1981 until 1993. It creates only three classes of networks for unicast communication. Chapter 8 discusses the limitations this imposes.**

In the next chapter, it will be important for you to be comfortable working with subnet masks in binary form, so let's take a look at what the three default subnet masks look like:

Class A (255.0.0.0)

11111111.00000000.00000000.00000000

Class B (255.255.0.0)

11111111.11111111.00000000.00000000

Class C (255.255.255.0)

11111111.11111111.11111111.00000000

DEFAULT SUBNET MASKS

A *default subnet mask* is one that conforms to the rules of classful subnetting. In Chapter 8, you will learn that other subnet mask possibilities exist and are used to create networks of the size desired. As you will learn, this removes the restriction of only having three sizes of networks to choose from in design.

As you already know, the computer evaluates everything in binary, so when the computer reads the subnet mask, 1s indicate the network portion and 0s indicate the host portion. It is also important to know that the string of 1s indicating the network portion is *never* interrupted by 0s, which means there will never be a subnet mask like this:

11100011.00000000.00000000.00000000

In each network or LAN, there are two IP addresses that can never be assigned to devices. These addresses are reserved for special roles in each network. The first is called the *network ID* and second is called the *broadcast address*. These two addresses can be identified in the LAN by the bits in the host portion of the IP address. If all of the bits in the host portion are 0s, then the address is the network ID. If all of the bits in the host portion are 1s (or 255s in decimal), the address is called the broadcast address. An example of a Class A network ID and broadcast address in both binary and dotted decimal form is shown here:

IP Address	Dotted Decimal Format	Binary Format
Network ID	1.0.0.0	00000001.00000000.00000000.00000000
Broadcast	1.255.255.255	00000001.11111111.11111111.11111111

The network ID is used to identify the network as a group. It is an important value that routers use in the routing tables. If this value were not available to identify the entire LAN, a router would have to have an entry for every host, which would make the routing tables huge and would slow the routing process to a crawl. By using this value, the router can route packets to any computer in a LAN, and then the router that physically connects to that LAN will locate the specific host at the Network Access layer by using the ARP broadcast method you learned about in Chapter 3.

The broadcast address is used any time a computer needs to send a packet to every host in its LAN. An example of a broadcast is an ARP broadcast. Hosts broadcast in other instances as well. Later in this chapter, you will learn about the operation of Dynamic Host Configuration protocol (DHCP). When DHCP is used, the computers broadcast to locate the DHCP server.

The number of possible networks per class is a function of the possible combinations of the number of bits dedicated to the network portion for the class. For example, if 2 bits were used for the network (which is not possible in classful

IP addressing, because 8 bits is the minimum, but consider this example just for illustration purposes) the possible combinations using 2 bits would be as follows:

00

01

10

11

Those are the only combinations using 2 bits. Because there are four possible combinations using 2 bits, it would mean you could have four networks, each identified by the values in the first 2 bits. To determine the number of possible networks given the number of bits dedicated to the network portion of the address, the following formula can be used:

2^n = number of possible networks
where n = the number of bits in the network portion

To prove this formula manually, we can use the previous 2-bit example. Because $2^2 = 4$, the formula works. That means that for a Class A network in which 8 bits (the entire first octet) are used for the network portion, the number of networks possible would be 2^8, which is 256. Using this formula and applying it to each of the three classes of networks, the number of possible networks for each is shown here:

Network Class	Number of Possible Networks
Class A	$2^8 = 256$
Class B	$2^{16} = 65,536$
Class C	$2^{24} = 16,777,216$

Just as the number of bits dedicated to the network portion of the address determines the number of possible Class A, B, and C networks, the number of host bits determines the possible number of computers in a Class A, B, and C network. The number of computers possible in each class network is a function of the number of possible combinations of numbers using the number of host bits. The formula for the number of possible computers in a network is

$2^n - 2$ = possible number of computers
where n is the number of host bits in the address

Using a Class C address as an example (which has 8 host bits, which is the entire last octet), the possible number of computers would be as follows:

$$2^8 - 2 = 254$$

Can you guess why we are subtracting 2 from the possible number of computers in each network? Remember the two IP addresses that are reserved in each network (network ID and broadcast). We must subtract those out to get the number of available IP addresses in each network. Using this formula and applying it to each of the three classes of networks, the number of possible computers for each is shown here:

Network Class	Number of Possible Computers
Class A	$2^{24} - 2 = 16,777,214$
Class B	$2^{16} - 2 = 65,534$
Class C	$2^8 - 2 = 254$

Because there are only three classes in classful IP addressing, there are only three sizes of networks. In the next chapter, you will learn the limitations that restriction introduces and how classless IP addressing solves those problems.

Describing Private IP Addresses and NAT

When IPv4 was created, it was thought that the number of possible IP addresses would be sufficient to serve the Internet. However, after a few years of incredible growth, it became apparent that this was not the case. The eventual solution was IPv6, which you will learn about later in this chapter. While the IPv6 system was still in development, two temporary solutions were implemented to delay the eventual exhaustion of the address space. These two solutions were classless IP addressing (which you will learn about in the next chapter) and private IP addressing used in conjunction with Network Address Translation (NAT) services.

Up until the time that private IP addressing and NAT services were introduced, all computers that were to connect to the Internet had to have a unique IP address issued from the entities managing the Internet. Therefore, a company with 500 computers that required Internet access would be issued a block of 500 unique addresses from their Internet service provider. Then the NAT server was introduced, which allowed a single server to be the gateway to the Internet for the entire company, to represent all 500 computers on the Internet with a single IP address.

When Network Address Translation is in use, the computers in the network have IP addresses that need not be unique on the Internet. When one of these computers needs to go to the Internet, their packet will go to the NAT server. The NAT server will remove the IP address of the computer and replace it with the IP address of the NAT server. Therefore, when the packet is sent to the web server on the Internet, the source IP address will be that of the NAT server. When the page is returned from the web server to the NAT server, the NAT server will forward the page back to the computer, using the IP address of the computer as the destination.

If you understand how Network Address Translation works, it really doesn't matter what IP addresses you use in your LAN as long as they are unique within the LAN. Because these IP addresses are never seen on the Internet (because they get translated to a public address that is unique on the Internet), you could use any addresses you like.

Having said that, three special ranges of IP addresses have been reserved for use inside LANs. The IP addresses in these ranges are called *private IP addresses*. These ranges were specified in Request for Comments (RFC) 1918.

There is a range in each address class. These addresses are not given out for use on the Internet. There is no requirement to use them in a LAN, but it has become a common practice to do so.

These ranges are as follows:

> Class A—10.0.0.0 to 10.255.255.255
>
> Class B—172.16.0.0 to 172.31.255.255
>
> Class C—192.168.0.0 to 192.168.255.255

Before a standard is adopted and published, it is presented to the standards body in a document called a Request for Comments (RFC).

Utilizing Diagnostic Tools

In the process of implementing and maintaining a network, there will be times when computers cannot communicate with one another and the problem must be isolated. There are a number of command-line tools that can be utilized to accomplish this. The purpose of these tools is to eliminate possibilities one by one until the smallest sets of possible causes exist, helping to determine and ultimately correct the problem.

Understanding the TCP/IP model can be a great aid when troubleshooting network problems. There are four possible layers where the problem can exist.

As a review, the four layers and the types of problems that exist at those layers are as follows:

Application Layer   Specific applications and services operate at this layer (DNS, SMTP, and so forth). If this layer functions, *all* other layers must be functioning, because this layer depends on all other layers for a connection. An example of a problem at this layer is the inability of computers to locate one another by name. This is a name resolution problem caused by the malfunction of DNS, an Application layer protocol.

Transport Layer   Port numbers are at this layer. If this layer functions, the Internet and Network Access layers *must* be functioning, because the Transport layer depends on them to function. Problems at this layer will prevent connection at both the Application and Transport layers, because the Application layer depends on this layer to function.

Internet Layer   IP addresses are at this layer. If this layer functions, the Network Access layer *must* be functioning, because the Internet layer depends on it to function. Problems at this layer will prevent connection at the Internet, Transport, and Application layers, because those layers depend on this layer to function.

Network Access Layer   MAC addresses, Frame Relay DLCIs, and PPP SPIDs are at this level. If this layer functions, the physical LAN or WAN connection is operational and devices are seeing each other at the Network Access layer. Problems at this layer will prevent connection at *all* layers, because all layers depend on this layer to function.

The command-line tools discussed in the remainder of this section can help determine on which of these layers the problem exists. Specifically, these tools and the layers they can troubleshoot are as follows:

> *Parameters*, also called *switches*, allow you to alter the execution of a command. Some commands will function with no switches, and some will not.

       `ipconfig`—Used to obtain information for troubleshooting every layer

       `ping`—Can troubleshoot Internet and Transport layers

       `arp`—Can troubleshoot Network Access layer

       `traceroute`—Used to troubleshoot the Internet layer

Executing the *ipconfig* Command

The ipconfig command can be used to view the current IP configuration of a computer. It can show the IP address, subnet mask, and default gateway. An example of the output is shown in Figure 7.3.

```
C:\Users\tmcmillan>ipconfig

Windows IP Configuration

Ethernet adapter Local Area Connection:

   Connection-specific DNS Suffix  . : alpha.kaplaninc.com
   Link-local IPv6 Address . . . . . : fe80::ada3:8b73:a66e:6bc0%11
   IPv4 Address. . . . . . . . . . . : 10.88.2.177
   Subnet Mask . . . . . . . . . . . : 255.255.254.0
   Default Gateway . . . . . . . . . : 10.88.2.6
```

FIGURE 7.3 ipconfig

When you are unfamiliar with the configuration of a computer (which in most cases, you will be), this command gives you a quick look at the settings currently in place.

Executing the *ping* Command

You learned about the ping command in Chapter 4, "Protocols." You learned it can be used to test connectivity at the Internet layer when you ping an IP address. It can test other operations at this layer as well. The following are some uses of the ping command listed in the recommended order of execution:

Ping 127.0.0.1   When you ping the loopback address and receive a response, you can rule out a problem with the TCP/IP protocol and with the network adaptor card. This is useful because network cards can become loose, their device drivers can become corrupted, and they can simply stop functioning. The TCP/IP protocol is typically installed by default with the operating system but it can be uninstalled, and if it is, a ping to 127.0.0.1 will also fail. Testing the loopback address is useful because if it fails, *none* of the other tests discussed in this section will succeed and will be a waste of time.

Ping the Local IP Address   If you can successfully ping the local IP address, you know that TCP/IP is installed, the network adaptor is functioning, and the IP address and subnet mask you are expecting has been assigned. This is not always a given because users have been known to change their IP addresses for all sorts of odd reasons. Another way to check the IP address is to execute the ipconfig command.

The ipconfig command will display the IP address, subnet mask, and default gateway if executed with no parameters, but if you add /all to the command, you will get much more information.

Although the most common address used is 127.0.0.1, any IP address in the 127.0.0.0 network is mapped to the loopback and will work. Try it!

Ping Another Computer on the Local LAN   If this succeeds, you know that TCP/IP is installed, the network adaptor is functioning, and the IP address and subnet mask of the two local computers are in the same subnet. Considering how unlikely it is that two users changed their IP addresses and managed to get in the same subnet, it probably means that both computers are configured correctly.

Ping the Default Gateway   As Chapter 11, "LAN Operations," explores further, the *default gateway* is the IP address of the router connected to the local LAN. To connect to anything outside of the local LAN, such as other LANs or the Internet, you must be able to ping the default gateway. If you can, you know that TCP/IP is installed; the network adaptor is functioning, and the IP address and subnet mask of the local computer is in the same subnet with the router.

Ping a Computer in Another LAN   If this ping fails and the ping to the default gateway succeeds, there is a routing problem. If this ping succeeds, routing is working properly (at least to that LAN). In that case, you know that TCP/IP is installed, the network adaptor is functioning, the IP address and subnet mask of the local computer is in the same subnet with the router, and the router is able to route to the remote network.

> Subnets are created with the subnet mask. If two computers use the same subnet mask, and the network portion of their address matches, they are in the same subnet.

> In Chapter 8, you will learn how to create subnets of a certain size by manipulating the subnet mask.

> The combination of the IP address and the port number is called a *socket*.

Ping can also be used to test the Transport layer. When you can ping a computer by its IP address but you can't connect to a service running on the computer, you can ping the port number of that service to see whether the port is blocked or the service is not functioning. For example, if you can ping the email server but you cannot connect to your email box, ping the port number for SMTP (25). This is done by pinging the IP address with the port number added to the same line after a colon. If the IP address of the email server were 192.168.6.6, the command would be as follows:

```
ping 192.168.6.6:25
```

If this fails, either the service is not functioning or the port has been blocked by an access list. Access lists are discussed in Chapter 13, "Configuring Routers."

Executing the *arp* Command

As you learned in Chapter 3, Address Resolution Protocol (ARP) is responsible for learning the MAC address that goes with an IP address. It does this by broadcasting in the local LAN. All computers will get the broadcast, but only the computer with the IP address will answer. There is also a command-line program called arp.exe that can be used to examine the local arp cache.

When a computer resolves a MAC address to an IP address, it stores that mapping in memory for a short period of time. This area of memory is called the *arp cache*. In some instances, when a network problem arising from an incorrect IP address has been corrected, other local computers in the LAN may still be caching an incorrect IP address. You can determine whether that is the case and if necessary delete the entry in the cache with the arp command.

The arp command requires that you also include a parameter (also called a switch) with the command. The following are the most useful parameters:

> arp -s <MAC address>—Adds a static entry to the ARP cache
>
> arp -N <Interface IP address>—Lists all ARP entries for the interface specified
>
> arp -a or arp -g—Displays all the current ARP entries for all interfaces

The arp command requires a switch to function. If you execute it alone, it will simply display the Help menu for the arp command.

◄

◄

The use of angle brackets indicates a variable. You replace the brackets and their contents with the appropriate information that is called for inside the bracket description.

Executing the *traceroute* Command

The traceroute command can be used on a Cisco router to determine the path to another network and can be used to determine where along that path the connection is broken. To execute this command on a Windows computer, you must execute tracert, rather than traceroute. It will display each hop (a *hop* is a router traversed and the time taken to cross the router). When connectivity does not exist between router A and router B, and you know there are a number of routers between them, this command will help determine where the communication stops. As explained in Chapter 4, the last router to report its hop will be the last router before the problem router.

Understanding DHCP

Dynamic Host Configuration Protocol (DHCP) is a service that can run on either a router or a server. Its function is to automate the process of assigning IP addresses, subnet masks, default gateways, and other settings to computers. It also helps prevent IP address conflicts by keeping track of which IP addresses have been issued and which have not. This section discusses the operation of DHCP in any form and then looks at how DHCP is implemented on a Cisco router.

Operations

Before a DHCP server or router can function, the service must be enabled and an IP address range or scope must be created. A *scope* is a set of IP addresses that the DHCP server or router will use to issue IP addresses. The DHCP server will issue these addresses on a first-come, first-served basis and will mark an address when it is assigned to prevent duplicates.

Computers must be set to participate in the DHCP process to obtain an address. This is done by selecting the check box to obtain an IP address automatically in the Properties of TCP/IP on the computers, as shown in Figure 7.4.

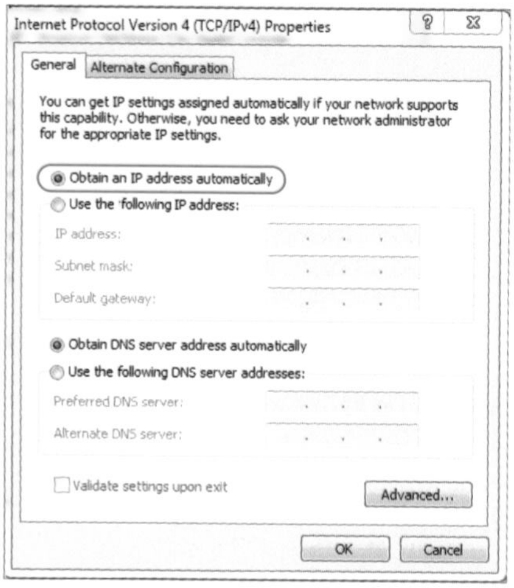

FIGURE 7.4 DHCP settings

You may have noticed that the computer is *not* configured with the IP address of the DHCP server or router. When a computer is set to use a DHCP server, it will broadcast to locate the DHCP server. The server will answer and offer an IP address if it has one, and the computer will accept the address and begin to use it. There are four packets that will go back and forth between the DHCP server or router and the DHCP client, as shown in Figure 7.5.

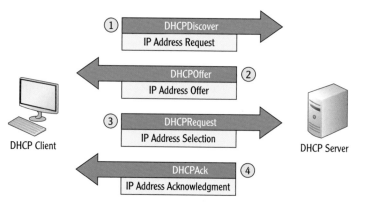

FIGURE 7.5 DHCP process

Many settings can be issued using DHCP. The most common are as follows:

► IP address

► Subnet mask

► Default gateway

► DNS server

Cisco DHCP

A Cisco router also has the ability to act as a DHCP server for the computers on the local LAN. As you learned earlier, routers connect LANs via physical Ethernet interfaces. The computers do not usually connect directly to this interface; instead, a switch is connected to the interface and computers are then connected to the switch, as shown in Figure 7.6.

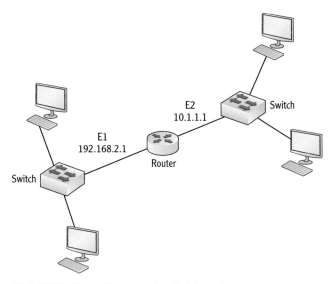

FIGURE 7.6 Router and switch layout

DHCP is configured on the router and will function on the interface that is the same LAN as the scope. For example, if the scope range is from 196.168.2.2–192.168.2.50 and the E1 interface has an IP address of 192.168.2.1, computers on the LAN connected to the switch connected to E1 will receive an answer to their DHCP request. Computers connected to the switch connected to E2, which has an IP address of 10.1.1.1, will not receive an answer unless a scope is configured for that network, such as 10.1.1.2–10.1.1.50. In Chapter 13, you will learn the commands to enable DHCP for an interface.

Introducing IPv6

IPv6 is an IP addressing scheme designed to provide a virtually unlimited number of IP addresses. It uses 128 bits rather than 32 as in IPv4, and it is represented in hexadecimal rather than dotted decimal format. Moreover, any implementation of IPv6 requires support built-in for Internet Protocol Security (IPsec), which is optional in IPv4. IPsec is used to protect the integrity and confidentiality of the data contained in a packet. This section covers the format and allowed expressions of an IPv6 address. This section also points out some special IPv6 addresses that are reserved for particular purposes.

IPv6 Address Format

An IPv6 address looks different from an IPv4 address. When viewed in non-binary format (it can be represented in binary and is processed by the computer in binary), it is organized into eight sections, or fields, instead of four as in IPv4. The sections are separated by colons rather than periods as in IPv4. Finally, each of the eight sections has four characters rather than one to three as in the dotted decimal format of IPv4. An IPv4 and IPv6 address are presented here for comparison:

> IPv4—192.168.5.6
>
> IPv6—2001:0db8:85a3:0000:0000:8a2e:0370:7334

The IPv6 address has two logical parts, a 64-bit network prefix and a 64-bit host address. The host address is automatically generated from the MAC address of the device. The host address in the preceding example consists of the rightmost four sections, or 0000:8a2e:0370:7334. The leftmost four sections are the network portion. This portion can be further subdivided. The first section to the left of the host portion can be used by organizations to identify a site within the organization. The other three far-left sections are assigned by the ISP or in some cases are generated automatically based on the address type (as you will see shortly).

There are some allowed methods of shortening the representation of the IPv6 address:

Leading zeros are any zeros that appear on the left side of a group. If any nonzero characters appear to the left of zeros within a group, those are *not* leading zeros.

1. Leading zeros in each section can be omitted, but each section must be represented by at least one character unless you are making use of rule 2. By applying this rule, the previous example IPv6 address could be written as follows:

   > 2001:0db8:85a3:0:0:8a2e:0370:7334

2. One or more consecutive sections with only a 0 can be represented with a single empty section (double colons), as shown here applied to the same address.

2001:0db8:85a3:: 8a2e:0370:7334

3. The second rule can be applied only once within an address. For example, the following IPv6 address, which contains two sets of consecutive sections with all zeros, could have rule 2 applied only once.

2001:0000:0000:85a3:8a2e:0000:0000:7334

It could *not* be represented as follows:

2001::85a3:8a2e::7334

IPv6 Address Types

There are three types of IP addresses in IPv6. One of the benefits of IPv6 is that there are no broadcasts in IPv6.

Unicast Addresses   A packet is delivered to one interface. This is the same concept as in IPv4.

Multicast Addresses   A packet is delivered to multiple interfaces. This is the same concept as in IPv4.

Anycast Addresses   A packet is delivered to the nearest of multiple interfaces (in terms of routing distance). This is unique to IPv6 and allows an IPv6 address to be applied to multiple interfaces, with the packet going to the interface that is closest.

A unicast address can be one of three types, and its type determines the scope of its uniqueness:

Global Addresses   These are publicly routable addresses. That means the prefixes were assigned by an ISP and the address is unique globally. Global addresses start with 2000:. The host portion is composed of the MAC address.

Link-Local Addresses   Both the network and host portions of these addresses are automatically generated and are unique only on the LAN or subnet on which they are generated. They always start with FE80:.

Unique Local Addresses   These addresses have a manually configured network portion (by an administrator), and the host portion is composed of the MAC address. The network portion can either be set computer by computer or it

◄

The single set of double colons for rule 2 applies even if you replace three or four sections with double colons. You wouldn't use three or four sets of colons.

◄

Addresses that are unique globally are unique on the Internet.

can be issued by a DHCPv6 server. These addresses operate much like private addresses in IPv4 in that they allow an organization to create LANs and route between the LANs. However, these addresses are unique only within the organization. The prefix for site-local addresses is FEC0:. The organization would use the section between FEC0 and the MAC address to identify different LANs in the organization.

Special IPv6 Addresses

Just as in IPv4, there are some IPv6 addresses that are reserved to represent specific things. These special addresses are listed here:

> 0:0:0:0:0:0:0:0 (also written as ::) —This is the source address of a host when it is trying to locate a DHCPv6 server.

> 0:0:0:0:0:0:0:1 (also written as ::1)—This the IPv6 loopback address (127.0.0.1 in IPv4).

> FF00:—Addresses that start with FF00 are in the multicast range.

Most operating systems today run IPv6 at the same time IPv4 is running. In the output of `ipconfig` in Figure 7.7, you can see the IPv6 address along with the IPv4 addresses. In this case, the IPv6 address was generated as a link-local unicast address. You can tell this by the FE80 at the beginning.

```
Ethernet adapter UMware Network Adapter UMnet8:

    Connection-specific DNS Suffix  . :
    Link-local IPv6 Address . . . . . : fe80::347a:e64c:6544:effcx18
    IPv4 Address. . . . . . . . . . . : 192.168.21.3
    Subnet Mask . . . . . . . . . . . : 255.255.255.0
    Default Gateway . . . . . . . . . :
```

F I G U R E 7.7 `ipconfig` IPv6

completely. IPv6 is an IP addressing scheme designed to provide a virtually unlimited number of IP addresses. Among the command-line tools utilized when troubleshooting network problems are ping, ipconfig, traceroute, and arp. DHCP is used to automate the process of assigning IP configurations to computers.

ADDITIONAL EXERCISES

1. Identify whether each of the following IP addresses can be assigned to a computer.

   A. 192.168.5.6

   B. 10.1.0.1

   C. 172.20.0.0

   D. 192.168.200.255

   E. 1.1.1.1

   F. 10.0.0.0

   G. 172.10.255.255

   H. 172.61.9.8

   I. 16.16.55.9

   J. 127.6.1.3

2. Execute the ipconfig command on your computer and make note of your IPv6 address. Look at the first section and determine what type of unicast address that it is.

3. Execute the following command and identify what you just pinged.

   ```
   ping ::1
   ```

REVIEW QUESTIONS

1. Which of the following is *not* a benefit of network segmentation?

   A. Better performance   **C.** Requires less hardware

   B. Security   **D.** Network expansion

2. True or False: With larger LANs unsegmented by routers, network problems are easier to isolate.

3. Which of the following is a Class B address?

   A. 192.168.5.5   **C.** 126.65.5.6

   B. 15.6.5.1   **D.** 172.69.5.1

(Continues)

THE ESSENTIALS AND BEYOND *(Continued)*

4. What are the most significant 3 bits of a Class C address?

   A. 000   **C.** 010

   B. 001   **D.** 110

5. Which of these are loopback addresses?

   A. 127.1.1.1   **D.** ::1

   B. 127.0.0.0   **E.** 0.0.0.0

   C. 127.0.0.1

6. What is the network portion of 192.168.5.6?

   A. 192   **C.** 192.168.5

   B. 192.168   **D.** 192.168.5.6

7. Which of the following is *not* a private IP address range?

   A. 10.0.0.0–10.255.255.255   **C.** 192.168.0.0–192.168.255.255

   B. 168.192.0–172.31.0.0   **D.** 172.16.0.0–172.31.255.255

8. If you ping the server but can't make an FTP connection, at what layer is the problem *most* likely to be found?

   A. Internet   **C.** Transport

   B. Network Access   **D.** Application

9. Which command displays the arp cache?

   A. `arp -d`   **C.** `arp -a`

   B. `arp -s`   **D.** `arp -b`

10. Which of the following packets is the second packet sent in the DHCP process?

   A. DHCPAck   **C.** DHCPOffer

   B. DHCPDiscover   **D.** DHCPRequest

CHAPTER 8

Classless IP Addressing

Chapter 7, "Classful IP Addressing," introduced IP addressing. One important aspect of IP addressing is that for two devices to communicate with one another, the devices must be in the same network. There are two parts of an IP address: the network part and the host part. The network portion of the IP address must match on the two devices for communication to be possible, even if they reside on the same physical segment.

Much of what was discussed in Chapter 7 is characteristic of *classful* networking. This was the original design of IPv4 networking. In classful networking, there are three classes of IP addresses that may be assigned to individual devices. The size of the network in which a computer resides is a function of the address class used for the network. Computers determine the network class from a second configuration value called the *subnet mask*.

In this chapter, you'll review the limitations of the classful networking design and discuss the benefits of departing from the restrictions of using the three default classes. Specifically, this chapter covers the following topics:

▶ **Understanding the limitations of classful networking**

▶ **Understanding the benefits of subnetting**

▶ **Describing the components of CIDR**

Understanding the Limitations of Classful Networking

When IPv4 addressing was designed in the 1970s, it was based on assumptions about the use of the network for which it was designed. These assumptions grossly underestimated the number of organizations to be connected, the number of end systems per organization, and the total number of end systems on the network. None of the designers could have foreseen the eventual growth of the Internet to its size in the 1980s, not to mention what it is today!

The design flaws resulted in three main issues:

▶ Exhaustion of the Class B network address space

▶ Unmanageable routing tables

▶ Exhaustion of the 32-bit IPv4 address space

Two of these flaws were addressed by the introduction of Classless Inter-Domain Routing (CIDR). The third was partially addressed but was not fully addressed until the development of IPv6, which was discussed in Chapter 7.

Exhaustion of the Class B Network Address Space

In the early days of the Internet, blocks of IP addresses were assigned by the Network Information Center (NIC). Only three sizes of network blocks were available (A, B, and C), and none of these was an appropriate size for a mid-sized organization. Class C, with a maximum of 254 host addresses, was too small. Class B, which allows up to 65,534 host addresses, was too large for most organizations but was the best fit available.

This not only resulted in the overuse of the Class B space, but also resulted in many wasted IP addresses in most cases. As an illustration, consider a company that requires 56,000 IP addresses. If the company was issued a Class B set, such as 175.60.0.0, it would be issued 65,534 host addresses, resulting in almost 10,000 wasted IP addresses!

CIDR, developed to address this problem, envisioned a system in which a network block such as 175.60.0.0 could be further subdivided and smaller pieces could be issued to stop the waste. Later in this chapter, you will learn how to manipulate the subnet mask to accomplish this network division, which is called *subnetting*.

Unmanageable Routing Tables

When a router reads a routing table, it will read the entire table, looking for the closest match to the network of which the destination address is a member. The larger the routing table, the longer it takes the router to read it, and the slower the routing process.

Any design change that can make the routing tables smaller is beneficial, and another design feature of CIDR was the introduction of route aggregation, or summarization. Route summarization may be seen as the opposite of

Parsing a table or file means the router reads the table from top to bottom until the router finds a match.

subnetting. Its details will not be clear until after the coverage of subnetting, but perhaps an analogy may give you a broad understanding of both concepts.

Consider a mother who has a pie that has been sliced into three slices: one that is very large, another that is about medium in size, and one that is very small. She has five children to feed, and they are ages 3, 7, 14, 16, and 18. Not only does she not have enough slices, but she has slices that are too large and too small. If she had the ability to slice the pie at her discretion, she could give each child the correct size slice and do so with no waste. This is what *classless subnetting* allows.

Now consider the same mother and the same pie. She has sliced the pie into 10 pieces of varying sizes but has not yet distributed them. Her husband, who is going to the store, inquires, "How much pie do we have right now?" After some work with paper and pencil, she hands him a list of each slice and its exact size. He looks at it and says, "Why didn't you just tell me we have one pie?" This is what *route summarization* allows.

Exhaustion of the 32-Bit IPv4 Address Space

As you learned in Chapter 7, the ultimate solution to the exhaustion of the 32-bit IPv4 address space is IPv6, but CIDR also introduced private IP addresses. When organizations started using these addresses within the organizational LANs and began to use Network Address Translation (NAT) servers, it helped to delay the exhaustion. When an organization with 5,000 computers requiring Internet access can be represented by a single public IP address, it surely helps save public IP addresses!

NAT introduces some problems in that certain applications and services will not operate through a NAT server. IPsec for a time would not function through NAT (although that problem has been addressed). The ultimate solution for address exhaustion is a global switch to IPv6.

Understanding the Benefits of Subnetting

Although certainly benefits have been derived on the Internet from CIDR and subnetting, there are solid reasons to deploy subnetting and CIDR in the design of LANs as well. When it is included in network design, subnetting can improve both performance and security. This section covers the problems presented by network congestion and the benefits possible with subnetting. The ways that network segmentation at the Internet layer can enhance security are also discussed.

Public IP addresses have been issued by the Internet authorities and are unique on the Internet. Private IP addresses cannot be routed to the Internet and are not unique.

◀

◀

IP Security (IPsec) is a network security protocol designed to protect the integrity and confidentiality of data while it is en route across an untrusted network.

Identifying Sources of Network Congestion

Network congestion occurs when the amount of traffic in the network exceeds the abilities of the physical infrastructure. In the same way that too many cars on a highway slow traffic to a crawl, too much traffic in the network dramatically decreases the data throughput. This occurs for two main reasons::

Collisions   Ethernet networks use Carrier Sense Multiple Access/Collision Detection (CSMA/CD) to arbitrate access to the network. By each host checking the wire for activity prior to transmission, the overwhelming majority of collisions are avoided. However, many are not, and thus the inclusion of the collision detection and retransmission mechanism. As you learned in Chapter 5, "Physical and Logical Topologies," collisions cause all hosts to stop transmitting while both hosts involved in the collision retransmit their packets. When this occurs frequently, the throughput of the network falls. When the number of computers in the network increases, the chance of collisions occurring increases as well.

Broadcast Traffic   Broadcast traffic is inevitable. It occurs when computers are attempting to locate a DHCP server and when IP addresses are being resolved to MAC addresses. When this traffic occurs, *all* hosts must process it, and it competes with unicast traffic for network time on the wire. As the number of computers increases, the amount and the frequency of broadcast traffic also increases. This increased broadcast traffic also decreases the effective throughput of the network.

When network congestion occurs, two options exist to address it. One is to upgrade the network infrastructure. This means upgrading all of the network cards and changing out all of the network cable so that both items support higher speeds. For example, you could install 10 GB network cards and change all the cabling to support 10 GB. However, this is an expensive option that will yield only a small improvement.

A better option is to break the larger network into a number of smaller *subnets*. This helps in the following ways:

- ▶ Reduces the number of computers per subnet, thereby lowering the chances of collisions

- ▶ Reduces the amount of broadcast traffic produced

This approach has the added benefit of isolating network problems to a smaller area, which aids troubleshooting.

Deploying Subnetting as a Segmentation Tool

Network segmentation implemented at the Internet layer (subnetting) can also be used to organize computers for security reasons. You already know that when computers are in different subnets, by definition they cannot communicate with one another. So simply placing two of four computers in a network in one subnet and the other two computers in a different subnet, without using routers, would effectively keep them from communicating, as shown in Figure 8.1.

But by organizing these two sets of computers by subnet and linking the subnets with a router, you not only can enable them to communicate, but can now deny the communication as well, as shown in Figure 8.2.

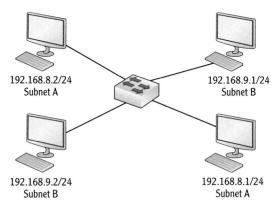

FIGURE 8.1 Subnets with no router

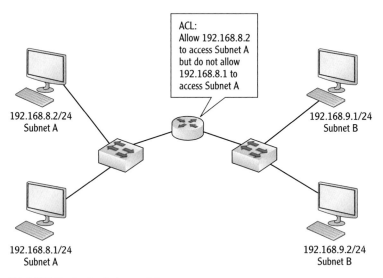

FIGURE 8.2 Subnet with router

Moreover, you can be selective about this process and allow some of the computers to communicate with the remote subnet while denying others. In this respect, segmentation at the Internet layer in combination with the use of routers and access control lists (ACLs) adds a whole new level of sophistication to the process of securing the network.

ACLs are used to control traffic that goes through a router. You will learn more about how they work in Chapter 13, "Configuring Routers."

Describing the Components of CIDR

In Chapter 7, you learned that the number of bits in the network portion of the subnet mask determines the number of possible networks, and that the number of host bits determines the number of hosts on those subnets. You also learned the formula to calculate these values given the numbers of bits. However, in classful subnetting, with only the three default subnet masks available, you can calculate those values as many times as you like and you always get the following answers:

Network Class	Number of Networks	Number of Hosts
Class A	256	16,777,214
Class B	65,536	65,534
Class C	16,777,216	254

In this section, you will learn how to create subnet masks that will yield the number of networks you need or the number of hosts you need on each network. You'll also be introduced to Variable-Length Subnet Masking (VLSM) and the additional benefits that can be derived by including this concept in the network design.

Introducing Classless Subnetting

The network or subnet that a computer resides in is a function of the interaction of two values: the IP address and the subnet mask. In Chapter 7, you learned that the three default subnet masks in dotted decimal notation are as follows:

Class A—255.0.0.0

Class B—255.255.0.0

Class C—255.255.255.0

These classes are shown in dotted decimal format. However, when we start manipulating subnet masks within octets or bytes, we must view and work with them at the bit level, which are shown as four binary octets.

OCTETS AND BYTES

In classful subnetting, the subnet boundaries occur between bytes, or on the byte boundaries. Subnetting within an octet means that the dividing line between the subnet portion and the host portion no longer occurs on a byte boundary. Instead, the dividing line is between bits within a byte, such as 11100000.

When viewed at the bit level, the three masks are as follows:

Class A—11111111.00000000.00000000.00000000

Class B—11111111.11111111.00000000.00000000

Class C—11111111.11111111.11111111.00000000

The network portion is where the bits are turned on (1s), and the host portion is where the bits are turned off (0). When a default network is subnetted, the routers and the devices *must* have some way to differentiate or identify each subnet. This is accomplished by creating a third part of the subnet mask called the *subnet portion*. After this is done, conceptually the subnet mask and the IP address that goes with it will now have three parts, as shown here:

Network portion   Subnet portion   Host portion

As an example, let's assume for moment that we subnetted a network into eight subnets. The network portion identifies the classful network from which the subnet was derived, the subnet portion identifies the specific subnet out of the eight possible subnets, and the host portion identifies the possible host addresses within that subnet.

A subnet mask has 32 bits, and we can neither add nor subtract from that number. This means that any bits we use for subnet identification purposes must come from existing bits. They cannot come from the network portion, because that portion identities the class network. Therefore, they will come from the host portion. We refer to this process as *borrowing* bits (which is an odd term to use, because we never give them back!).

Steps to designing and implementing CIDR

To apply the principles of CIDR and subnetting to correctly size each network and maximize the use of the IP address space, follow these steps:

Calculating the Mask for a Required Number of Subnets   The number of bits that are borrowed depends on the number of subnets required. As you may remember from Chapter 7, the number of networks that are possible for Class A, B, and C networks are a function of the number of bits in the network portion (1s) of the mask. You'll also remember that the number of hosts possible in each network is a function of the number of bits in the host portion of the mask (the 0s). Then you probably won't be surprised to learn that the number of subnets is a function of the number of bits in the *subnet portion* (additional 1s added to the network portion).

Consider this example: We have a Class C network that we would like to subnet for better performance. The network ID is 192.168.5.0 (with the network portion comprising the first three octets), and the subnet mask is 255.255.255.0 (with each octet holding a value of 255, indicating a part of the address that is the network portion), as shown here:

192.168.5.0

255.255.255.0

First, let's look at the subnet mask in binary because we already know we need to work with it on the bit level:

11111111.11111111.11111111.00000000

We have 24 bits in the network portion and 8 bits in the host portion. So how many bits should we borrow if we want 16 subnets? The same formula to calculate the number of networks (2^n = number of networks) can also be used to calculate the number of bits to borrow to get a required number of subnets.

What Do I Plug In ⁿ Again?

If you are calculating the mask for a required number of subnets, you put in the number of bits you are borrowing or the subnet bits. If you are calculating the mask for a required number of hosts, you put in the number of host bits that will remain at the end of the mask.

When used for this purpose, the formula becomes 2^n = number of subnets, with *n* being the number of bits borrowed. So if we plug the number of subnets that we need (16) into the formula, we get $2^n = 16$. By counting up in powers of 2 until we get to 16 (2, 4, 8, 16), we discover that $2^4 = 16$.

COUNTING IN POWERS OF 2: IT'S OK TO USE YOUR FINGERS!

Counting up in powers of 2 is a skill you should work to become comfortable doing. Many even count on their fingers, starting with 2 as the first finger, then 4 for the second, and so on. Just keep doubling the number as you add a finger. When you arrive at the number of networks or the number of hosts you are trying to supply, the number of fingers will tell you the number of bits to add to the mask (in the case of networks) or the number of bits to leave as zeros at the end of the mask (in the case of hosts).

So borrowing 4 bits will yield the desired number of subnets. Once we know the number of bits required, these bits are added to the 24 bits that are already there to identify the Class C network we started with. After we do that, the mask looks like this in binary:

11111111.11111111.11111111.11110000

If we convert this to dotted decimal, the new mask that divides the 192.168.5.0 network into 16 subnets is as follows:

255.255.255.240

The 240 in the last octet is simply the value of that octet in binary (11110000), converted to decimal. If we also wanted to know the number of computers that could be on each one of those 16 subnets, we could determine that in the same fashion we did in Chapter 7. That is, plug the number of host bits left in the mask (four 0s) into the formula for hosts ($2^n - 2$ = number of hosts) and we would find that $2^4 - 2 = 14$. So each network would have 14 hosts. There are actually 16 IP addresses in each subnet, but remember that two of these addresses (network ID and broadcast address) cannot be assigned to any hosts.

CIDR Notation: It's Nothing New!

One of the vexing issues that have faced network designers and engineers is fitting all the IP address and subnet masks onto a network diagram. CIDR also introduced a new way of notating the IP address and subnet mask. Instead of writing out both values like this

192.168.5.5

255.255.255.0

CIDR notation allows you to write the IP address and then a forward slash followed by a number that represents the number of bits in the subnet mask. In the case of the preceding IP address, because there are 24 bits in the subnet mask of 255.255.255.0, we could write this address as 192.168.5.5/24.

Calculating the Mask for a Required Number of Hosts   In some cases, the design requirement is in terms of subnet size rather than number of subnets. In this example, we have a Class B network that we would like to subnet in such a way that each subnet has at least 35 IP addresses In the example network, the /16 indicates that there are 16 bits in the subnet mask:

172.18.0.0/16

The mask as it now stands is as follows:

11111111.11111111.00000000.00000000

If we need each subnet to have at least 35 IP addresses, we will have to leave enough 0s, or host bits, on the end of the mask to yield at least 35 when plugged into the formula $2^n - 2$ = number of hosts. So if we plug in the required number, we get this:

$2^n - 2$ = at least 35

If we count up in powers of 2 until we reach a number that is greater than 35 after subtracting 2, that will be the number of host bits to leave at the end of the mask. Once we know that, we can simply turn on all other bits (1s) and we have our mask. By counting up in powers of 2 (2, 4, 8, 16, 32, 64), we find that $2^6 - 2$ = 62. That means there needs to be 6 host bits on the end of the mask:

11111111.11111111.11111111.11000000

When we convert that to dotted decimal format, the subnet mask used with a class B address such as 172.18.0.0 to yield at least 35 IP addresses per subnet would be 255.255.255.192 (11000000 = 192).

Determining the Boundaries of Each Subnet   When it comes time for actually placing the IP addresses on the devices either manually or by creating a scope in DHCP, you must know where each subnet begins and ends and which IP addresses cannot be used (that is, which addresses in each subnet are the network ID and the broadcast address).

Creating a scope in DHCP is discussed in Chapter 7.

To illustrate this procedure, let's work with an example that yields a small number of subnets. (The concepts are the same when you need to yield thousands of subnets.) In this example, let's suppose that your boss has already determined the subnet mask. He has given you the following Class C network and subnet mask:

192.168.6.0
255.255.255.128

First, can you determine how many subnets this will give you? You can use the same formulas to determine that. You have a Class C network, which tells you that the default mask was 255.255.255.0, and you can see that all that has been added is 128 in the last octet. So how many bits were "borrowed" to make this 128 in decimal? Well, think about the value of each bit in the 8-bit pattern for 128 as shown here:

128	64	32	16	8	4	2	1
1	0	0	0	0	0	0	0

As you can see, it took only one "borrowed" bit to make 128. If we plug that into our formula for the number of networks (2^n = number of networks), we get 2^1 = number of networks. Because any number to the first power is itself, that means we will get two subnets if we use the 255.255.255.128 mask with a Class C network such as 192.168.6.0. So where do these two networks begin and end, and which addresses are off limits?

Each subnet begins with its network ID and ends with its broadcast address, and all IP addresses in between the two are in the same subnet and are legitimate to assign to hosts. Therefore, if you find your network IDs and your broadcast addresses, the IP addresses between the two are in the same subnet. The following sections will show how this is done.

Finding Your Network IDs   The first network ID will always be the classful network you are subnetting. In this case, the first network ID is 192.168.6.0. To determine the next network ID, you must identify a value that is sometimes called a *block size* (Cisco terminology) and sometimes called an *interval* (Microsoft terminology). This value is always the value of the last bit in the mask. In this case, that value is 128.

WARNING: DON'T ADD BIT VALUES TOGETHER TO DETERMINE THE INTERVAL!

When you are determining the value of the interval (or block size), it will be equal to the value of the single far-right bit.

You do *not* add together the entire bit values in the octet. For example, consider this mask in binary:

11111111.11111111.11100000.00000000

The far-right bit in the example 11100000 is the third bit from the left and is worth 32:

128	64	**32**	16	8	4	2	1
1	1	**1**	0	0	0	0	0

You do *not* add together all of the bit values in the octet (192 + 64 + 32 = 224).

Increment the number in the octet where you stopped borrowing bits, and that will give you the next network ID. In this case, that means you are incrementing from 192.168.6.0 upward by the value of 128, so the other network ID is 192.168.6.128. We now have our two network IDs:

> 192.168.6.0
>
> 192.168.6.128

MAKE SURE YOU INCREMENT YOUR INTERVAL IN THE CORRECT OCTET!

The octet in which you increment the interval is *not* always the first octet where you borrowed bits. Consider the following network:

> 172.16.0.0/27

With a 27-bit mask, it means the mask in binary is as follows:

> 11111111.11111111.11111111.11100000000

Therefore, the octet where you stopped borrowing was not the third octet but the fourth octet. So you increment the interval in that octet to determine the network IDs. In this case, the interval is 32, so the first three network IDS are as follows:

> 172.16.0.0/27
> 172.16.0.32/27
> 172.16.0.64/27

They are *not* these:

> 172.16.0.0/27
> 172.16.32.0/27
> 172.16.64.0/27

Finding Your Broadcast Addresses   Each broadcast address is one number less than the next network ID or the next classful network, whichever comes first. In this case, for the 192.168.6.0 network, the broadcast address (one less than the next network ID or the next classful network, whichever comes first) will be 192.168.6.127 (192.168.6.128 – 1 = 192.168.6.127). For the 192.168.6.128 network, the broadcast address (one less than the next network ID or the next classful network, whichever comes first) will be 192.168.6.255 (192.168.7.0 – 1 = 192.168.6.255).

WHERE DID THAT 255 COME FROM?

It is important that you understand that 1 less than 1.0 is 0.255. Make note of the following consecutive IP addresses:

192.168.6.253
192.168.6.254
192.168.6.255
192.168.7.0

Notice that when you add 1 to 255, it is 256, but in dotted decimal notation there is no 256. That means you increment the next left-hand position by 1 and go back to 0 in the current position, just as you would if you were adding 1 to 19 to get 20.

Therefore, when your next network ID is *x.x.x*.0, the broadcast address will be *x.x.x* − 1.255. For example, if the next network ID is 192.168.55.0, the broadcast address for the previous network will be 192.168.54.255.

Identifying the IP addresses in the subnet   Now that we know the two network IDs and broadcast addresses, we have the following ranges of IP addresses:

Network 192.168.6.0 is from 192.168.6.1 to 192.168.6.126.

Network 192.168.6.128 is from 192.168.6.129 to 192.168.6.254.

IP Addresses between the two are in the same subnet.

SO WHY IS THIS ALL SO IMPORTANT?

One of the skills you need is the ability to recognize when two IP addresses are *not* in the same subnet. Sometimes it's obvious, as with these two addresses:

10.6.5.4/8 and 192.158.6.3/24

But sometimes the *only* way you can tell is by performing the operations we just discussed. Take a look at these two addresses:

192.168.6.126/25 and 192.168.6.129/25

These IP addresses are only three addresses apart. Wouldn't you be tempted to say they are in the same network? Well, these two addresses come from

(Continues)

So Why Is This All So Important? *(Continued)*

the network we just finished subnetting into two networks. The two ranges that we got were as follows:

Network 192.168.6.0 is from 192.168.6.1 to 192.168.6.126.

Network 192.168.6.128 is from 192.168.6.129 to 192.168.6.254.

Notice that one address is in the first subnet, and the other is in the second. So, yes, this is all very important if you were trying to determine why these two computers could not ping one another!

Understanding VLSM

Variable-Length Subnet Masking (VLSM) is the use of subnet masks of varying lengths in the network design. It is this concept that really allows you to leverage the power of "right sizing" each subnet with as little waste of IP addresses as possible. In its simplest form, as shown in Figure 8.3, VLSM allows each interface on the router to host a network with a different mask length. In this example, a Class A, Class B, and Class C network are located on interfaces E0, E2, and E1, respectively.

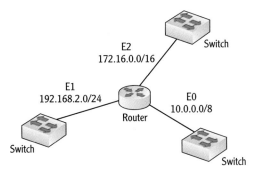

FIGURE 8.3 Simple VLSM

However, to really save addresses, you must use subnet masks that are designed to meet the size needs of each interface without wasting addresses. Consider the following design requirements presented to you by your boss in Figure 8.4. Your job is to determine the network IDs and subnet masks for each interface that would waste the fewest addresses. Moreover, you must use networks derived from the 172.16.0.0/16 network.

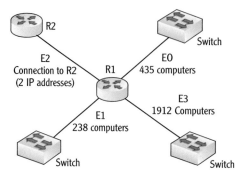

FIGURE 8.4 Network design

First, determine the mask for each interface that when used with the 172.16.0.0 network ID provides the smallest subnet possible to meet the requirement of each connection:

E0 435 Computers   You need $2^n - 2$ = at least 435, so count up in powers of 2 until you meet or exceed 435 (2, 4, 8, 16, 32, 64, 128, 256, 512). That's 9 bits. Leave nine 0s on the end of the mask, turn all other bits on, and you have 255.255.254.0 (or /23).

E1 238 Computers   You need $2^n - 2$ = at least 238, so count up in powers of 2 until you meet or exceed 238 (2, 4, 8, 16, 32, 64, 128, 256). That's 8 bits. Leave eight 0s on the end of the mask, turn all other bits on, and you have 255.255.255.0 (or /24).

E2 Connection to R2 (Two IP Addresses)   First, realize that on a point-to-point connection to another router, you have a network where you need only two IP addresses. You need $2^n - 2$ = at least 2, so count up in powers of 2 until you meet or exceed 2 (2, 4). That's 2 bits. Leave two 0s on the end of the mask, turn all other bits on, and you have 255.255.255.252 (or /30).

WHY DIDN'T WE STOP AT 1 BIT?

We need two addresses for the connection to R2. The reason we did not stop at 1 bit even though we have two addresses is that $2^1 - 2 = 0$. The network would have two addresses, but they would be the network ID and the broadcast address, and there would be no addresses left for the interfaces on the routers!

E3 1,912 Computers You need $2^n - 2 =$ at least 1,912, so count up in powers of 2 until you meet or exceed 1,912 (2, 4, 8, 16, 32, 64, 128, 256, 512, 1024, 2048). That's 11 bits. Leave 11 0s on the end of the mask, turn all other bits on, and you have 255.255.248.0 (or /21).

Now we know the masks required for each interface. For each of those networks, we could pick from a number of different IP address ranges, because when you apply those masks, multiple networks of that size will be possible. The number of choices possible for each of the masks we calculated to meet the requirements are as follows:

Network ID and Mask	Number of Networks	Bits Borrowed	Calculating Bits Borrowed	Calculating Number of Networks
172.16.0.0/23	128 networks	7	23 − 16 = 7	$2^7 = 128$
172.16.0.0/24	256 networks	8	24 − 16 = 8	$2^8 = 256$
172.16.0.0/30	32,768 networks	15	30 − 16 = 15	$2^{15} = 32,768$
172.16.0.0/21	32 networks	5	21 − 16 = 5	$2^5 = 32$

So we need four slices of the 172.16.0.0/16 pie. It's best to start with the largest slice and then move to the next largest and so on. The /21 mask provides the fewest number of networks, but they are the largest networks (or slices of the pie). So first let's look at *some* of the possible /21 network IDs.

Let's review this. With a /21 mask against a /16 classful network, we borrowed 5 bits (21 − 16). That means we borrowed into the third octet. Our interval is 8; the value of the far-right bit is shown here in binary:

11111111.11111111.11111000.00000000.

So the first network ID is our starting classful network ID (192.168.0.0), and then we increment by 8 in the third octet, as shown here:

172.16.0.0
172.16.8.0
172.16.16.0

The /21 network IDs are the largest slices because each slice (or network) is capable of $2^{11} - 2$ or 2,047 IP addresses. The other networks, or slices, are smaller (/24 = $2^8 - 2$, or 254 IP addresses; /23 = $2^9 - 2$, or 511 IP addresses, and /30 = $2^2 - 2$, or 2 IP addresses).

This continues on until the last one, which is as follows:

172.16.248.0

Let's use the first one for the E3 network: 172.16.0.0/21.

Now we need a /23 slice. We will start at 172.16.8.0 because we have already used all the addresses up to that point for E3. Because we are using a /23 instead of a /21, our interval will not be 8. It will be 2, the value of the far-right bit, as shown here:

11111111.11111111.11111110.00000000.

We still have borrowed into the third octet, however, so that will be where we increment.

If we look at some of the /23 network IDs starting from 172.16.8.0 on, we get this:

172.16.8.0
172.16.10.0

And so on, until the last one, which is this:

172.16.254.0

Let's use the first one for the E0 network: 172.16.8.0/23.

Now we need a /24 slice. We will start at 172.16.10.0 because we have already used all the addressees up to that point for E3 and E0. Because we are using a /24 instead of a /23, our interval will not be 2. It will be 1, the value of the far-right bit, as shown here:

11111111.11111111.11111111.00000000.

We still have borrowed into the third octet, however, so that will be where we increment.

If we look at some of the /24 network IDs starting from 172.16.10.0 on, we get these:

172.16.10.0
172.16.11.0

And so on, until the last one, which is this:

172.16.255.0

Let's use the first one for the E1 network: 172.16.10.0/24.

Finally, we need a /30 slice. We will start at 172.16.11.0 because we have already used all the addresses up to that point for E3, E0, and E1. Because we are using a /30 instead of a /24, our interval will not be 1. It will be 4, the value of the far-right bit, as shown here:

11111111.11111111.11111111.11111100.

We still have now borrowed into the *fourth* octet, so that will be where we increment.

If we look at some of the /30 network IDs starting from 172.16.11.0 on, we get these:

172.16.11.0.0
172.16.11.0.4

And so on, until the last one, which is this:

172.16.255.252

Let's use the first one for the E2 network: 172.16.11.0/30.

By choosing the slices in the order of largest to smallest and keeping them as numerically close as possible, we left the largest possible pieces of the 172.16.0.0/16 network for future expansion. As a matter of fact, we used only the 172.16.0.0/21 network and a part of the 172.16.8.0/21 network! Now we can label the diagram with the address ranges as shown in Figure 8.5.

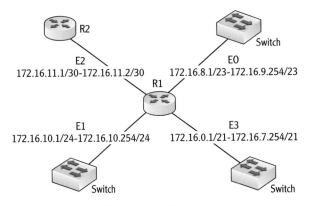

FIGURE 8.5 Network solution

Summarization

Now we can talk about *summarization*. Look at Figure 8.5. When router R1 advertises (informs) R2 about the routes in its routing table, the route advertisement could include all of the networks we just created. If that were the case, R2's routing table would include these networks:

> 172.16.0.0/21
> 172.16.8.0/23
> 172.16.10.0/24
> 172.16.11.0/30

These networks end in 0 because they started at the beginning of a parent subnet. If we select the second /30 network in the parent 172.16.11.0 subnet, the network ID for the network between R1 and R2 would be 172.16.11.4/30.

As you learned earlier in the "Unmanageable Routing Tables" section, anything we can do to reduce the number of routes in a routing table will enable the router to read the routing table faster and make faster routing decisions. We can use network summarization to do this. Because we subnetted the 172.16.0.0/16 network to begin with, we could configure R1 to advertise the 172.16.0.0/16 network to R1, and then any packets destined for *any* subnet of 172.16.0.0/16 would be sent to R1. Then R1 could make the routing decision based on its more specific knowledge of the subnets.

THE ESSENTIALS AND BEYOND

Classless Inter-Domain Routing (CIDR) addresses the exhaustion of the 32-bit IPv4 address space by introducing flexibility to network sizing and by reducing the number of public IP addresses required by organizations. CIDR also reduces the size of unmanageable routing tables by using summarization. When subnetting is included in a network's design, it can improve both performance and security. CIDR is implemented by manipulating the subnet mask. Variable-Length Subnet Masking (VLSM) is the use of subnet masks of varying lengths in the network design. Summarization is the aggregation of subnets to the classful network of which they were commonly derived and is used in router advertisements to reduce the number of networks in the routing table, thereby improving router performance.

ADDITIONAL EXERCISES

1. Using Figure 8.6 and the network ID of 158.59.0.0/16, determine the mask and network ID for each interface that provides the smallest subnet possible to meet the requirement of each connection. Then list the range of addresses for each network.

(Continues)

THE ESSENTIALS AND BEYOND (Continued)

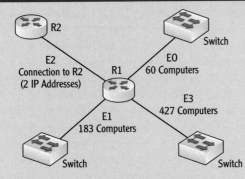

FIGURE 8.6 VLSM exercise

2. For each of the following IP addresses, identify the network ID of the network in which it lies.

   A. 10.99.57.15/24

   B. 192.168.6.9/30

   C. 17.69.48.3/15

   D. 56.57.58.60/22

   E. 172.156.30.14/27

REVIEW QUESTIONS

1. Which of the following is *not* an issue resulting from the design flaws of classful IP addressing?

   A. Inefficient use of the of the Class C network address space

   B. Exhaustion of the 32-bit IPv4 address space

   C. Unmanageable routing tables

   D. Exhaustion of the Class B network address space

2. Which of the following issues resulting from the design flaws of classful IP addressing was only partially addressed by CIDR?

   A. Inefficient use of the of the Class C network address space

   B. Exhaustion of the 32-bit IPv4 address space

   C. Unmanageable routing tables

   D. Exhaustion of the Class B network address space

3. In which IP address class was the wasted address problem most severe in classful IP addressing?

   A. Class A

   B. Class B

   C. Class C

   D. Class D

(Continues)

THE ESSENTIALS AND BEYOND (Continued)

4. Which design feature of CIDR helps to make routing tables more manageable?

    A. Classless subnetting   **C.** Network summarization

    B. NAT   **D.** Network pruning

5. Which of the following issues resulting from the design flaws of classful IP addressing are addressed by NAT?

    A. Inefficient use of the Class C network address space   **C.** Unmanageable routing tables

    B. Exhaustion of the 32-bit IPv4 address space   **D.** Exhaustion of the Class B network address space

6. How does breaking a larger network into a number of smaller subnets increase performance?

    A. Reduces the number of computers per subnet, thereby lowering the chances of collisions   **C.** Increases the amount of broadcast traffic produced

    B. Increases the number of computers per subnet, thereby reducing the chances of collisions   **D.** Increases the number of computers per subnet, thereby reducing the broadcast traffic

7. Which of the following subnet masks is equivalent to /20?

    A. 255.255.224.0   **C.** 255.255.240.0

    B. 255.192.0.0   **D.** 255.255.255.128

8. Which mask would yield at least 39 subnets?

    A. 172.16.0.0/17   **C.** 172.16.0.0/19

    B. 172.16.0.0/18   **D.** 172.16.0.0/22

9. Which mask would create subnets large enough for 78 hosts without wasting IP addresses?

    A. 192.168.5.0/25   **C.** 192.168.5.0/28

    B. 192.168.5.0/27   **D.** 192.168.5.0/29

10. What is the range of IP addresses for the network 172.16.8.0/23?

    A. 172.16.8.1/23– 172.16.8.254/23   **C.** 172.168.8.1/23– 172.168.11.254/23

    B. 172.16.8.1/23– 172.168.9.254/23   **D.** 172.168.0.1/23– 172.168.31.254/23

Media

One of the first things done when setting up a network of routers, switches, and host devices is the creation of connections between the devices. This connection is done via *media*. The media can be either bounded (cables) or unbounded (wireless).

When data is transmitted across media, operations are occurring at the Network Interface layer. This layer includes both the physical implementation (cable type, wireless frequency, connectors, and so on) and the communication method employed by the media (Ethernet, 802.11, Frame Relay, PPP).

This chapter covers all aspects of media with a particular emphasis on cabling, as bounded media is usually used to connect infrastructure devices such as switches and routers. Moreover, the management of infrastructure devices is typically done via wire, and not wirelessly in accordance with security best practices.

Specifically, this chapter covers the following topics:

▶ **Selecting the proper media type**

▶ **Understanding cabling**

▶ **Describing wireless standards**

Selecting the Proper Media Type

When choosing a media type, the main characteristics to consider are as follows:

> ▶ Bandwidth
>
> ▶ Security
>
> ▶ Convenience
>
> ▶ Cost

> **Cisco defines three layers (access, distribution, and core) of devices in the enterprise network. This model is discussed in more detail at the end of Chapter 10, "Network Devices."**
>
> ▶

In the past, a trade-off existed between convenience/cost and bandwidth/security. If you wanted low cost and convenience, you could deploy wireless and give up security and bandwidth. If you needed security and bandwidth, you sacrificed convenience and cost. That largely remains true, but wireless has made huge strides in both security and bandwidth. It may never be fast enough or secure enough for a network backbone, but it could serve a larger role at the distribution layer at some point.

In this section, the media types are compared and contrasted with regard to these characteristics. Each media type can have a useful role in the enterprise. By taking advantage of the unique strengths of each in the network design, the characteristics can be delivered in the appropriate mix for every scenario.

Bandwidth

You will learn more about 802.11n in the section "Understanding 802.11 Amendments" later in this chapter.

Wired media delivers much more bandwidth at this time than any type of wireless. Wireless rates have gone from 54 Mbps to 150 Mbps using 802.11n, which is certainly an impressive gain.

But wired media, which can be commonly found running at 100 Mbps and 1 Gbps in the enterprise, will probably be operating in data centers at between 40 and 100 Gbps in the next five years. The IEEE 802.3ba Task Force is developing this gear and cabling as we speak.

The demand for this amount of bandwidth is coming from the types of applications that run in the enterprise and the need to continue the migration of LANs from 100 Mbps to 1 Gbps to the desktop. These megaspeeds will be occurring in the data centers and on the backbone, not to the desktops. Nevertheless, 1 Gbps to the desktop is almost 10 times what wireless can currently deliver at its best to the desktop.

Security

The IEEE standard for wireless LANs is called 802.11. You will learn more about it and its amendments in the section "Understanding 802.11 Amendments."

Wired media is considered more secure than wireless because the media is bounded. If you control the physical access to the cabling, you can control access to the transmission, which cannot be done with wireless. With wireless, transmissions can be captured by anyone with a transceiver. With wireless transmission, it must be assumed that privacy does not exist and that any data that is sensitive must be encrypted.

In the early years of 802.11, wireless was avoided because it was thought that it could not be secured.

Rogue access points are access points not under your control or management. You will learn more about them later in this section.

But over time, administrators realized that not only did users demand this service, but a "no wireless policy" became more difficult to enforce as rogue access points began to show up in the network, not placed there by sophisticated hackers but by the users themselves!

Today wireless systems under your control can be secured and monitored with the same level of confidence as wired networks. However, there are still wireless security threats that are unique to its operation. These threats are detailed throughout the rest of this section.

Ease of Data Collection

When data is transmitted wirelessly, there is very little you can do to control who can receive it. You can use semidirectional antennas to shape the direction of the transmission, and you can control the range of transmission. However, someone who has a high-powered antenna connected to a device may still be able to receive your transmission. Moreover, in many cases wireless networks need to be available in all directions from the access point.

Some wireless gear makers have given many the false impression that "hiding" the Service Set Identifier (SSID), or network name, from the signal that is used to announce the presence of the network (called a *beacon frame*) can stop hackers from connecting to the network because when this is done, the hacker must have a wireless profile created specifying the SSID. But the hacker doesn't need to be connected to the network to capture and view the packets.

◄

***Access points* are devices that can transmit and receive data in radio form and can connect to the wired network through a cabled network interface.**

WIRELESS PACKET CAPTURES

You may remember in Chapter 7, "Classful IP Addressing," that you looked at a network capture to identify IP addresses and MAC addresses. That capture was done with a wired capture tool, but wireless tools also exist that capture wireless packets. By viewing these raw data captures, the SSID can be seen in all frame types other than the beacon frame, and MAC addresses of stations that are on the allowed list can be viewed on any frame that these stations transmit.

Moreover, if a hacker is even casually interested in connecting to the network, it is simple to locate the SSID in the transmissions going between the access point and legitimate users. After determining the SSID, the hacker can create a wireless profile to connect to the hidden network.

Even some administrators think that creating a list of allowed MAC addresses and disallowing all other MAC addresses is an effective way to control access. But the hacker can use the same method used to learn the SSID to learn an allowed MAC address. By capturing some packets and then recognizing a successful authentication sequence in the capture, a hacker can learn an allowed MAC address. Then he can change his MAC address to the allowed MAC address and connect.

CHANGING YOUR MAC ADDRESS

At one time, changing your MAC address required advanced knowledge of the Registry on a Windows computer, which is dangerous to edit if you don't know what you are doing. Now it is quite simple to do this in the properties of your network card in Device Manager. On the Advanced tab of the properties of the network card, the desired MAC address can be entered. When you use either method to change your MAC address, you are not actually changing the address on the card, which is burned in; you are simply changing what the computer places in the frames that it sends out.

The bottom line is that even if you have an effective security solution that prevents a hacker from connecting to your wireless network, he can capture your packets. The only way you can make the transmission unavailable to hackers is to also make it unavailable to your users.

Rogue Access Points

A WIPS is a radio-equipped device that scans the wireless area looking for other access points. It can notify you of other APs in the area.

▶

As noted earlier, *rogue access points* are those that you do not control and manage. There are two types: those that are connected to your wired infrastructure and those that are not. The ones that are connected to your wired network present a danger to your wired and wireless network. They may be placed there by your own users without your knowledge or they may purposefully be put there by a hacker to gain access to the wired network. In either case, they allow access to your wired network. Wireless Intrusion Prevention System (WIPS) devices are usually used to locate rogue access points and to alert administrators of their presence.

Rogue access points that are not connected to your wired infrastructure are usually used as a part of a highjacking attack, which is discussed next.

Highjacking Attacks

A *peer-to-peer attack* is one that occurs between two computers that are on the same subnet. The hacker identifies open ports and exploits weak passwords to gain control of the computer.

▶

A *highjacking attack* is one in which the hacker gets one or more of your users' computers connected to his network for the purpose of a peer-to-peer attack.

The attack begins with the introduction of an access point that is under the hacker's control. This access point will be set to use the same network name or SSID as your network, and it will be set to require no authentication (which is called an *open network*).

Moreover, this access point will be set to use a different channel than the access point under your control, as shown in Figure 9.1.

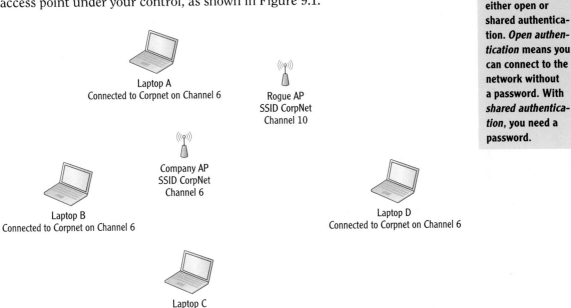

FIGURE 9.1 Rogue access point 1

To understand how the attack works, you must understand how wireless stations (laptops, PDAs, and so on) choose an access point with which to connect. It is done by SSID and not by channel. The hacker will "jam" the channel on which your access point is transmitting. When a station gets disconnected from an access point, it scans the area for another access point with the same SSID. The stations will find the hacker's access point and will connect to it.

Once the station is connected to the hacker's access point, it will receive an IP address from a DHCP server running on the access point, and the user will now be located on the same network as the hacker. At this point, the hacker is free to commence a peer-to-peer attack. The entire process is shown in Figure 9.2.

WLANs can employ either open or shared authentication. *Open authentication* means you can connect to the network without a password. With *shared authentication*, you need a password.

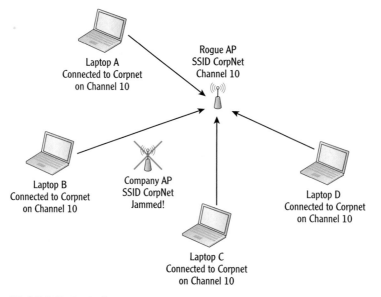

FIGURE 9.2 Rogue access point 2

Wired networks also suffer from security problems, but not of the types listed here, which are unique to the wireless domain. In summation, when security is important, wired networks are more secure.

Convenience

When it comes to convenience, wireless media wins hands down. Users love the ability to roam around and still use the network. Just as wireless media will probably never equal wired media in bandwidth or security, wired networks will never be as convenient for users as wireless networks.

In a time of reliance on mobile devices, plugging into a network will increasingly feel restrictive to users. This may drive continued development of wireless security and bandwidth to satisfy the needs of the mobile worker.

Cost

From a cost standpoint, deploying a wireless LAN is a less-expensive alternative. Deploying wireless results in the following:

► Elimination of cabling costs

► Elimination of access switch costs

► Reduction in installation costs

► Reduction in maintenance costs

In many cases, the hardware and installation costs of a wireless LAN serving the same number of users can be as little as 20 percent of the cost of a wired LAN. Add to that the ability to pick up the network and take it with you—lock, stock, and barrel at any time—and wireless provides a lot of cost savings!

Understanding Cabling

Cabling is inescapable in networking. It is critical to understand cabling to correctly connect Cisco routers, switches, and the hosts they serve. Moreover, you must understand the security, performance, and compatibility issues surrounding the selection of cables.

This section provides the characteristics of various cable types, along with a description of each type and the strengths and weaknesses of each. Finally, the factors that determine the type of cable to use between devices are explained.

Describing Cable Behavior and Characteristics

Cables come in a variety of thicknesses and materials and can operate using either electrical or optical signals. Cables can differ in the following ways:

- ▶ Transmission technology

- ▶ Maximum length

- ▶ Susceptibility to radio frequency interference (RFI)

- ▶ Susceptibility to electromagnetic interference (EMI)

- ▶ Susceptibility to eavesdropping

- ▶ Half-duplex or full-duplex (with twisted-pair cabling)

- ▶ Wiring pattern (with twisted-pair cabling)

- ▶ Cost

In the "Describing Physical Implementations" section, cable types are described in terms of these characteristics, and you will learn the factors that determine the type of cable to use between various device types. But first you need to understand some important behaviors and characteristics of cabling:

Attenuation   When an electrical signal travels down a wire or an optical signal travels down a glass tube as it does in fiber-optic cabling, the signal meets resistance and loses energy. This loss of energy translates to a weakening of the signal. The resistance that a cable introduces to the signal can be measured in ohms. When the signal becomes too weak, the receiving device is unable to successfully tell the difference between an on (1) signal and an off (0) signal. If the receiver misreads even 1 bit, the packet will not pass the frame check sequence (FCS) and will be dropped. Even if somehow it was to pass FCS, the misread bit would result in an entirely different bit pattern, resulting in garbled data.

The weakening of the signal as it travels down the cable is called *attenuation*. All cable types have a maximum cable length. The maximum length describes the longest length of cable that can be run without suffering from attenuation. This is one of the considerations when choosing a cable type. A device called a *repeater* can be introduced to extend a cable run, but if you think about it, it really doesn't alter the limits, it simply ties together two compliant lengths by amplifying the signals.

EMI   Sources of electromagnetic interference are present in most situations. These include electric power transmission lines, electric motors, thermostats, and so forth. The devices we use create this EMI constantly. Anywhere electrical power is being rapidly turned off and on is a potential source. The question is whether it is enough to interfere with the electrical communication in a cable.

If the EMI is very strong, it can corrupt the data in the cable. In these cases, it is advisable to use shielded cable, which adds a layer of protection. You will learn more about shielded cable in the section "Describing Physical Implementations."

RFI   Radio frequency interference (RFI) causes the same problems as EMI; it just comes from a different source. These problems are caused by strong radio signals. The solution is the same as for EMI, which is shielding. RFI is usually more of a problem in a wireless network, as you will learn in the last section of this chapter.

Eavesdropping   Eavesdropping occurs when a hacker physically taps into the cable and connects a device to the cable run. When possible, hiding cabling in walls, under carpets, or in other enclosures reduces the possibility of this happening.

Describing Physical Implementations

There are three main types of cabling used in networking: coaxial, twisted-pair, and fiber-optic. Each type has strengths and weaknesses. Each type can be the appropriate type for a given situation. None is correct in every situation.

Coaxial Cable

Coaxial cabling is familiar to anyone who has had cable TV. It has either a solid copper wire or a stranded copper wire in the center and comes in two forms. The two differ in rigidity, cable length, and cost. Both types are impervious to RFI and EMI because of the braided shielding that is used in them. They use Ethernet at the Network Interface layer, and their physical implementations are referred to as 10Base2 and 10Base5. Both operate at 10 Mbps. Coaxial can be susceptible to eavesdropping, so physical security of the cabling is a consideration. Coaxial cabling is less expensive than fiber cabling, more expensive than unshielded twisted-pair (UTP), and equal to the cost of shielded twisted-pair (STP).

IEEE SHORTHAND

When describing Ethernet cable types, a system called *IEEE shorthand* is used to describe the speed, cable type, and cable size. The first number indicates the speed in Mbps. Then the word *Base* refers to the transmission type, which is baseband (as opposed to broadband). The last number indicates the cable type or cable size. Some examples of the final value are as follows:

2—The smaller of the two coaxial cables

5—The larger of the coaxial cables

T—Twisted-pair

F—Fiber

10Base2 (Thinnet)   Thinnet coaxial is the more flexible of the two implementations because of its use of stranded copper wire, but it will not go as far without attenuation. It also costs less than thicknet. Thinnet can go about 185 meters. The connectors that are used with 10Base2 are called *BNC connectors* and usually connect to each station with a T-connector.

10Base5 (Thicknet)   Thicknet coaxial is the less flexible of the two implementations because of its use of a solid copper wire, but it will go farther without attenuation. It also costs more than thinnet. It can go about 500 meters. 10Base5 transceivers are connected to cable segments with either N-connectors or via a vampire tap. A vampire tap clamps onto the cable, forcing a spike to pierce through the outer shielding to contact the inner conductor while other spikes bite into the outer braided shield.

Both 10Base2 and 10Base5 operate in a bus topology. This means that each end of the network must use a connector that is terminated. It is not very likely that you will encounter any new network implementations using coaxial, but you may find some existing ones.

Twisted-Pair Cable

Twisted-pair cabling is probably the type of cabling that you will encounter most often. It uses four pairs of wires that are twisted or braided inside the outer covering. The twisting mitigates a behavior called *crosstalk* that occurs when the twisting is not in place. Crosstalk is interference of signals on one wire with those on another wire.

There are several types of twisted-pair, and all come in either shielded (STP) or unshielded (UTP) varieties. The shielded versions cost more and should be used only when EMI or RFI is present, as nothing else is gained by using it. Twisted-pair cabling uses an RJ-45 connector, which resembles a telephone connector, only slightly larger. Twisted-pair can be susceptible to eavesdropping, so physical security of the cabling is a consideration. UTP is less expensive than coaxial, while STP is equal to the cost of coaxial. Both types of twisted-pair are less expensive than fiber.

Twisted-pair uses Ethernet at the Network Interface layer and has a maximum cable length of 100 meters. The following are some of the most common types:

> **10BaseT** operates at 10 Mbps.
>
> **100BaseT** operates at 100 Mbps and is the most common.
>
> **1000BaseT** operates at 1 Gbps and will soon be the most common.
>
> **10000BaseT** operates at 10 Gbps and is already becoming common as a connection between infrastructure devices.

Twisted-pair cabling also is capable of two types of transmission: half-duplex and full-duplex, as discussed next.

Half-Duplex Communication   Cables are somewhat like roads. They can operate two ways (in two directions), or they can operate one-way, in one direction, part of the time and one-way, in the other direction, part of the time. *Half-duplex* describes a cable that can send or receive, but cannot do both at the same time.

Half-duplex cables have two pairs of wires but use only one of the pairs and in only one direction at a time. Some characteristics of half-duplex are as follows:

▶ Uses CSMA/CD to detect collisions

▶ Uses one pair of wires and can send or receive at only one time, not both at once

▶ Is the only type of connection that a hub is capable of using

Full-Duplex Communication   Full-duplex transmission uses both pairs of wire, one dedicated to sending and the other to receiving. It uses a point-to-point connection between the two devices. In this type of connection, there is only one device (or network interface) on either end.

Full-duplex transmission requires a network interface card (NIC) on either end of the connection. Therefore, full-duplex is not available on hubs because the hub interfaces don't have the functionality of a NIC.

These are some characteristics of full duplex:

▶ No collisions on the point-to-point link

▶ A dedicated switch port (not hub) required for each full-duplex host

▶ Both ends set to do full-duplex

▶ Better throughput because each end can send and receive at once

Full duplex can be used in any situation where the preceding requirements can be met. This can include the following:

▶ A host to a switch

▶ A switch to a switch

▶ A host to a host (using a crossover cable)

▶ A router to a router

▶ A switch to a router

> ◀
>
> **Point-to-point connections are not always between two separate physical devices. They can be made between any two interfaces that are capable of full-duplex.**

> ◀
>
> **Crossover cables are covered in the section "Choosing the Correct Wiring Standard."**

Fiber-Optic Cable

Fiber-optic cable has a glass tube rather than a wire at its center and uses beams of light created by a laser to transmit bit patterns. Because it is not electrical in nature, it is susceptible to neither EMI nor RFI. It does, however, have a maximum cable length that is partly dependent on its mode (discussed later in this section). From a cost standpoint, fiber-optic is the most costly option of all. Not only is the cable more expensive, but working with fiber cabling requires special skills that increase the cost of installation. It is nearly impossible to eavesdrop on a fiber cable because tapping into the connection requires cutting it, which interrupts the connection. The extra cost does buy the following:

▶ No susceptibility to EMI or RFI

▶ No susceptibility to eavesdropping

▶ Longer cable runs

Fiber-optic cables come in versions that support 100 Mbps, 1 Gbps, and 10 Gbps, as twisted-pair cabling does. The exact length supported depends on the mode used in the cable. Multimode fiber is much less expensive than single mode and uses lower-cost light sources (LEDs and less-expensive lasers), but it cannot be extended as far as single mode. Distances vary depending on speed; 100 Mbps can be extended up to 2 kilometers, while 10 Gbps can be extended only 300 meters. Single mode costs more because of its use of more-expensive lasers, but can go up to 80 km.

The most common fiber-optic cabling has two connector models: straight tip (ST), and small form-factor pluggable (SFP). SFP (the most common) can use either subscriber connectors (SC) or lucent connectors (LC). In Figure 9.3, the SC is on the left and the LC is on the right.

Choosing the Correct Wiring Standard

When making connections to and between network infrastructure devices, the cabling standard must be considered. There are three cable types you will be working with in this regard. They differ in how they are wired and in their application. This section presents their differences and the situations in which they can be used.

Utilizing Straight-Through Cables

Straight-through cables are the most common cables you will use. The wiring pattern connects the send on one end of the cable to the send on the other end.

The exact pattern is illustrated in Figure 9.4. The eight horizontal bars represent the eight wires in the cable. These wires are numbered 1–8. Each wire is individually wrapped in a plastic covering that is a specific color assigned to that wire number. Wires 4, 5, 7, and 8 are not used in 10BaseT and 100BaseT. The other four wires (1, 2, 3, and 6) are used, and they either send (TX for transmit) or receive (RX). You will notice that in this straight-through cable, send goes to send and receive goes to receive. Terminal devices such as computers need to have the signals crossed over so that send goes to receive on the receiving devices. The hub or switch will perform that crossover function internally.

FIGURE 9.3 SFP SC and LC

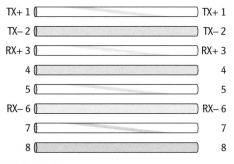

FIGURE 9.4 Straight-through cable

Straight-through cables are used in the following situations:

▶ Computer to hub

▶ Computer to switch

▶ Switch to router

Utilizing Crossover Cables

Crossover cables switch wires 2 and 6, and wires 1 and 3. These cables are used whenever the crossover function is missing, such as when a computer is connected directly to another computer. It is also required when two devices that are performing the crossover function are connected together because they are canceling each other out. The wiring pattern is shown in Figure 9.5.

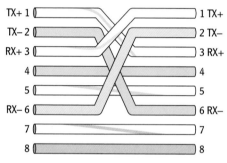

FIGURE 9.5 Crossover cable

Crossover cables are used in the following situations:

▶ Computer to computer

▶ Hub to hub

▶ Switch to switch

▶ Router to router

Utilizing Rolled Cables

Rolled cables are completely different from the other two cables discussed in this section and are used in only one situation: when connecting to a router from a computer for the purpose of managing the router. When this cable is used, it will not be connected to an Ethernet port on the router or switch. It will be connected to the console port. The console port will be labeled as such and

---

In the real world, many devices and interfaces can perform *automatic crossover*, which eliminates the need for crossover cables even between like devices.

In 1000BaseT, all four pairs are used bidirectionally. Because those network adaptors perform automatic crossover, the wiring pattern is not important.

When trying to sort out the crossover/straight cable issues, remember this: to connect like devices, use a crossover cable, and to connect unlike devices, use a straight cable.

will accept an RJ-45 connector but is wired differently than a twisted-pair cable and will be a flat cable. A console port is shown in Figure 9.6.

FIGURE 9.6 Console port

You will learn more about how to use a rolled or console cable in Chapter 13, "Configuring Routers." One end connects to the serial port on a computer and the other to the console port on the router or switch. There are two types; one has a serial connector on one end and an RJ-45 connector on the other, as shown in Figure 9.7.

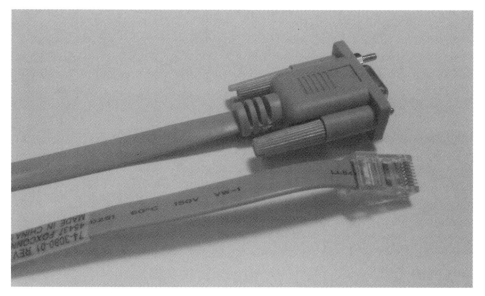

FIGURE 9.7 Console 1

The other type has RJ-45 connectors on both ends (which means you will need a transformer to connect to the serial port on the computer). This type is shown in Figure 9.8.

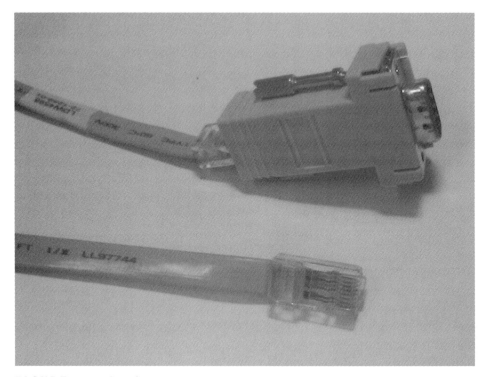

FIGURE 9.8 Console 2

There are eight wires in these cables, and although not all of them are used, the ends switch the wiring completely (that is 1 to 8, 2 to 7, 3 to 6, 4 to 5, 5 to 4, 6 to 3, 7 to 2, and 1 to 8). Typically, these cables are purchased, but if you were creating one, you would wire one end exactly the opposite of the other.

Describing Wireless Standards

Wireless networks operating according to the 802.11 standard are becoming more and more common. You will need to understand not only how to incorporate them into the larger network design but also the components involved, the terminology used, and the operation of the contention mechanism that is used. This section explains all of those topics.

Identifying Standards Bodies

Several organizations have an impact on the wireless world. Some of the organizations create regulations that must be followed, while others simply create standards that are voluntary. The following are the main bodies in the United States:

Institute of Electrical and Electronics Engineers (IEEE)   The IEEE is a professional association dedicated to advancing technological innovation and excellence. A part of what it does is to create standards for networking. The IEEE created the standards you learned about in Chapter 5, "Physical and Logical Topologies," for Ethernet (802.3) and Token Ring (802.5). It created the original 802.11 standard and has since amended the standard a number of times to account for technological advances. These standards are entirely voluntary but are usually followed by the major manufacturers to ensure interoperability with other equipment.

Federal Communications Commission (FCC)   Whereas the standards created by the IEEE are voluntary, the regulations created and enforced by the FCC are not. This organization controls the use of the radio spectrum. Some parts of this spectrum are licensed, and some parts are not. The range of the spectrum that is used by 802.11 is unlicensed.

Wi-Fi Alliance   The Wi-Fi Alliance is an industry group that encourages cooperation and standardization among its members. One of its larger contributions was the introduction of a security solution called Wi-Fi Protected Access (WPA), which addressed security weaknesses that were hampering the adoption of 802.11 in the enterprise. WPA served as a temporary solution while the IEEE completed work on the 802.11i security standard. The Wi-Fi Alliance logo is used to indicate that a piece of equipment is interoperable with other equipment bearing the same logo.

◄

A licensed band of the radio spectrum is one that an entity has exclusive access to, such as a radio station. Unlicensed bands are free to use.

Understanding 802.11 Amendments

In 1997, the *802.11 standard* was adopted by the IEEE. It describes a standard that uses either of two technologies: direct-sequence spread spectrum (DSSS) or frequency-hopping spread spectrum (FHSS). Starting with the 802.11a amendment and going forward, FHSS is no longer a part of the standard. DSSS operates on a fixed frequency, while FHSS changes frequencies in a pattern known by the transmitter and receiver. It operates in the 2.4 GHz frequency and is capable of 1 and 2 Mbps.

FREQUENCIES

To communicate, two devices must be operating at the same frequency. Just as you must tune your radio to the frequency of the radio station you want to listen to, wireless stations and the AP must be using the same frequency. When we speak of the 2.4 and 5.0 frequencies, we are referring to a range of frequencies, with each specific frequency within that range representing a channel. Two devices can be 2.4 GHz devices, but if they are not operating on the same channel (exact frequency), they cannot communicate.

As time went by and technical advancements occurred, many amendments were made to the standard. These amendments are indicated by letters added to the right of the 802.11 name. The major amendments and their main characteristics are listed here:

802.11a   The 802.11a amendment was not widely adopted when it was initially released as it operated in a different frequency, necessitating a hardware upgrade. Many thought that the extra performance gained by upgrading would not be worth the extra expense. Operating in the 5.0 GHz frequency it was inoperable with the current 802.11 devices, which operated in the 2.4 GHz frequency. Later, after the spread of 802.11g, it became more widely accepted. 802.11a operates in the 5.0 GHz frequency and supports up to 56 Mbps.

802.11b   The 802.11b amendment was pretty much an upgrade of the 802.11 standard in that it uses the same frequency, is backward compatible with 802.11, but supported up to 11 Mbps. Although not as fast as 802.11a, 802.11b was more widely embraced because it required no hardware upgrades as did 802.11a.

802.11g   By departing from the use of DSSS as its modulation technique and using orthogonal frequency-division multiplexing (OFDM), 802.11g is able to achieve 56 Mbps while still operating in the 2.4 GHz frequency to maintain compatibility with both 802.11 and 802.11b.

802.11n   802.11n uses multiple antennas, which is not new, but the way in which it uses them is. Multiple antennas had been used before to prevent a behavior called *multipath*, whereby the signal reflects off an object and arrives slightly out of sequence with the main signal, corrupting the main signal. By using two antennas and constantly sampling each for the cleanest signal, this could be avoided. When multiple antennas are used in this fashion, it is called *antenna diversity*.

802.11n uses the multiple antennas (as many as eight) working together in a process called multiple-input multiple-output (MIMO) to transmit multiple frames at once that are then sequenced after transmission. 802.11n also uses a 40 MHz channel, which is double that of the other 802.11 standards and thereby doubles the speed. Finally, changes to the CSMA/CA contention method allow blocks of frames to be acknowledged (instead of individual frames, as the other 802.11 standards require). You will learn more about CSMA/CA later in this section.

Understanding Wireless LAN Components and Terminology

You must be able to identify the main components of wireless LANs (WLANs), understand how they work together, and use correct terminology when discussing WLANs. This section first identifies the components, then covers some terminology, and finally explains the manner in which the parts communicate.

Access points Wireless access points (APs) and wireless routers transmit and receive signals and are a required piece in all network types except ad hoc networks (covered later in the "Service Sets" list item). The access point is the point of connection to all the wireless stations and usually connects them to the wired LAN. When stations communicate with one another, they do not do so directly. The transmission is relayed through the AP.

This relationship is depicted in Figure 9.9. In the figure, laptop C is transmitting to laptop B wirelessly through the AP, and laptop A is transmitting wirelessly through the AP back to WS 1 on the wired network. The transmissions of all the wireless stations are relayed through the AP.

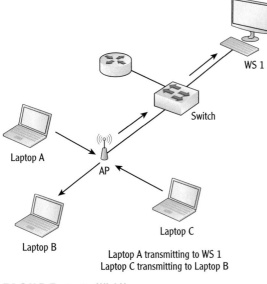

Laptop A transmitting to WS 1
Laptop C transmitting to Laptop B

FIGURE 9.9 WLAN

The AP is also responsible for announcing the presence of the network, if desired, in frames called *beacon frames.* In a secured network, the AP controls access to the network by authenticating stations before allowing them to connect.

Wireless Stations   Wireless stations can be any devices capable of using 802.11. This could include laptops, barcode scanners, PDAs, tablet computers, and smartphones.

Service Sets   The service set defines the wireless objects that are a part of the same wireless network. The three types of service sets are as follows:

> **Basic Service Set (BSS)**   This includes a single AP and its associated stations. This is the type of set illustrated in Figure 9.9; the set includes the AP and laptops A, B, and C.
>
> **Independent Basic Service Set (IBSS)**   This is also called an ad hoc or peer-to-peer network. It has no AP, and the wireless devices communicate directly with one another. An IBSS requires the first station to create the network and others to join. It is shown in Figure 9.10.

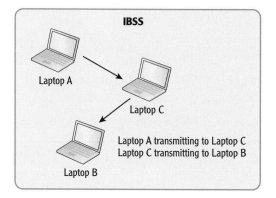

FIGURE 9.10 IBSS

> **Extended Service Set (ESS)**   An extended service set is one that has a single SSID but multiple APs. It may use the multiple APs in a small space to provide more bandwidth, or they may be placed apart from one another to extend the range of the wireless network. When a station moves out the range of one of the APs, it will scan for APs with the same SSID in the area and "roam" to the next AP in the ESS. This is shown in Figure 9.11.

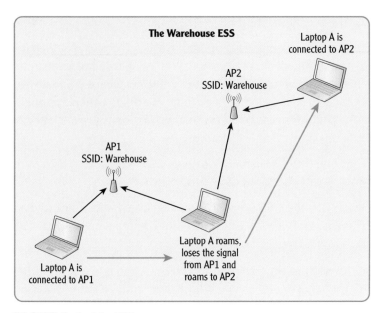

FIGURE 9.11 ESS

Describing CSMA/CA Operation

Because it is impossible for wireless stations to detect collisions, another contention method is required to arbitrate access to the network. The method is called *Carrier Sense Multiple Access/Collision Avoidance (CSMA/CA)*. It requires a more involved process of checking for existing wireless traffic before a frame can be transmitted wirelessly. The stations (including the AP) must also acknowledge all frames. The steps in the process are as follows:

1. Laptop A has a frame to send to laptop B. Before sending, laptop A must check for traffic in two ways. First, it performs carrier sense, which means it listens to see whether any radio waves are being received on its transmitter.

2. If the channel is *not* clear (traffic is being transmitted), laptop A will decrement an internal countdown mechanism called the *random back-off algorithm*. This counter will have started counting down after the last time this station was allowed to transmit. All stations will be counting down their own individual timers. When a station's timer expires, it is allowed to send.

3. If laptop A checks for carrier sense and there is no traffic and its timer hits zero, it will send the frame.

4. The frame goes to the AP.

5. The AP sends an acknowledgment back to laptop A. Until that acknowledgment is received by laptop A, all other stations must remain silent. The AP will cache the frame, where it already may have other cached frames that need to be relayed to other stations. Each frame that AP needs to relay must wait its turn to send using the same mechanism as the stations.

6. When the frame's turn comes up in the cache queue, the frame from laptop A will be relayed to laptop B.

7. Laptop B sends an acknowledgment back to the AP. Until that acknowledgment is received by the AP, all other stations must remain silent.

When you consider that this process has to occur for every single frame and that there are many other frame types used by the AP to manage other functions of the network that also create competition for air time, it is no wonder that actual throughput on a wireless LAN is at best about half the advertised rate.

For example, if two wireless stations were the only wireless clients and they were using 802.11g, which is capable of 56 Mbps, the *very best* throughput experienced would be about 25–28 Mbps. Moreover, as soon as a third station arrives, throughput will go down again because the stations are dividing the air time by 3 instead of 2. Add a fourth, and its gets even worse! Such is the challenge of achieving throughput on a wireless LAN.

THE ESSENTIALS AND BEYOND

Connections are created between devices with media. Media can be either bounded (cables) or unbounded (wireless). Wireless provides lower cost and more convenience, while cabled networks deliver higher security and more bandwidth. Cables come in a variety of thicknesses and materials and can operate using either electrical signals or optical signals. When choosing cabling, factors such as maximum length, cost, and susceptibility to RFI, EMI, and eavesdropping must be balanced against the needs of the design. Straight-through cables are used to connect unlike devices, and crossover cables connect like devices. Rolled cables are used only to make a connection to the console port on a router or switch. Wireless LANs may be deployed using 802.11, 80211a, 802.11b, 802.11g, or 802.11n, each having a unique set of capabilities. Access points are used to create service sets, which include the APs and the stations that are connected to the APs. WLANs use CSMA/CA to arbitrate access to the network, which creates challenges to achieving high throughput.

(Continues)

THE ESSENTIALS AND BEYOND (Continued)

ADDITIONAL EXERCISES

You work as a network consultant for a network design firm. For the following two clients, choose which type of media (cabled or wireless) should be used in each of the sections of the client network.

1. Client A

   A. Warehouse network in which barcode scanners are used to check merchandise in and out. Security and bandwidth needs are low because only bar codes are being transmitted. Cost should be minimized if possible.

   B. Office network that has large and frequent data transfers. High-security customer information is also transmitted.

   C. Guest network in the reception area, where only Internet access is provided.

2. Client B

   A. Outdoor garden sales area, where sales are recorded and transmitted back to the main office. Customer information such as credit card information will be transmitted back to the office network. Bandwidth needs are low. Sales stations are some distance from the main building.

   B. Office network in which sales and customer information from the inside and outside sales areas are consolidated and transmitted to the main office. Bandwidth needs are high.

   C. Guest network that allows customers Internet access so they can access the web-based catalog for special orders. Convenience is important. Financial information will not cross this network as payments occur at pickup. Throughput needs are low.

REVIEW QUESTIONS

1. Which of the following is *not* a security concern unique to WLANs?

   A. Rogue access points

   B. Ease of access to data

   C. Ease of connection to an unauthenticated network

   D. Stolen login passwords

2. Which of the following represents the correct ratio of current wired bandwidth to the desktop, to current wireless bandwidth to the desktop?

   A. 2 to 1

   B. 3 to 1

   C. 5 to 1

   D. 10 to 1

(Continues)

THE ESSENTIALS AND BEYOND *(Continued)*

3. Why is hiding the SSID *not* an effective access control method?

   A. The SSID is displayed in the beacon frames.

   B. The SSID is displayed in transmissions between legit-imate users and the AP.

   C. The SSID is the MAC address of the AP, which is displayed in the beacon frames.

   D. If the hacker can identify the "hidden" channel (the channel on which the SSID is displayed), he can learn the SSID.

4. Which of the following is *not* a component a hacker must have in place to execute a highjacking attack?

   A. DHCP

   B. Rogue access point

   C. Knowledge of the SSID

   D. Port-scanning software

5. In which of the following areas is wireless *not* superior to a cabled network?

   A. Security

   B. Convenience

   C. Cost

   D. Ease of installation

6. Which of the following describes the loss of energy as an electrical signal travels down a wire or an optical signal travels down a glass tube?

   A. EMI

   B. Attenuation

   C. RFI

   D. Crosstalk

7. What is EMI?

   A. Electromagnetic interference

   B. Sources of strong radio signals

   C. Tapping into the cable and connecting a device to the cable run

   D. When the signals on one wire interfere with those on another wire

8. What cabling type comes with either a solid copper wire or a stranded copper wire in the center?

   A. Fiber-optic

   B. Twisted pair

   C. Coaxial

   D. Full duplex

9. Which of the following connector types is used for coaxial?

   A. SC

   B. RJ-45

   C. Vampire tap

   D. SFP

10. What behavior is the twisting used in twisted-pair cabling designed to prevent?

    A. EMI

    B. RFI

    C. Crosstalk

    D. Attenuation

CHAPTER 10

Network Devices

Various hardware devices can be deployed to connect a network. Knowledge of how they work and where to place them is critical to designing the network. A poorly designed network will be difficult to optimize, regardless of the quality of the equipment.

This chapter is dedicated to the understanding of the role played by each device and the principles that drive the positioning of each. Specifically, this chapter covers the following topics:

▶ **Describing device functions**

▶ **Understanding device placement principles**

Describing Device Functions

Infrastructure devices are those devices that connect sections of the network together, like road systems that connect cities and towns. Some of the devices create connections that operate like limited-access interstate highways connecting cities, while others create connections that are more like secondary highways that connect smaller towns and provide access to the interstate highway at specified entrance ramps. Finally, using the same analogy, some of the devices create connections that might be considered local roads, connecting neighborhoods to the secondary roads.

If you've ever driven in an area where the road system developed over time without a master plan and experienced the headaches that result from this, you can understand why proper network design in the front end is critical. Besides designing for the immediate performance of the network, you need to consider the ability of the network to absorb growth over time without sacrificing performance. Before you can properly design the network and place the devices, you must have an understanding of the functions of the devices, the concepts that guide their operation, and the interrelationships that exist.

One of the best ways to frame the discussion of each device is to map the device to the TCP/IP model. When we do this, it helps to make clear the layers at which the devices operate, and this in turn helps us understand which devices should create interstate highways and which should create secondary roads and so forth from a design perspective.

This section covers the major devices with respect to the following:

▶ The TCP/IP layers at which they operate

▶ The roles they can play in the Cisco three-layer model

▶ The position they occupy in the LAN hierarchy

Understanding Repeaters

Repeaters operate at the Network Access layer of the TCP/IP model, but to say they operate at that layer is really to overstate the intelligence of these devices. The Network Access layer includes both the Network Access layer technology (which in the case of a LAN is Ethernet using MAC addresses) and the physical implementation of that technology. A repeater operates on only the physical part of this layer, so it is sometimes referred to as a *physical device.*

A repeater simply takes the original signal and amplifies, or boosts, the signal. As you may remember from the discussion about cable length and attenuation in the preceding chapter, after the signal has traversed a certain length of cable, the signal strength is gradually weakened by the resistance in the cable (which is called *attenuation*). At some point (at the maximum cable length), the signal becomes so degraded that it cannot be understood when it arrives at the destination device. A repeater can be used to connect two lengths of cable that together would exceed the maximum length. It simply amplifies the signal and transmits it.

Repeaters really should be avoided in network design. You should plan the location of the access switches in such a way that no runs of cable over 100 meters are required. You should view repeaters as a solution to a network design problem that you inherited, not one you created. If a bad network design causes a repeater to be included in the network, this device would be considered to be operating on the Access layer of the Cisco three-layer model. This model is discussed in more detail at the end of the chapter.

Understanding Hubs

Hubs operate at the same layer as repeaters and are sometimes referred to as *multiport repeaters*. They have no intelligence. When a signal is received by a hub on one of its ports, it simply repeats the signal to all other ports. This is illustrated in Figure 10.1. A signal arriving in port 1 is simply sent out all other ports.

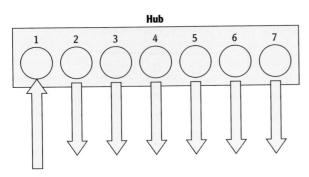

FIGURE 10.1 Hub operation

The problem with this operation is that all of the ports are on a shared network. They all exist in one collision domain. You will learn more about collision domains later in this chapter, but for now understand that when signals are regenerated to every port as with a hub, the frequency of collisions is greatly increased. As you learned, collisions lead to retransmissions, which lead to reduced data throughput (that is, a slow network).

Hubs should never be a planned piece in a network design. Over and above the performance problems they introduce, they also create security concerns. If a protocol analyzer or sniffer is connected to a port on the hub or is operating as software on a computer connected to the hub, traffic from all computers connected to the hub can be captured. As explained in the next section, switches segregate devices into separate collision domains (one for each port) and in the process make capturing packets from all devices impossible. If a sniffer is connected to a port on a switch or is running as software on a computer connected to a port on a switch, only the traffic between the sniffer or computer and the switch port can be captured. If a hub is included in the network, it would be considered to be operating on the Access layer of the Cisco three-layer model.

Understanding Bridges

Bridges operate on the Network Access layer of the TCP/IP model, but unlike repeaters and hubs, they go beyond the physical half of the layer and use Ethernet information (MAC addresses) to make forwarding decisions. When a bridge is first started, it acts as a hub does. It sends a frame out every port except for the one on which it arrived. However, in a very short period of time, it learns the MAC address of every device connected to every port. It stores these addresses in a table called the *MAC address table*. Then, when it receives a frame (these are frames, remember, because we are using information at the Network Access layer), it sends that frame only out the port where the destination MAC address is located, as shown in Figure 10.2. This process is called *transparent bridging*.

◄

The Cisco three-layer model is discussed at the end of this chapter.

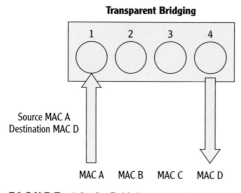

FIGURE 10.2 Bridging operation

The result of this is that each bridge port resides in its own *collision domain*. The traffic on each bridge port is *only* traffic destined for that device (or network). That greatly decreases the chance of collisions and in turn lowers the retransmission rate, which increases performance by leaps and bounds.

Bridges have typically been used in the past to connect network segments, rather than devices. So when bridges are used in this manner, each network segment is a collision domain, as shown in Figure 10.3.

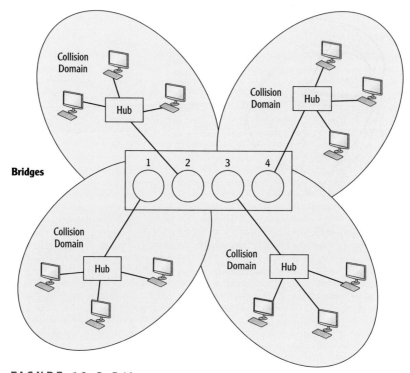

FIGURE 10.3 Bridges

Switches provide a port and a collision domain to each device, as shown in Figure 10.4.

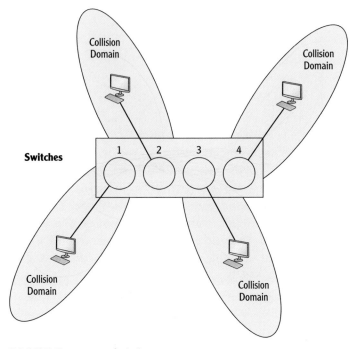

FIGURE 10.4 Switches

Bridges are rarely used anymore in networks because the same transparent bridging can be provided by switches, which have many advantages over bridges. These advantages are discussed in the next section. If a bridge is included in the network, it would be considered to be operating on the Access layer of the Cisco three-layer model.

Understanding Switches

Switches also operate on the Network Access layer of the TCP/IP model and use Ethernet information (MAC addresses) to make forwarding decisions. There are all sorts of functions that you can configure on a Cisco switch by connecting to it with a console cable and using the Cisco command-line interface (CLI). But even if you never touch this interface and use the switch as it comes straight out of the box, it will provide the same transparent bridging provided by an Ethernet bridge.

◄

The Cisco three-layer model is discussed at the end of this chapter.

Advantages of Using Switches

The main advantages of a switch over a bridge are as follows:

Software vs. Hardware   Bridges perform the bridging function by using software. Switches, on the other hand, are hardware based. The switching is done using ASIC chips. When hardware is used for this function, the forwarding process is much quicker.

ASICs

Application-specific integrated circuits (ASICs) are those that are dedicated to a specific function, as opposed to a general-purpose integrated circuit. An example is a chip designed solely for a cell phone (you can use it for only that purpose). By using this customized circuitry for the switching function, rather than using the CPU or other more general-purpose circuitry in the switch, performance is greatly enhanced. This is sometimes referred to as switching in the hardware rather than switching in the software.

▶

Port density simply refers to the number of ports. A device with 24 ports would exhibit more port density than one with 8 ports.

Port Density   Because bridges are designed to connect network segments, they tend to have fewer ports. Switches, on the other hand, normally come in 16-, 24-, and even 52-port models.

Spanning-Tree Instances   Bridges are limited to a single instance of Spanning Tree, while switches can have many. Spanning Tree Protocol (STP) is discussed in Chapter 14, "Configuring Switches." This protocol is used to prevent switching loops that can occur when switching path redundancy is present in the network.

PATH REDUNDANCY AND LOOPS

If designing path redundancy creates switching loops, why would you include them in the design, anyway? The reason for this is fault tolerance. Just as multiple routing paths between two destinations allows for a backup route if one of the routes becomes unavailable, switching path redundancy provides the same benefit. It is such a beneficial design characteristic that the Spanning Tree Protocol (STP) was designed to prevent loops when switching path redundancy exists. Moreover, you don't even have to enable this; it operates automatically!

So as you can see, there are many reasons that switches are used rather than bridges even though they perform the same function.

Types of Switches

Switches come in two versions: those that operate at the Network Access layer only and those that are called multilayer switches. Multilayer switches operate at both the Network Access and the Internet layers, which means (as you will learn in the next section) they do switching and routing. The rest of this section presents the characteristics of both Network Access layer switches and multilayer switches.

Network Access Layer Switches   These switches make forwarding decisions based only on MAC addresses and do not use Internet layer information (IP addresses). They typically act as the connection point to the network for workstations, printers, and other devices on the LAN. A Network Access layer switch is shown in Figure 10.5.

FIGURE 10.5 Network Access layer switch

Because this is the case, these types of switches are said to be operating on the Access layer of the Cisco three-layer model. The functions of switches that operate at this layer are listed here:

> **MAC Address Learning**   The switch identifies the source MAC address whenever a frame enters one of the ports and places this in its MAC address table.
>
> **Forward/Filter Decisions**   When a frame enters a port, the switch identifies the destination MAC address. If it finds that MAC address in its table, it sends the frame out the port listed for that MAC address *only*. If it doesn't find the MAC address listed in its table, it will flood the frame out every port except the one on which it arrived.
>
> **Loop Avoidance**   If switch path redundancy exists in the network, it is the job of the switch to avoid loops. Loops occur when a frame doesn't find its destination and (because of loops that exist in the

◄

The Cisco three-layer model is discussed at the end of this chapter.

◄

Port flooding refers to the process of sending a frame out every port except the one on which it arrived.

network for redundancy purposes) continues around the network over and over again. Loops are avoided by the switches communicating with one another using STP to close these loops. You will learn more about STP and its operations in Chapter 14.

SWITCH PATH REDUNDANCY

So what does switch path redundancy look like? The following graphic shows that because of the way switches A, B, and C are connected, there is redundancy between A and C if the direct link between them fails. They can still have a switching path by going through switch B. By building in this fault tolerance, however, a potential switching loop is introduced around switches A, B, and C. STP is used to prevent these loops from causing problems, as you will learn in Chapter 14.

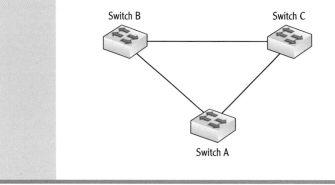

MLS Switches   Multilayer switches perform routing and switching, but what is most impressive is the way in which they combine these functions. To appreciate the operation of these devices, consider that when one device is sending data to another device, it is a not a transmission made up of a single packet. It can be made up of hundreds and even thousands of individual packets in the same transmission.

Rather than simply routing each packet (which is what you would expect if this were simply a box containing both a router and a switch), it routes the first packet (routing is a much slower process than switching) and then by maintaining an awareness of that route, it switches all of the other packets in the transmission. This concept has come to be known in the Cisco world as *route one and switch many*. The result is an impressive increase in speed of the delivery of the entire transmission. Multilayer switches can operate on the Access layer of the Cisco three-layer model. However, in most cases they operate on the Distribution layer, where most routers operate, or on the Core layer of the model, where their speed is one of the main requirements of devices at that layer.

◄

The Cisco three-layer model is discussed at the end of this chapter.

Understanding Routers

Routers operate at the Internet layer of the TCP/IP model and make routing decisions based on IP address information. A router is shown in Figure 10.6.

FIGURE 10.6 Router

The IP address information is stored in routing tables. Routing tables contain routes, or pathways, to networks (called *network routes,* usually maintained in the form of the network ID) and if configured as such, routes to specific devices (called *host routes*). They also can contain a type of route called a *default route.* The router uses the default route to send all traffic for which it has no route in its table. A default route can be thought of as the default gateway for the router because it uses that route much like a host uses its default gateway (that is, a host will send any traffic that is not in its local network to the default gateway). If a router is configured with a default route and you issue the command to show all routes (show ip route), this route is referred to as the *gateway of last resort.*

Routing tables of the routers can be populated in two ways. When an administrator connects to the router and manually uses commands to program the routes into the routing table, the router will be using *static routing.* When the router is configured to use a routing protocol, the router will be using *dynamic routing.* Each of these methods has advantages and disadvantages, which are discussed in the following sections.

Dynamic Routing

When a routing protocol is enabled on a router, it will exchange routing information with other routers that have been enabled with the same routing protocol. Before a router has learned any information from other routers, it will have only routes in its table to networks to which it is directly connected. In Figure 10.7, router R1 has routes in its table only to the 192.168.5.0/24 and 192.168.6.0/24 networks. This is because it is directly connected to only those networks. It does not, however, know about the 192.168.7.0/24 network because it is not directly connected to that network.

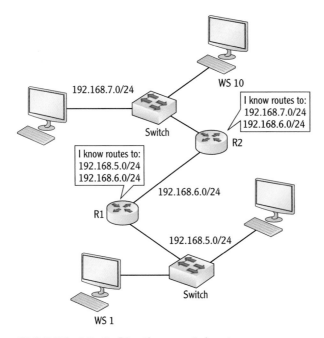

FIGURE 10.7 Directly connected routes

Likewise, before any routing information is exchanged between R1 and R2, router R2 will know about only the 192.168.6.0/24 and 192.168.7.0/24 networks, because those are the only networks to which it is directly connected. After the two routers have exchanged their routing tables, both routers will have all three routes in their tables, as shown in Figure 10.8, and *only then* will a packet from WS 1 destined for WS 10 be routed successfully.

The advantages of dynamic routing are that the remote routes (the routes that are not directly connected) will not have to be entered manually but will be placed in the table automatically as the routers exchange information. The disadvantage is that for this to occur, the routers create traffic on the network called *routing update traffic*. In some cases, this traffic can be significant and competes with normal data traffic on the network.

Another advantage of dynamic routing is that if multiple paths exist to the same network, as shown in Figure 10.9, the router can use metrics to choose the best route. A *metric* is a value that is used to determine the best route that can be based on the number of routers on each path (called hops) or on more-sophisticated combinations of information such as hop count and bandwidth. The routers in Figure 10.9 are using hop count (number of routers on the path) as their metric, and so R1 will send any information from WS1 to WS10 through R4 because it's a shorter path in terms of hop count.

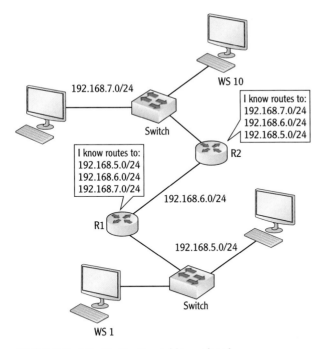

FIGURE 10.8 Routing tables updated

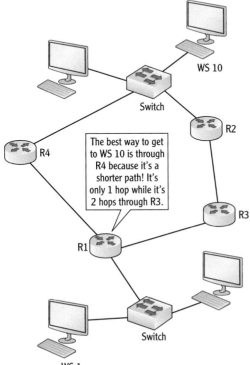

FIGURE 10.9 Multiple routes

Moreover, if the best route becomes unavailable (because of link outages, for example), the router can use the other route to still reach the remote network, as shown in Figure 10.10.

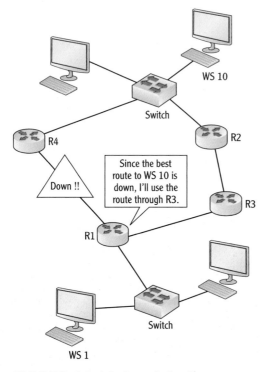

FIGURE 10.10 Route fault tolerance

Static Routing

The advantage of using static routing is that there is no routing update traffic created. In some situations where the network is very small and the equipment and connections are very reliable and stable, it may be the best choice. The disadvantages of static routing are as follows:.

▶ The routes must be entered manually.

▶ Any changes that occur from a link outage, from a change in design, or from the addition of devices must be made manually.

▶ The best route choice must be made by the administrator and manually configured.

Understanding Wireless Access Points and Wireless Routers

Wireless access points (APs) can be of two types. Some APs are simply switches that provide logical wireless ports to multiple wireless devices, while others are also routers. In an enterprise network, there is a role for both. Depending on the role of the AP and where it is located in the network, it may not be required for it to be a router, and wireless routers cost more than simple APs. In this section both are discussed.

Wireless APs

An AP that is not a router is acting as a switch. It doesn't look like a switch because it doesn't have physical switch ports that you can see and touch (although some models may include one or two of those). The ports are wireless and they are logical. When a device connects to an AP (which may or may not require authentication), it is said to be *associated* with the AP.

The AP maintains this information in an association table that is much like the MAC address table in a switch. If a wireless device needs to send traffic that goes through the AP and then on to the wired part of the network, the device will have to have an IP address that is on the same subnet as the network to which the AP is connected. This is the same concept that would apply if a wired device were connected to a switch. This process is shown in Figure 10.11. In this scenario, because AP 20 is operating as a switch and is *not* a router, laptop 1 will not be able to connect to the router R3 because its IP address is not in the same subnet as the interface on the connection from router R3 to the AP (which is the 192.168.5.0/24 network). The other laptops will not have that problem because their IP addresses are in the same subnet as the router.

SAY THAT AGAIN?

How do we know that router R3 and laptop 1 are not in the same subnet, and what is that 192.168.5.0/24 address all about? Laptops 2 and 3 and the router all have 24-bit subnet masks (255.255.255.0 or /24). That means that if the first three octets of their IP addresses match, they are in the same subnet. Because they all have 192.168.5 in the first three octets, they are all in the same network, which is the 192.168.5.0/24 network. Laptop 1 also has a 24-bit mask, but its first three octets are 192.168.56, so it is not in the same network as laptops 2 and 3 and the router.

When the AP is connected to a router that can provide routing, as shown in Figure 10.11, it is not necessary for the AP to be a router.

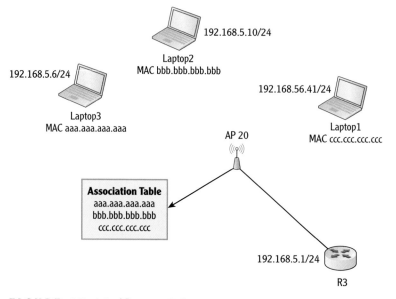

192.168.5.10/24

Laptop2
MAC bbb.bbb.bbb.bbb

192.168.5.6/24

Laptop3
MAC aaa.aaa.aaa.aaa

192.168.56.41/24

Laptop1
MAC ccc.ccc.ccc.ccc

AP 20

Association Table
aaa.aaa.aaa.aaa
bbb.bbb.bbb.bbb
ccc.ccc.ccc.ccc

192.168.5.1/24

R3

FIGURE 10.11 AP as a switch

Wireless Routers

In some situations, it is beneficial or even required for the AP to also be a router. The best example of this is a wireless AP that provides access to the Internet in a home. In this situation, the wireless clients in the home will be using private IP addresses. Because these addresses cannot be used to access the Internet, those addresses must be converted to a public IP address using Network Address Translation. This is a function performed by a router.

Moreover, the AP in this situation will also probably be acting as a DHCP server for the wireless clients. Therefore, it will assign them a private IP address, maintain both the MAC address and the IP address in the association table, and when Internet access is required, it will convert the private IP address to a public IP address. This entire process is shown in Figure 10.12. When laptop 2 sends traffic to the Internet, the AP will convert the IP address 192.168.5.10/24 to the public IP address 202.62.31.9/24.

Regardless of whether the AP is acting as a switch only or as a wireless router, these devices are acting on the Access layer of the Cisco three-layer model.

◀

The Cisco three-layer model is discussed at the end of this chapter.

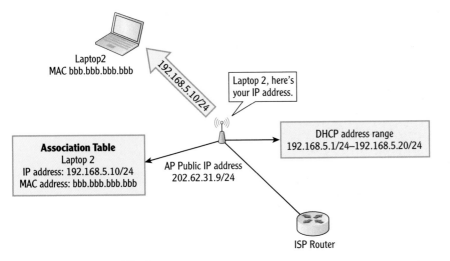

FIGURE 10.12 Wireless router

Understanding Device Placement Principles

Once you understand the operations of the various devices and their roles in the network, it's time to put the pieces together. In this section, a review of collision and broadcast domains will be followed by a more complete description of the three-layer Cisco hierarchical model.

Defining Broadcast Domains

A *broadcast domain* is a set of devices that will receive one another's broadcast packets. If these devices have physical connectivity with one another and are in the same subnet, they are in the same broadcast domain. One of the main functions of routers is to separate or create broadcast domains. In Figure 10.13, the router has four interfaces, and each interface is a separate broadcast domain.

Creating broadcast domains is an integral part of the function of a router. If you attempt to put an IP address on a router interface that is in the same subnet as another interface on the same router, you will receive an error message. For example, if you tried to put an IP address on FastEthernet1 located in the same subnet as the IP address used on Fastethernet0/0, the error message would say `overlaps with FastEthernet0/0`. This basically means that you cannot do that. Each interface is supposed to host a different broadcast domain, which is not possible if they are in the same subnet. In Figure 10.13, hosts in one broadcast domain will never receive broadcast packets from other broadcast domains.

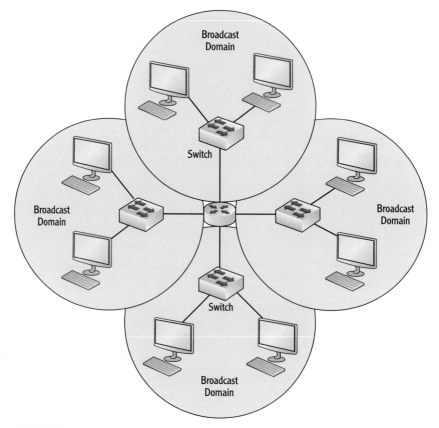

FIGURE 10.13 Broadcast domains

Defining Collision Domains

A *collision domain* is a set of devices whose packets could potentially collide with one another. By definition, devices that are in the same collision domain are also in the same broadcast domain. One of the purposes of a switch is to place each device in its own collision domain so that collisions are reduced. Because a hub cannot provide that, all devices connected to a hub are in the same collision domain. This relationship is illustrated in Figure 10.14.

In this scenario, each switch port provides a collision domain. However, because a hub is connected into one switch port, and then three computers are connected into the hub, those three devices are forced to share the collision domain—in contrast to the other devices that have their own collision domains.

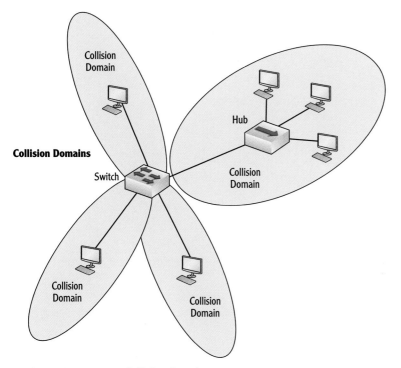

FIGURE 10.14 Collision domains

When we put the routers, switches, and hubs together in one network diagram, you can more easily grasp the relationship between collision and broadcast domains (see Figure 10.15).

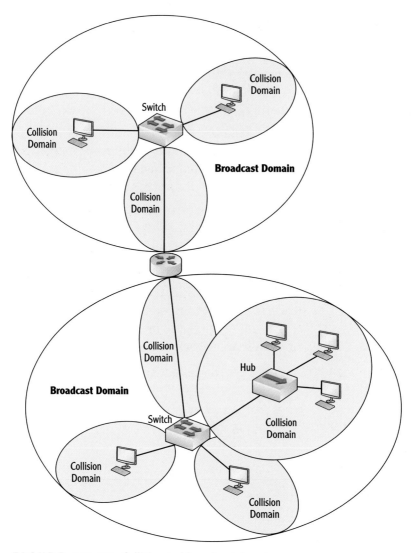

FIGURE 10.15 Collision and broadcast domains

Understanding the Cisco Three-Layer Model

The *Cisco three-layer model* is used to describe the way in which infrastructure devices such as routers and switches should be organized to maximize the performance and security of the network. Certain functions should be performed on certain levels, and certain devices should be placed on certain levels.

Access Layer   The access layer is the connection point for workstations, printers, wireless computers, and any other devices that operate on the network with an IP address. These devices usually make this connection via a switch, hub, and wireless AP or wireless router. This is also called the *network edge*.

Distribution Layer   This layer is where routers and multilayer switches connect the access switches together. This layer is typically where security is applied in the form of access control lists. It is also where the routing function takes place.

Core Layer   This is the backbone of the network, where the emphasis should be on speed. Functions that do anything to impede this goal, such as routing and security, should not be performed on this layer. Devices on this layer are usually high-speed multilayer switches. Fault tolerance is also important on this layer, because problems on this layer generally are felt across the entire network.

The three layers and their relationships are shown in Figure 10.16.

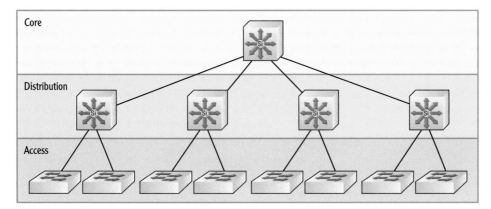

FIGURE 10.16   Three-layer model

THE ESSENTIALS AND BEYOND

Infrastructure devices are those devices that connect sections of the network together, such as repeater, hubs, bridges, and switches. Repeaters, hubs, and bridges operate at the Network Access layer. Repeaters amplify, or boost, the original signal. Hubs create a single collision domain for all ports. Bridges use MAC addresses to make forwarding decisions. Switches create a separate collision domain for each port. Multi-layer switches operate at both the Network Access and the Internet layers by performing routing and switching and can route the first packet and switch all of the other packets in the transmission. Routers operate at the Internet layer. Routers make routing decisions based on IP address information located in routing tables that can be populated either manually or by using dynamic routing protocols. Routers define broadcast domain borders at each interface of the router. Wireless access points can be either switches or routers, and depending on their function operate on the Network Access and Internet layers, respectively.

A broadcast domain is a set of devices that will receive one another's broadcast packet. A collision domain is a set of devices whose packets could potentially collide with one another. The Cisco three-layer model is used to describe the way in which infrastructure devices such as routers and switches should be organized to maximize the performance and security of the network. The model consists of an Access, Distribution, and Core layer.

ADDITIONAL EXERCISES

1. Using Figure 10.17, determine the number of collision and broadcast domains in the network.

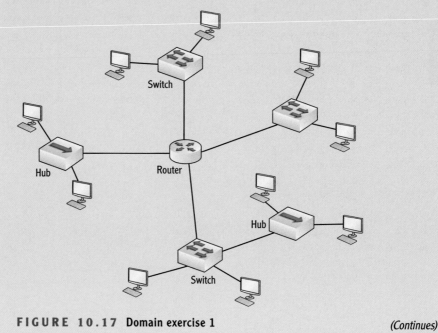

FIGURE 10.17 Domain exercise 1   *(Continues)*

THE ESSENTIALS AND BEYOND (Continued)

2. Using Figure 10.18, label each of the seven domains as either collision or broadcast.

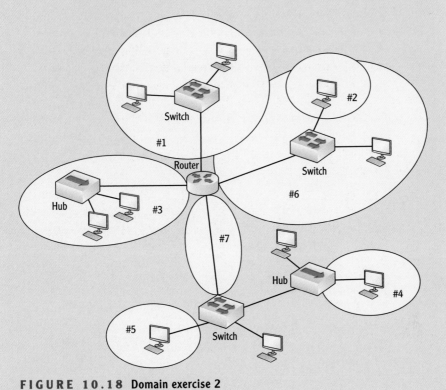

FIGURE 10.18 Domain exercise 2

REVIEW QUESTIONS

1. Repeaters operate at which layer of the TCP/IP model?

   A. Internet

   B. Network Access

   C. Application

   D. Transport

2. What cable behavior are repeaters designed to mitigate?

   A. EMI

   B. RFI

   C. Crosstalk

   D. Attenuation

3. Which of the following devices operates on the Internet layer of the TCP/IP model?

   A. Repeater

   B. Hub

   C. Bridge

   D. Router

(Continues)

THE ESSENTIALS AND BEYOND *(Continued)*

4. With which of the following devices are all of the ports in the same collision domain?

   A. Hub   C. Switch

   B. Bridge   D. Router

5. Which if the following is *not* an advantage of switches over bridges?

   A. MAC address learning   C. Port density

   B. Hardware bridging   D. More Spanning Tree instances

6. Which of the following is *not* a function of Network Access layer switches?

   A. IP address filtering   C. Forward/filter decisions

   B. MAC address learning   D. Loop avoidance

7. Which device operates on both the Network Access and the Internet layer?

   A. Switch   C. MLS switch

   B. Router   D. Bridge

8. Which of the following is *not* a type of route contained in a routing table?

   A. Default   C. Network

   B. Multicast   D. Host

9. What type of route is also known as the gateway of last resort?

   A. Default   C. Network

   B. Multicast   D. Host

10. Which of the following is *not* an advantage of using a dynamic routing protocol?

   A. Less network traffic   C. Best router selection

   B. Route fault tolerance   D. Automatic table population

CHAPTER 11

LAN Operations

Although an understanding of the cabling and other physical aspects is important, designing and troubleshooting networks require an understanding of what goes on at the upper part of the Network Access layer and the Internet layer of the TCP/IP model. In this chapter, topics that have already been covered to some extent are reviewed and in some cases taken to another level of detail. But the real intent of this chapter is to put all of the pieces together so you can get the big picture of how a LAN operates. Specifically, this chapter covers the following topics:

▶ **Understanding the routing process**

▶ **Describing the switching process**

▶ **Describing end-to-end communications**

Understanding the Routing Process

Routers and multilayer switches tie subnets together and use IP addresses to locate destinations on behalf of hosts that are in directly connected networks and on behalf of hosts that may be located many routers, or hops, away. That's because no single router performs the routing process for a host unless the source and destination networks are directly connected, as shown in Figure 11.1.

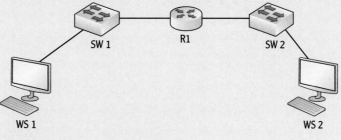

FIGURE 11.1 Local routing

In Figure 11.1, the router R1 can perform the entire routing job because the source and destination computers are connected to switches that are directly connected to R1. This is possible because routes to networks that are directly connected to a router are automatically placed in the routing table. In this section, the structure, methods of population, and the use of routing tables are discussed.

Describing Routing Tables

Routers use routing tables to store information about remote networks, but they don't store this information as you might expect. When you ask someone for directions or you use a GPS to determine how to get somewhere, the answer usually comes as a series of steps, such as turn left at Elm, go 5 miles, turn left on Oak, and so forth.

Routers do *not* store information that way. Routers keep track *only* of the next step in the directions, or the next router in the path to the destination. So if directions worked this way, you might ask how to get to a certain location, and the person giving you the directions would simply say, "Go to Elm Street, and when you get there, ask the guy standing on the corner, and he'll tell you the next step." In a network, that guy standing on the corner represents the next router.

So when you examine a routing table, the information you will see for each entry will consist of the following listed items per route. As the items are explained and added, the entries will become increasingly complete. One item, metrics, is not discussed here but rather in the "Understanding Population Methods" section.

Network (or Network ID)　This identifies the destination network. If the classful or major network has been subnetted, all of those subnets will be grouped together under the classful network and the mask used to subnet. For example, if the 10.0.0.0/8 Class A network had been subdivided into four Class C networks, 10.0.1.0/24, 10.0.2.0/24, 10.0.4.0/24, and 10.1.6.0/24, the entry would look as follows:

```
10.0.0.0/24 is subnetted, 4 subnets
      10.0.1.0
      10.0.2.0
      10.0.4.0
      10.0.6.0
```

> **This is not a complete routing table. To see the routing table, use the `show ip route` command.**

Population Method　Routes can find their way into the table in one of three ways: they can be directly connected (these go into the table automatically), they can be configured manually by the administrator from the command line (static), or they can be learned from another router by using a dynamic routing protocol. These methods are discussed in more detail in the "Understanding Population Methods" section. The method will be indicated by a letter next to the network ID: *C* indicates directly connected, *S* indicates static, and if the route came from another router, a letter that represents that particular routing protocol (such as *R* for Routing Internet Protocol, or RIP) will be used.

These letters go to the left of the network ID. The following is an example of a static route:

◄

RIP is covered later in this chapter.

```
S    192.168.5.0/24
```

Next Hop   This value indicates the IP address of the next router along the route to the destination network. If the next hop is the same router as was shown in Figure 11.1, it will read, *directly connected*. If it is an IP address, it will read, *via ip address*. When you add this information to an entry, the entry looks like this:

```
10.0.0.0/24 is subnetted, 4 subnets
C    10.0.1.0 is directly connected
R    10.0.2.0 via 10.1.6.1
R    10.0.4.0 via 10.1.6.1
C    10.0.6.0 is directly connected
```

In the preceding entry, two of the four subnets are directly connected (10.0.1.0 and 10.0.6.0), and two were learned from another router by using RIP (10.0.2.0 and 10.0.4.0). The next hop to both networks learned through RIP is the router with the IP address of 10.1.6.1.

Exit Interface   The exit interface is the interface on the local router used to connect to the next hop. When that is added to the same entries, they appear as follows:

```
10.0.0.0/24 is subnetted, 4 subnets
C    10.0.1.0 is directly connected Serial 0
R    10.0.2.0 via 10.1.6.1 Serial 1
R    10.0.4.0 via 10.1.6.1 Serial 1
C    10.0.6.0 is directly connected Serial 1
```

In the preceding entry, the exit interface to the directly connected network (10.0.1.0) is the Serial 0 interface, and the exit interface to the directly connected network (10.0.6.0) is the Serial 1 interface. The exit interface to the two that were learned from another router using the RIP routing protocol (10.0.2.0 and 10.0.4.0) is also Serial 1.

Elapsed Time Since Last Routing Update   For routes that have been learned via another router, the elapsed time since the last update is indicated in between the next hop IP address and the exit interface. As it relates to this set of networks in the table, the table is complete, as shown here:

```
10.0.0.0/24 is subnetted, 4 subnets
C    10.0.1.0 is directly connected Serial 0
R    10.0.2.0 via 10.1.6.1 0:01:00 Serial 1
R    10.0.4.0 via 10.1.6.1 0:01:00 Serial 1
C    10.0.6.0 is directly connected Serial 1
```

In the preceding entry, the two routes learned from the router at 10.1.6.1 (10.0.2.0 and 10.0.4.0) were last updated exactly one minute ago (the elapsed time since the last update was 0:01:00).

Additional information can be found in the routing table, and that is covered later, in the section "Understanding Population Methods." But before moving on to that, Figure 11.2 illustrates the router that owns this table (R1), with its physical interfaces labeled and the connection to the router at 10.1.6.1 labeled. The physical interfaces of R2 and R3 are not labeled, as they would not appear in or be relevant to the routing table in R1. Study this figure and ensure before moving on that you can relate the diagram to the table entries.

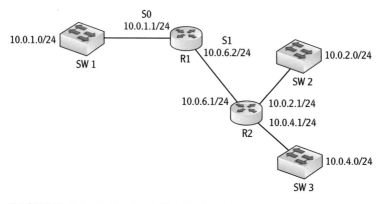

FIGURE 11.2 Routing table visualized

It is important that you can look at a routing table and create the diagram that goes with the table. This helps you to see where problems are. Remember, you may have a network diagram that shows the way things should be, but the routing table tells you what the router's reality is!

There is some information that was added to the diagram for clarity that you could *not* have discerned from the routing table. Specifically, with the exception of the 10.0.6.1/24 interface of R2, the IP addresses of the router interfaces could not be known specifically, but their networks could have been identified.

The diagram also shows the R2 router with two additional interfaces other than the interface that connects it to R1. Whether or not that is the case cannot be determined with the information you have been given. Both of those networks could have been located off a single interface if R2 were connected to a third router. Later, in the section "Understanding Population Methods," you will learn about information not present in the simplified routing table you were given that could have helped to make this determination.

Here is a list of the information in the table that you should have been able to gather:

▶ There are two routers involved: the local router, which owns this table, and the router from which the local router learned of two networks (10.0.2.0/24 and 10.0.4.0/24) by using a routing protocol.

▶ The remote router is located at 10.0.6.1/24. This means that the local router's interface that connects to the remote router at 10.0.6.1/24 must have an IP address in the 10.0.6.0/24 network.

▶ The local interface that connects to the remote router is Serial 1.

▶ The local router has an interface Serial 0, to which the network 10.0.1.0/24 is directly connected. This means that the IP address of the S0 interface must be in the 10.0.1.0/24 network.

▶ The routing protocol that was used to learn the two routes from the remote router was RIP (because there is an *R* next to the route in the table).

The next section focuses on the methods by which routes are inserted into the table, specifically focusing on dynamic routing protocols. Once you have some understanding of these protocols, you will be able to make sense of some additional information found in the routing table that you could have used to make your diagram more detailed with more certainty.

Understanding Population Methods

Three ways that routes are populated to the routing table are:

▶ Directly connected, which are placed in the table automatically

▶ Static, which are configured manually from the command line

▶ Routing advertisements, which are received from other routers running the same routing protocol

An *autonomous sys-tem (AS)* is a group of routers that are managed by the same group of administra-tors, usually for the same enterprise (company). An enterprise can have multiple ASs.

There's not much more to add about static and directly connected routes (although in Chapter 15, "Configuring Static Routing," you will learn how to configure and verify static routes). However, there is much to know about the population of the routing table by dynamic routing protocols. The rest of this section is dedicated to the use of these protocols. There are two basic types of routing protocols:

Exterior Routing Protocols   These protocols are used to route between autono-mous systems, such as the routing that occurs on the Internet.

Examples are Border Gateway Protocol (BGP) and the now-obsolete Exterior Gateway Protocol (EGP). Exterior routing protocols are beyond the scope of this book.

Interior Routing Protocols   These routing protocols are designed to be used within an autonomous system. The configuration, monitoring, and trouble-shooting of a set of routers running one of these routing protocols will usually be handled by the same company or entity. There are two types of these pro-tocols: distance vector routing protocols and link state routing protocols. The two types differ mainly in the metric used to make routing decisions. Each is described next.

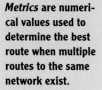

Metrics are numeri-cal values used to determine the best route when multiple routes to the same network exist.

Distance Vector   Distance vector routing protocols use a very simple metric called *hop count*. Hop count simply describes the number of routers between the source and the destination using that router. In Figure 11.3, if the router R1 received a packet from WS 1 that was destined for WS 2, it would have two routes available, through R2 or R3. The route through R2 would be two hops, and the route through R3 would be one hop. If a distance vector routing protocol were in use, the route through R3 would be chosen.

When examining a network diagram and discussing hop count, switches do not count as hops. Only devices that route are considered to be hops.

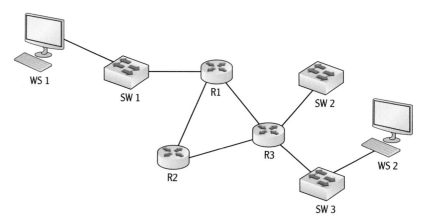

FIGURE 11.3 Distance vector route selection

Link State   Link state routing protocols use a combination of factors when deciding the best route. They certainly consider hop count, but they also consider the bandwidth of the links involved and the delay that is being reported by traffic already sent in a particular direction. Then all of the information is run through an algorithm that generates a numerical value used as the metric.

ALGORITHMS

Algorithms such as the ones discussed in this book (DUAL, Dijkstra, and so forth) are mathematical formulas that assign weight to certain variables. When a route's variables such as hop count, bandwidth, and delay are entered into the formula, it generates a value that represents the metric.

With link state protocols, it is entirely possible that a router may choose a route that is more hops simply because the bandwidth on the links along the way of that route is superior to that of the route with fewer hops.

Both link state and distance vector routing protocols may place routes to the same network in the routing table. These routes may also be competing with static routes and directly connected routes to the same network.

Understanding Administrative Distance

Before metrics are even considered in router choice, an additional value is considered before a route is chosen. This value is not used to compare routes learned from the same routing protocol but to consider the relative desirability of routes from all sources, including static, directly connected and from various routing protocols. This value is called administrative distance.

Administrative Distance

We discuss three types of routing protocols in this book: distance vector, link state, and a Cisco proprietary routing protocol that exhibits characteristics of both types (which is why it is sometimes called a *hybrid protocol*). But first, you need to know that a router will consider one other item when it has multiple routes to the same network. This item is called administrative distance, or AD.

Cisco routers are programmed to consider certain sources of routing information to be more trustworthy than other sources. For example, if a route was learned because the network is directly connected to the router, that information is considered to be more reliable than information about the same network learned from a routing protocol. Each of the route population methods has a default numerical value that is called the administrative distance (EIGRP, OSPF, and RIP are detailed later in this chapter):

▶ Directly connected: 0

▶ Static: 1

▶ EIGRP: 90

▶ OSPF: 110

▶ RIP: 120

So if a router had two routes in its table to the same network, and one was a static route and the other was learned by OSPF, the router would use the static route because its administrative distance is 1, whereas the AD of the OSPF route is 110. The values in the preceding list are the default values, but they can be changed at the command line if desired.

So the router has two things to consider, and it makes these considerations in a particular order:

1. If it has two routes to the same network from different routing information sources (for example, one from OSPF and another from RIP), it will pick the route with the smallest AD.

2. If there are two routes from the chosen routing source (say, two routes learned from OSPF), the route with the lower metric will be chosen.

AD and the Routing Table

Now that we have discussed hops and AD, we can put the finishing touches on our discussion of the routing table. Both hop count and AD are placed in each routing table entry. Look at the following table, which is similar to the one used for Figure 11.2, but when examined for clues, reveals that it is for a different network:

```
10.0.0.0/24 is subnetted, 4 subnets
C    10.0.1.0 is directly connected Serial 0
R    10.0.2.0[120/1] via 10.0.6.1 0:01:00 Serial 1
R    10.0.4.0[120/2] via 10.0.6.1 0:01:00 Serial 1
C    10.0.6.0 is directly connected Serial 1
```

In the preceding table, the information in the brackets between the destination network and the next hop router IP address represents the AD and the hop count,

You don't see 10.0.0.0 in the network diagram in Figure 11.2 because that is the classful network from which the subnets 10.0.1.0 and 10.0.6.0 are derived.

respectively. In this case, [120/1] means that the AD is 120 and the hop count is 1 for 10.0.2.0, and [120/2] means the AD is 120 and the hop count is 2 for 10.0.4.0.

Static and directly connected networks do not display the AD and hop count. These values are displayed only for routes learned from other routers through routing advertisements.

This table contains information that can be used to identify the number of interfaces on R2. You may remember that we said that with the information given in the first example (Figure 11.2), it could not be determined whether R2 had additional interfaces beyond the connection with R1. If the hop count from R1 to the 10.0.6.0 network is 2 (as is indicated in this table), that means that there are two routers between R1 and the destination network. In that case, the diagram must be as shown in Figure 11.4.

When a router sends routing updates to another router, it is called a *router advertisement*.

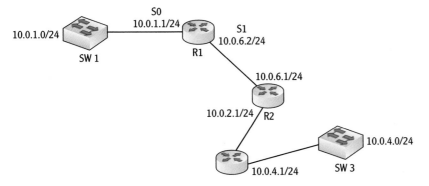

FIGURE 11.4 Routing table visualized 2

Remember that if R2 had any additional interfaces up and running, they would show up in R1's table learned from RIP with a hop count of 1. The fact that this is not the case tells us that the network must be as shown in Figure 11.4. You can tell a lot by studying the routing table!

Using Routing Protocols

Three routing protocols are the most widely used within the autonomous system. These protocols are Routing Internet Protocol (RIP), Enhanced Interior Gateway Routing Protocol (EIGRP), and Open Shortest Path First (OSPF). In the following sections, each is discussed in detail. At the end of the "Understanding Population Methods" section, a table provides a side-by-side comparison of the three that summarizes their specific capabilities and/or shortcomings.

Routing Internet Protocol

Routing Internet Protocol (RIP) is a distance vector protocol that uses only hop count as a metric. It has two versions, and the most significant difference between the two versions is that version 1 is classful and version 2 is classless. A classful routing protocol will not send subnet mask information in its routing advertisements. This means that the use of variable-length subnet masks is not possible with version 1.

A RIP router will always send a route advertisement with the assumption that the mask is the default mask for that class. So if the network 10.5.6.0/24 was advertised, it would be advertised only as 10.0.0.0, and the receiving router would assume that the mask is the default for a Class A network, which is 8 bits, not 24. Version 2 does advertise subnet mask information, which makes the use of variable-length subnet masks possible.

It also means that summarization of subnets in router advertisements is possible. As you learned in Chapter 8, "Classless IP Addressing," summarization allows a router to advertise a summary of a set of subnets rather than advertising all of the subnets. For example, instead of advertising 192.168.5.0/24, 192.168.6.0/24, and 192.168.3.0/24, it could simply advertise 192.168.0.0/16, which would include all of the subnets of 192.168.0.0/16.

HOW DOES THAT WORK AGAIN?

To understand how 192.168.6.0/24, 192.168.5.0/24, and 192.168.3.0/24 are summarized by 192.18.0.0/16, consider that if you subnetted 192.168.0.0/16 with a subnet mask of 255.255.255.0 (/24), your interval would be 1 (the value of the far-right bit in the mask) and it would be applied in the octet where the borrowing stopped (third) and the first six subnets would be as follows:

▶ 192.168.1.0

▶ 192.168.2.0

▶ 192.168.3.0

▶ 192.168.4.0

▶ 192.168.5.0

▶ 192.168.6.0

Subnets can always be summarized with the classful network from which they were derived.

Like RIP version 1, RIPv2 will automatically summarize subnets, but you can disable this if it is advantageous to advertise the subnets rather than advertise a summarization. You can also specify exactly how the summarization is to be done, a feature which is called *manual summarization*.

Other features of RIP are presented throughout the rest of this section.

Routing Update Process

RIP is said to be a *chatty* protocol because it sends updates every 30 seconds, and when it does so, it sends its entire routing table. This is true even if no changes have occurred. When a RIP router receives an update about a route from another router, before it includes the route as a part of its update to other routers, it will increment the hop count by 1. If a RIP router has more than one route to a network in its table, it will include only the best route in the routing updates it sends to other routers. Finally, when a RIP router learns about a new route or learns of a change such as a route lost due to a link outage, it will immediately send an update independent of the regular 30-second updates.

Loop Prevention

Just as switching loops can occur when switch path redundancy exists, routing path redundancy can result in routing loops. RIP uses several features that prevent these loops from occurring. These mechanisms are as follows:

Maximum Hop Count Any hop count over 15 is considered unreachable, and any routes with a hop count of 15 or greater will not be placed in the table or acted upon. The result is that a RIP network cannot exceed 15 routers in diameter. This is the reason RIP is not appropriate for large networks.

Split Horizon Split horizon is a routing rule built into the protocol (no need to enable it or anything) that prevents a router from advertising a route to the same interface on which it was learned. The assumption is that if a router is attempting to advertise a route back in the direction from whence it came, a loop is occurring.

The *diameter* of a network is the number of hops required to cross it at its widest point.

RIP Timers

All routing protocols use timers to control update intervals and to control the length of time that entries remain in the routing table. RIP has timers for the following operations:

Routing Update Frequency The amount of time between regular routing updates

Route Timeout Timer   The amount of time a route remains in the table until it is marked invalid

Route Flush Timer   The amount of time after a route had been marked invalid until it is deleted or flushed from the routing table

> *Flushing* the route means removing it from the routing table.

RIP is the easiest routing protocol to use, as you will see in Chapter 16, "Configuring Dynamic Routing," when you will learn how to get RIP running in a small network.

Enhanced Interior Gateway Routing Protocol

Enhanced Interior Gateway Routing Protocol (EIGRP) is known as a hybrid routing protocol because it exhibits some characteristics of both link state and distance vector protocols. It is a classless routing protocol, so VLSM can be used. Unlike RIP and OSPF (discussed later in this section), EIGRP is Cisco-proprietary, which means it can be used only between two Cisco routers. EIGRP uses routing updates and routing tables like RIP but also has number of unique features.

Neighbor Table

EIGRP routers keep track of their directly connected neighbors and monitor their continued existence with regular hello packets. When hello packets go unanswered, an EIGRP router knows the neighbor is down (or the link to it is down) and that routes learned from that neighbor are no longer available. This is one of three tables that EIGRP uses to maintain a more detailed awareness of the network than RIP. Before an EIGRP router can exchange routing updates with another EIGRP router, the neighbor must be discovered and placed in this table. The neighbor discovery is also done using hello packets. When a new EIGRP router is brought online and it receives a hello packet, it will answer, and the two EIGRP routers will become neighbors.

Routing Table

Unlike a routing table in a RIP router, which theoretically could contain four or five routes to the same destination network, the routing table in an EIGRP router will contain at *most* two routes for each network. It will contain the best route, and if a second-best route exists, that route will be included. The best route is called the successor route, and the second best is called the *feasible successor.*

Not all second-best routes can be feasible successors, however. There are strict rules that control the admissibility of a route as a feasible successor. These rules are explained in the "EIGRP Metrics" section.

Topology Table

The second table that EIGRP uses is called a *topology table*. It includes *all* routes that exist to a destination network along with the router that sent the route and the metric of the route. It is this table that is acted upon by the DUAL algorithm. This algorithm uses metric information to determine the successor and feasible successor routes that are then placed in the routing table.

Reliable Transport Protocol (RTP)

EIGRP uses a special protocol for guaranteed (think TCP) delivery of messages between routers and in any non-point-to-point network that will use multicasting rather broadcasting for its messages. Multicasting creates much less traffic than broadcasting, without all the overhead of unicasting.

EIGRP Metrics

In EIGRP, the metric is not hop count but a composite value that is based on delay and bandwidth on each link on the path to the remote network. Additional factors can be included, but the core EIGRP metrics are usually sufficient and are the only ones used by default. After the metric for each link along the path is calculated, the metrics are totaled, arriving at the total metric for the route.

Each route has two metric values calculated: advertised distance and feasible distance. *Advertised distance* is the metric as it was stated in the advertisement that was received by the local router. That does *not* include the additional metric for the connection from the advertising router to the local router. *Feasible distance* is the advertised distance plus the metric for the connection between the advertising router and the local router.

This rule helps to prevent routing loops. Let's look at a single entry in an EIGRP topology table for an illustration of this:

```
P 172.168.0.0/24, 1 successor, FD is 217416
    Via 172.168.1.1 (217416/205156), Fa0/0
    Via 172.168.10.2 (209336/208156), Fa0/1
```

This is the entry in the topology table for the successor or best route to the 172.168.0.0/24 network and a second route. The two routes are listed in lines 2 and 3 and indicate the router that advertised the route, the metrics in parentheses (*feasible distance/advertised distance*), and the exit interfaces. The P next to the first line indicates that the route in use is in a passive state, which is good. The other state is active, which means something is wrong and the algorithm is actively trying to reestablish the route or find a replacement route.

The entry also indicates that the route to the network 172.168.0.0/24 via the router at 172.168.1.1 is the best and has a feasible distance of 217416 and an advertised distance of 205156. Let's see if we can figure out whether the second route is eligible as a feasible successor. To be considered, the route's advertised distance must be less than the feasible distance of the route that was chosen as the successor route. Because the advertised distance of the route via 172.168.10.2 is

The *Diffusing Update Algorithm (DUAL)* is used by EIGRP to ensure that a given route is recalculated globally whenever it might cause a routing loop.

A route cannot be considered a feasible successor if its advertised distance must be less than the feasible distance of the route chosen as the successor route.

To see the full topology table, execute the show ip eigrp topology command.

208156, and the feasible distance of the route via 172.168.1.1 (the successor or "best" route) is 217416, and 217416 is greater than 208156, this route *does* qualify and will be placed into the routing table as a feasible successor.

WHY DOES THIS MATTER?

The result of EIGRP maintaining a feasible successor route is that if the best router becomes unavailable, the second-best route is already known. That means the algorithm does not have to be executed again to identify the next-best route. This results in faster convergence. *Convergence* is the amount of time it takes for all routers to adapt to a change in the network.

Summarization

Because EIGRP is a classless routing protocol, it will summarize subnets in its routing advertisements. As in RIPv2, this behavior can be disabled. You can instruct the router exactly how you want the subnets to be summarized as well. By default, they are summarized to the classful major network. As with RIPv2, you can use manual summarization.

When all of the routers are Cisco, EIGRP is a great routing protocol to use because of its scalability, its fast convergence, its maximum hop count of 255, and its simplicity, as you will see in Chapter 16, when you will learn how to enable it for a small network.

Open Shortest Path First

The routing protocol most suitable for a large network (and as a result, the most complex) is *Open Shortest Path First (OSPF)*. It is a true link state routing protocol and is an industry standard, which means it can be used with a mix of Cisco and non-Cisco routers. The most obvious departure from the operation of RIP and EIGRP is OSPF's use of *areas* and its designation of certain routers as *designated, border,* and *autonomous system border* routers. Before the details of OSPF can be discussed, these basic concepts of OSPF must be understood.

Areas

OSPF routers are organized into areas. Even if you envision having only a single area, the routers must still be designated to be in the same area. The benefit of this is that when you *do* have many areas, detailed routing information about an area will be confined to *that* area, and only a summary of information will be advertised to other areas. This has the benefit of keeping OSPF routing tables smaller.

Autonomous Systems

A group of areas can be grouped into an autonomous system (AS), creating another level of hierarchy. Just as one area will advertise only a summary of information about its networks to another area, an AS will advertise only a summary of all of its areas to another AS. Again, the result is a smaller number of entries in the routing tables related to other ASs (these are called *exterior routes*).

Router Roles

In OSPF, certain routers are designated to perform certain functions on behalf of all routers in an area or all routers in an AS. These router roles and their functions are as follows:

Designated Router   Each shared network segment will select a designated router (DR). The other routers on the segment will exchange updates only with the DR. This will occur after each non-DR establishes an adjacency with the local DR. OSPF routers will still exchange hellos and become neighbors with other OSPF routers with which they share a segment, but will establish adjacency and exchange information with only the DR. A DR and BDR will be elected on every multi-access segment. If two OSPF routers share a point-to-point link, there is no advantage to having a DR, and one will not be elected. The election process will be based on the priority of each OSPF router. By default, the priority of each router is 1. When there is a tie between two routers (which there will be if this issue is left to its default), the tie is broken with the router ID (RID). By default, this value is the highest IP address that exists on the router.

◄

A shared network segment is one in which all the devices are connected to the switch.

Area Border Routers   Areas apply to interfaces, which means that a router can have all interfaces assigned to the same area, or it can have one interface assigned to one area and another interface assigned to another area. When a router has interfaces in different areas, it is acting as an area border router (ABR). It will control the route advertisements between the two areas. It will exchange full routing information with the DR in the area to which the interface has been assigned, but will send only summary advertisements about the area to which the interface has not been assigned, as shown in Figure 11.5.

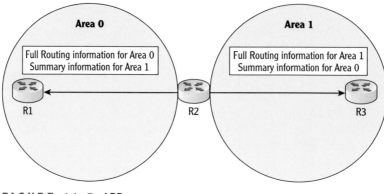

FIGURE 11.5 ABR

In Figure 11.5, R2 is the ABR between Area 0 and Area 1. R2 will exchange full routing information for Area 0 and summary information for Area 1 with R1, and full routing information for Area 1 and Summary information for Area 0 with R3. This is beneficial because if Area 0 has, for example, 15 subnets in it, a summary network could be advertised to R3, resulting in a single entry in R2's routing table rather than 15 entries.

Autonomous System Border Routers   Areas can be grouped into an autonomous system (AS). When a router has interfaces in different ASs, it is acting as an autonomous system border router (ASBR). It will control the route advertisements between the two ASs. It will exchange full routing information with the DR in the AS to which the interface has been assigned, but will send only summary advertisements about the AS to which the interface has not been assigned, as shown in Figure 11.6. Keep in mind as you look at Figure 11.6 that each AS (AS 20 and 30) is made up of at least one area.

OSPF is classless, which means VLSM can be enabled, and it uses a metric called *cost*. Each interface has a cost value that is determined based on its bandwidth. OSPF routers send what are called link state advertisements (LSAs). Link states are collections of information about each interface (or link) on a router. An LSA includes the IP address network type and routers to which it is connected. Each router stores these link states in a link state database.

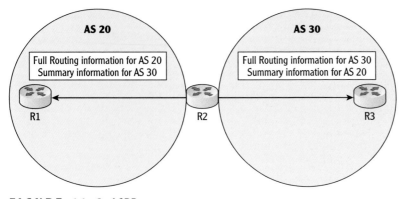

FIGURE 11.6 ASBR

There are 11 LSA types, which contain different types of information and are sent by different types of routers. Some of the more important types are as follows:

Router links are sent by each router about its links to the area. These are called Intra-area or Type 1 LSAs.

Network links are sent by a DR to describe all routes attached to the segment. These are also called Type 2 LSAs.

Summary links are sent by ABRs to other ABRs with summary information about the networks in the area. These are also called Type 3 LSAs.

ASBR Summary links are sent by ASBRs to other ASBRs with summary information about the networks in all of the areas in its AS. These are also called Type 4.

OSPF routers that are not DRs receive LSAs from the local DR, which in turn receives LSAs from the ABR, which in turn receives LSAs from the ASBR. When all of these link states have been stored in the local link state database and again any time a change occurs (addition, deletion, or change of a link state), the routers use an algorithm called the Shortest Path First (SPF), also called the Dijkstra algorithm, to create a view of the network from the perspective of the local router that is called the *SPF tree*.

This process is unlike RIP or EIGRP, in that in OSPF, each router maintains its own complete view of the network, not a partial view. Other advantages include an unlimited hop count and fast convergence. In Chapter 16, you will learn to configure a simple OSPF network.

TALE OF THE TAPE

The following table compares the three routing protocols:

Protocol	Metric	Convergence	VLSM	Configuration
RIP	Hop count	Slow	v1 no, v2 yes	Simplest
EIGRP	BW and delay	Fast	Yes	More difficult
OSPF	Cost	Fast	Yes	Most difficult

Describing the Switching Process

As a frame is moved from one interface to another interface, either on a point-to-point link or on a shared medium, the operation occurs at the Network Access layer. Even as a packet is relayed across a network from router to router and eventually to the destination subnet, at each point where it is transferred from the interface of one device (either host NIC to router interface, or router interface to router interface), the transfer is made in terms of MAC addresses, not IP addresses.

This section describes the process by which a packet is placed on the cable by the source device and received by the next interface. First, you will review the relationship between IP addresses and MAC addresses. Then you will review the CSMA/CD and CSMA/CA contention methods. You will explore the role of the switch and its use of the MAC address table in acting as an intermediary between the host device and the router. Finally, you will learn three possible methods that a switch can use to forward frames, and the costs and benefits of each. Keep in mind that this entire process will occur each time the frame must go from the host NIC to a router interface or from a router interface to router interface.

Reviewing MAC and IP Addresses

Packets are routed on the basis of IP addresses, and frames are switched on the basis of MAC addresses. This is why it is said that routers operate and routing occurs on the Internet layer of the TCP/IP model and that switches operate and switching occurs on the Network Access layer of the TCP/IP model. In a TCP/IP packet, there is a section called the Network Access layer header, where the source and destination MAC addresses go, and a section called the IP header, where the source and destination IP addresses go. When a packet is being assembled, the IP header is built first and the Network Access layer header is built and attached in front of the IP header, resulting in the structure shown in Figure 11.7.

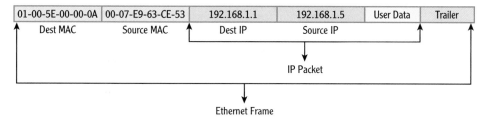

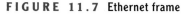

FIGURE 11.7 Ethernet frame

The part of this frame that will change every time the frame is switched from one interface to another will be the front portion, where the source and destination MAC addresses are located. The IP header where the source and destination IP addresses are located will not change. Each time the frame must be switched from one interface to another on its journey, a new source and destination MAC address will need to be placed in the frame, because a new set of source and destination interfaces will be involved in the transfer and each has a unique MAC address. This process is called *rebuilding the MAC header*. Each time this process is done, a new frame check sequence (FCS), used to verify the integrity of the MAC header, will be created and placed in a new trailer that will go on the end of the Ethernet frame.

When a frame needs to be switched from one interface to another, the new source and destination MAC addresses will need to be identified and placed in the MAC header. This is the job of the Address Resolution Protocol (ARP). In the "Describing End-to-End Communications" section, you will learn how this process occurs both on a local LAN and when a packet is being relayed through many routers across a network.

Reviewing Contention Methods

There are two contention methods used to get the frame onto the local network. Which one is used depends on whether the frame needs to be placed on an 802.3 (Ethernet) network or an 802.11 (WLAN) network. A brief review of each follows.

CSMA/CA

When the device sending the frame is transmitting onto a wireless network, the CSMA/CA contention method is used. The method starts with a check of the medium (in this case, a check of the radio frequency) for activity called *physical carrier sense*. If the medium is not clear, the station will implement an internal countdown mechanism called the *random back-off algorithm*. This counter will have started counting down after the last time this station was allowed to transmit. All stations will be counting down their own individual timers. When a station's timer expires, it is allowed to send. If the physical carrier is clear and the countdown timer is at zero, the station will send.

The frame will go to the AP. The AP will acknowledge reception of the frame. If the frame is destined for another wireless station located on this wireless LAN, the frame will be forwarded to it by the AP. When this occurs, the AP will follow the same CSMA/CA contention method to get the frame onto the wireless medium.

If the frame is destined for a station on the wired LAN, the AP will drop the 802.11 MAC header (which is structured differently from an Ethernet MAC header) and build a new Ethernet MAC header by using its MAC address as the source address and the MAC address of the default gateway as the destination. The LAN router will receive the frame and normal LAN routing to the destination will continue from there, using the CSMA/CD contention mechanism (covered in the next section) to place the frame in the wire at each step. If frames are returned to the station, the AP will receive them, drop the Ethernet MAC header, build an 802.11 MAC header, and return the frame to the wireless station. When this occurs, the AP will follow the same CSMA/CA contention method to get the frame onto the wireless medium.

CSMA/CD

When the device sending the frame is transmitting onto a wired network, the CSMA/CD contention method is used. This method is somewhat more efficient because it is possible for wireless computers to detect collisions while wireless stations cannot. When a host's or router's interface needs to send a frame, it checks the wire, and if no traffic is detected, it sends without checking a random back-off timer.

However, it continues to listen, and if it detects that a collision has occurred, it sends out a jam signal that requires all stations to stop transmitting. Then the two computers that were involved in the collision will both wait a random amount of time (that each arrives at independently) and will resend. So instead of using a random break-off algorithm every time a transmission occurs, Ethernet uses its ability to detect collisions and uses this timer only when required, which makes the process more efficient.

Describing MAC Address Tables

When a frame is switched from one router interface to another, no switch is involved, but when a computer sends to its default gateway or to another computer in its same subnet, the frame usually goes through a switch before it is switched on to the router interface or to the other local computer. As you learned in the preceding chapter, switches learn the MAC address of each device that is connected to each port and stores this information in a MAC address table.

The MAC address table shows the MAC address of each device on each port. The table can be displayed by executing the show mac-address-table command. When this is done, the output looks like this:

```
VLAN    MAC Address       Type       Port
1       0018.b967.3cd0    dynamic    Fa0/1
1       001c.b05a.5380    dynamic    Fa0/2
```

The output indicates that there are two devices connected to the switch. Both devices are in VLAN1. (By default, all devices are in VLAN1.)

The device connected to switch port 1 (Fast Ethernet 0/1) has a MAC address of 0018.b967.3cd0. The address was registered dynamically when the first frame was received from the device.

The device connected to port 2 has a MAC address of 001c.b05a.5380. As indicated by the Type column (which describes the way in which the address was

Virtual LANs (VLANs) are discussed in Chapter 14, "Configuring Switches."

◄

◄

MAC entries can also be manually assigned to a port if desired.

registered, static or dynamic), this address was also acquired the first time the device connected to port 2 sent a frame.

If a MAC address in the table is not refreshed by the device sending a frame for a certain period of time (which is configurable or can be left to the default value, called the *aging time*), the address will be purged from the table.

Understanding Frame Forwarding

When a switch first starts up, even if it has 20 devices connected to its ports that are up and running, its MAC address table will be empty and it will operate as a hub. The reason for this behavior (which will not last very long) has to do with normal rules of operation. These same rules will ensure that quite quickly the MAC address table will be populated and the switch will send frames *only* to their destination port.

The frame-forwarding operation can be summed up in a couple of steps:

1. If the switch finds the MAC address to be in its table, it will send the frame to that port only.

2. If the switch does not find the MAC address to be in its table, it will send the frame to every port except the port on which it arrived. This is called *frame flooding*.

When the switch is turned on, as hosts begin to send frames through the switch, the switch will read the source MAC address in the frame when the frame enters the switch and will record this address in the table. In the example at the beginning of this section, after all 20 devices have sent frames, all 20 addresses will be recorded, and after that point, no more unicast frame flooding will take place.

When the switch is reading the frame, it can perform this operation in one of three ways. Different models use different methods. These three ways are listed and explained here:

Store-and-Forward   When this frame-processing method is enabled, the switch will receive the entire frame and validate the FCS before making the forwarding decision. This method results in the slowest forwarding process, but the lowest number of corrupted frames because the FCS is checked. This is usually the default method on a switch.

Cut-Through   When a switch uses this method, it will read only the MAC header and forward the frame. This provides the fastest switching, but because it does not read the entire frame and verify the FCS, its can result in the highest number of corrupted frames.

Fragment-Free   This method will read the first 64 bits of the frame before forwarding. Although this does not provide a check of the FCS, which would require reading the entire frame before forwarding, it does read enough of the frame to avoid forwarding frames that were damaged because of collisions. You might consider this to be a compromise between the other two methods. It does not have the speed of cut-through, but neither does it produce the levels of corrupted frames. It is faster than store-and-forward and it results in more corrupted frames than store-and-forward, but certainly not as many as with cut-through.

Describing End-to-End Communications

In this section, the switching and routing processes are integrated. The contents of the MAC and IP headers are monitored as a packet is transferred from one computer to another through the switch(es) and router(s). Because the process is slightly different (and less complicated) if the source and destination computers are in the same LAN than if they are in different LANs (or subnets), each process is given its own section.

Understanding the Local LAN Process

Using Figure 11.8, if WS 1 needs to send a packet to WS 2, the following steps will occur for each packet:

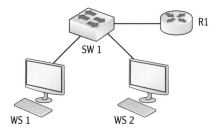

FIGURE 11.8 Local LAN process

1. WS 1 examines the destination IP address of WS 2 with respect to its own IP address and determines whether the two computers are in the same network. It comes to the conclusion that they are.

2. If WS 1 had come to the conclusion that WS 2 was in a different network, it would have performed an ARP broadcast for the MAC address that corresponds to the IP address of its default gateway (the R1 router interface). However, because they are in the same network, it performs an ARP broadcast in the local LAN for the IP address of WS 2.

3. All computers connected to the switch SW 1 (including the router interface) receive the ARP broadcast, but only WS 2 responds with its MAC address.

4. WS 1 places the MAC address of WS 2 in the MAC header and sends the frame to the switch SW 1. The switch reads its MAC address table, identifies the switch port to which WS 2 is connected, and switches the frame to WS 2.

Understanding the Remote Communication Process

Using Figure 11.9, if WS 1 needs to send a packet to WS 2, the following steps will occur for each packet:

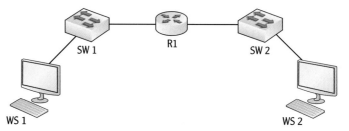

FIGURE 11.9 Remote communication process

1. WS 1 examines the destination IP address of WS 2 with respect to its own IP address and determines whether the two computers are in the same network. It comes to the conclusion that they are not.

2. Because WS 1 came to the conclusion that WS 2 is in a different network, it performs an ARP broadcast for the MAC address that corresponds to the IP address of its default gateway (the R1 router interface).

3. All computers connected to the switch SW 1 (including the router interface) receive the ARP broadcast, but only the R1 router interface responds with its MAC address.

4. WS 1 places the MAC address of the R1 router interface in the MAC header and sends the frame to the switch SW 1. The switch reads its MAC address table, identifies the switch port to which the router interface to R1 is connected, and switches the frame to R1.

5. R1 examines its routing table to see whether it has a route to the network to which WS 2 belongs. If it does not and the router has been configured with a default route, it will send the packet to that interface. If it does not have a route to the network in which WS 2 resides and it has not been set with a default route, R1 will drop the packet and send a destination unreachable message back to WS1. In this case, because WS 2 resides in a network that is directly connected to R1, the network *will* be in the routing table.

6. R1 performs an ARP broadcast in the network to which WS 2 belongs, sourced from the interface that connects to that subnet.

7. All computers connected to the switch SW 2 receive the ARP broadcast, but only WS 2 responds with its MAC address.

8. R1 places the MAC address of WS 2 in the MAC header and sends the frame to the switch SW 2. The switch reads its MAC address table, identifies the switch port to which WS 2 is connected, and switches the frame to WS 2.

THE ESSENTIALS AND BEYOND

Designing and troubleshooting networks requires an understanding of what goes on at the upper part of the Network Access layer and the Internet layer of the TCP/IP model. Routers and multilayer switches use IP addresses to locate destinations. As a frame is moved from one interface to another interface, the operation occurs at the Network Access layer. Routers use routing tables. Routes in the routing table are either directly connected, static, or dynamic. A routing table entry will include network, population method, next hop, exit interface, and metric information. Routers select the best route based on the metric and administrative distance. Routing protocols can be either exterior (used between autonomous systems) or interior (used within an autonomous system). Distance vector routing protocols use a very simple metric called hop count, and link state routing protocols use a combination of factors when deciding the best route. RIP is a distance

(Continues)

THE ESSENTIALS AND BEYOND (Continued)

vector protocol that uses only hop count as a metric, and maximum hop count and split horizon to prevent routing loops. EIGRP exhibits some characteristics of both link state and distance vector protocols. By using three tables (the neighbor, routing, and topology tables), EIGRP can converge faster than RIP. The most complex interior protocol is OSPF, which uses areas and a designation of certain routers as designated, border, and autonomous system border routers to achieve fast convergence. There are two contention methods used to get the frame onto the local network. The one used depends on whether the frame needs to be placed on an 802.3 (Ethernet) network (CSMA/CD) or an 802.11 (WLAN) network (CSMA/CA). Switches learn the MAC address of each device that is connected to each port and store this information in a MAC address table. When the switch is reading the frame, it can perform this operation in one of three ways: store-and-forward, cut-through, and fragment-free.

ADDITIONAL EXERCISES

Using the following output of the show ip route command, answer questions 1–5.

```
75.0.0.0/24 is subnetted, 4 subnets
C   75.0.1.0 is directly connected Serial 0
R   75.0.2.0[120/1] via 10.1.6.1 0:01:00 Serial 1
R   75.0.4.0[120/2] via 10.1.6.1 0:01:00 Serial 1
C   75.0.6.0 is directly connected Serial 1
```

1. What is the administrative distance of the route to the network 75.0.4.0?

2. How many hops away is the network 75.0.2.0?

3. What population method got the 75.0.1.0 network into the routing table?

4. How many active interfaces does the router connected to this router on interface Serial 1 have?

5. If this router needs to send a packet to the IP address 75.0.1.9, what will be the exit interface?

REVIEW QUESTIONS

1. Which of the following is *not* contained in a routing table entry?

A. Source network	**C.** Population method
B. Destination network	**D.** Metric

2. Which of the following is *not* a method of populating the routing table?

A. Direct connections	**C.** Dynamic routing protocols
B. DHCP	**D.** Manual route entry

(Continues)

THE ESSENTIALS AND BEYOND *(Continued)*

3. How did the following entry get into the routing table?

    S 192.168.5.0/24

    A. Direct connection   **C.** Dynamic routing protocols

    B. NAT   **D.** Manual route entry

4. How long has it been since the following routing table entry has been refreshed?

    R 10.0.4.0 via 10.1.6.1.0:01:50 Serial 1

    A. 1 hour and 50 minutes   **C.** 1 minute and 50 seconds

    B. 10 hours and 50 minutes   **D.** Cannot be determined with this
                                                   information

5. Which of the following is *not* an interior routing protocol?

    A. OSPF   **C.** EIGRP

    B. RIP   **D.** BGP

6. Which routing protocol uses hop count as its sole metric?

    A. OSPF   **C.** EIGRP

    B. RIP   **D.** BGP

7. What is the default AD of EIGRP?

    A. 90   **C.** 120

    B. 110   **D.** 150

8. If a router has numerous routes to the same network, learned from the following methods, which route will be chosen?

    A. An OSPF route   **C.** An EIGRP route

    B. A RIP route   **D.** A static route

9. How often does RIP send regular routing updates?

    A. Every 15 seconds   **C.** Every 30 seconds

    B. Every 20 seconds   **D.** Every 45 seconds

10. What routing rule built into RIP prevents a router from advertising a route to the same interface on which it was learned?

    A. Maximum hop count   **C.** Feasible distance

    B. Split horizon   **D.** SPF tree

CHAPTER 12

Managing the Cisco IOS

Cisco routers and switches have an operating system, just as computers have operating systems. This operating system is used to access and manage the hardware on the router or switch and is used as the interface to change and view settings on the device. Although most Cisco devices are now capable of being managed through a web interface that presents a graphical user interface (GUI) to the administrator, management of routers and switches traditionally is done through the Cisco command-line interface (CLI).

Until recently, Cisco switches could have one of two operating systems installed. The CAT OS, which was inherited when Cisco purchased another switch manufacturer, continued to be an option until just recently. Cisco issued its final maintenance release in 2009 and will end support of this operating system in 2013. The Cisco Internetwork Operating System (IOS) has been the operating system in Cisco routers all along, and over the years Cisco replaced the CAT OS with the Cisco IOS on its switch models.

It is important to understand not only the Cisco IOS and how to use it, but also the various hardware, software, and firmware locations on Cisco devices, what information is stored in each location, how the boot process uses the information in these locations, and how changes to the device are handled. That is the focus of this chapter. Specifically, this chapter covers the following topics:

► **Describing components**

► **Describing IOS navigation**

► **Understanding and managing the boot process**

Describing Components

A Cisco router or switch uses an operating system and a number of configuration files to perform its tasks. These components are stored in various locations on the device. Some components can even be located on a different device in the network and accessed as required across the network. The device also requires some general memory to use as a working space, as any computing device does.

This section presents the various types of storage that exist on a router or switch, with a particular emphasis on the type of information that is stored in these locations. This section also covers the ability of each type to retain information and the operations required to harness these capabilities.

Defining the Contents of RAM

All Cisco routers and switches have *random access memory (RAM)*. This very fast memory is used in the same fashion as RAM in a computer or server. This type of memory requires power to the device to retain its information. When the router or switch boots up, it will place some information in RAM, specifically the IOS tables, and it will dedicate some of this RAM to be used as buffers. This is not unlike the operating system on a computer, which will "load" itself into memory from the hard drive at bootup and operate from that location.

Additionally, the device will use RAM as an area to store a copy of the configuration file at startup. When edits are made to this file—for example, the addition of an IP address to one of the interfaces—the change will be reflected *only* in the version stored here (called the *running configuration*) unless it is copied to the version stored in NVRAM (covered in the next section).

To understand this, consider the relationship between memory and the hard drive in a computer. If you are working on a Microsoft Word document and making edits, the changes you are making are being applied to the copy stored in memory. Those changes will be lost if power is lost to the computer *before* you have "saved" them to the hard drive. This is the relationship between items stored in RAM and those stored in NVRAM in a Cisco router or switch.

In summation, the contents of RAM in a Cisco router or switch are as follows:

▶ The Cisco IOS tables

▶ The running configuration file

▶ Buffer space

RAM for a Cisco router or switch plugs into a memory slot, just as it does in a computer. An example of Cisco router RAM is shown in Figure 12.1. This RAM is located in a slot in a Cisco 2501 router.

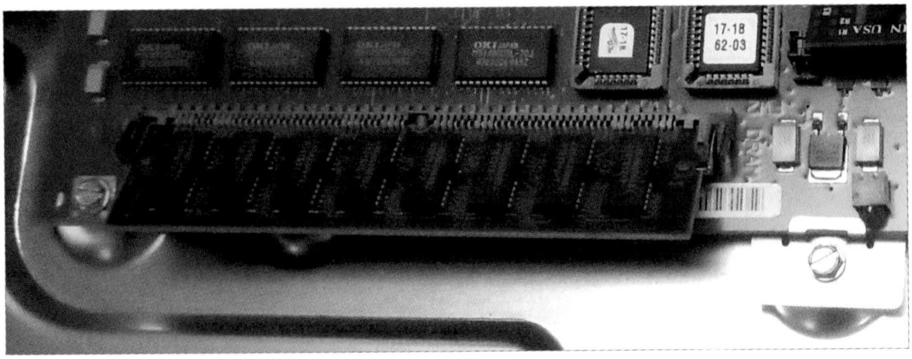

FIGURE 12.1 Router RAM

Defining the Contents of NVRAM

Cisco routers and switches do not have hard drives. Information that needs to be retained when power is off is stored in *nonvolatile random access memory (NVRAM)* or in flash memory (covered in the next section). In this extremely fast memory, the saved version of the configuration file is stored. In this location, it is called the *startup configuration*.

NVRAM resides on the motherboard of the router or switch in the form of a chip. It looks somewhat different from the RAM in a router or switch.

NVRAM is not very large, because its only content is the relatively small configuration file. It also contains a set of four hexadecimal digits called the *configuration register*. The settings in the configuration register determine the locations that will be searched for the IOS and for the startup configuration file. If the device boots up and no startup configuration file is present (or you have instructed the device to ignore the file that is present by using the settings in the configuration register), the device will present you with a menu-based set of prompts (called *setup*) designed to create one. This is discussed in the "Understanding and Managing the Boot Process" section later in this chapter.

Defining the Contents of Flash

The third type of memory present in a Cisco device is called *flash memory*. Flash memory can come in several formats in a Cisco device. It can be in a slot or single inline memory module (SIMM), it can reside in a flash card format, or it can be placed in a Personal Computer Memory Card International Association (PCMCIA) slot. The latter two form factors are typically used to supplement the

◄

Why ignore the startup configuration file? If you need to perform a password recovery, you first tell the device to ignore the file where the passwords are! Once you have accessed the device, then you can delete or change the passwords.

amount of flash memory present on the board in the SIMMs. Regardless of its format, flash memory differs from regular RAM in that it does not lose its content when the power goes off.

Flash memory is used to hold the operating system, which is typically referred to as the *IOS image*. It is possible, however, to store configuration files here as well. You might think of this as the hard drive of the device, because it has much more capacity than the NVRAM and can be used to hold whatever you want to copy there. Some devices store the bootstrap code there as well, which otherwise is usually stored in the ROM (covered in the next section). Flash memory in a Cisco 2501 router is shown in Figure 12.2. The router contains flash memory in two slots and has an empty slot available to add more flash memory in flashcard format.

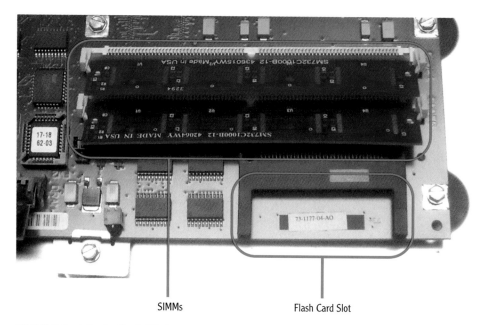

SIMMs   Flash Card Slot

FIGURE 12.2 Flash SIMMs and card slot

Defining the Contents of ROM

Read-only memory (ROM) is the same type of chip on which the Basic Input/Output System (BIOS) of a computer is often stored. It is read-only and contains what is called *bootstrap code*. As you will learn in the "Understanding and Managing the Boot Process" section, when the device starts, this is the very first place that it looks for instructions. Even if the router or switch has no IOS in flash memory, you will see output on the screen, and this is where that output is coming from. The ROM chips on a Cisco 2501 board are shown in Figure 12.3.

FIGURE 12.3 ROM

If you've ever booted a computer with no operating system, you know that the computer will appear to be booting up to a point when it will ask, "Where's the operating system? I can't find it." The instructions that got the computer to that point came from the BIOS of the computer stored on the BIOS chip. Those chips are the same type of ROM.

In the case of the Cisco device, the same type of instructions (bootstrap code) is there and will also get the device to the same point where it will need the operating system. Moreover, just as you can set the computer to boot to *setup* (which means you have instructed the computer to *not* proceed to the loading of the operating system but to stop and present you with a menu enabling you to make changes to or view the instructions held in the BIOS), you can instruct the Cisco device to boot into *ROMmon mode*. Once in this mode, you can make changes to the way in which the device boots and view information about those settings. There is more information on this special mode in the section "Managing the Configuration Register" later in this chapter.

The various storage locations in a Cisco router or switch and the *key* contents of each are summarized here:

Location	Type	Contents
NVRAM	Nonvolatile	Startup config/config register
Flash	Nonvolatile	Cisco IOS
RAM	Volatile	Running configuration
ROM	Nonvolatile	Bootstrap code

Although the locations can vary by device, Figure 12.4 shows how these storage locations might appear in the board of a device.

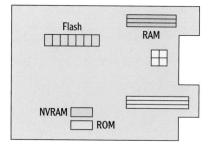

FIGURE 12.4 Cisco storage

Describing IOS Navigation

To manage a Cisco device, you must understand how the interface that is used to control it operates, how to make a physical or network connection to the device, and how to navigate through the various levels of access available in the IOS. In this section, you will learn how to perform these operations and you will learn some shortcuts that can make managing the CLI easier.

Connecting to the Device

There are two ways to make a connection to a Cisco router or switch. You can make a physical connection to the device by using a HyperTerminal program installed on a computer, or you can connect to the device over the network by using Telnet or a Telnet-like program. The second option is available only if the device has an interface enabled and has been configured with an IP address. Moreover, certain functions can be performed only with a direct connection using a HyperTerminal program (such as the password recovery procedure covered in the upcoming section "Managing the Configuration Register"). In this section, you will learn how to make both connections.

Physical Connection Using HyperTerminal

Making a physical connection obviously requires physical access to the device. It also requires that the computer from which you are accessing the Cisco device has a HyperTerminal program installed. Microsoft computers used to come with a HyperTerminal program installed but no longer do. Free

HyperTerminal programs for Windows XP, Windows Vista, and Windows 7 are available online at `http://download.cnet.com/HyperTerminal-Private-Edition/3000-2155_4-10966768.html`.

In the "Additional Exercises" section at the end of this chapter, you will have a chance to install this program.

This procedure also requires a connection to the device using a console or rolled cable. As you learned in Chapter 9, this cable has an RJ-45 connector on one end and an RS-232, or serial, connector on the other end. The RJ-45 connector is plugged into the console port on the Cisco device, and the serial end connects to the serial port on the computer, as shown in Figure 12.5.

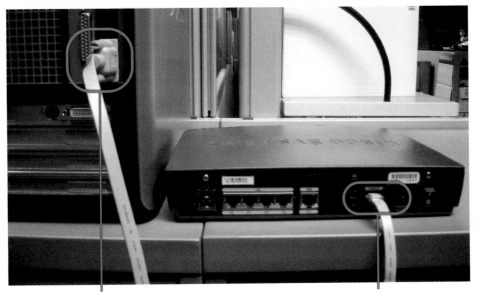

Serial connector to the serial port
on the computer

RJ-45 connector to the console port
on the router

FIGURE 12.5 Console port to serial port

Most new laptops (which are the tool of choice for Cisco technicians) do not have a serial port. When that is the case, you will need a serial-to-USB adaptor.

After the connections are in place, start the HyperTerminal program on the computer. The opening dialog box will require you to answer a few questions about the settings in the program, as shown in Figure 12.6. In the Location Information dialog box, set an area code. This is really of no consequence because we will not be using the HyperTerminal program with a modem, but you must enter an area code to proceed. Click OK, and the Phone And Modem dialog box appears.

FIGURE 12.6 Location Information dialog box

In the Phone And Modem dialog box, accept the default location and click OK (again, this has relevance only when using a modem, but the box must be addressed to move forward). The Connection Description dialog box appears.

In the Connection Description dialog box, you can name the connection. (I have named mine *Router*.) Naming it is not required, and if you click OK, the connection will be named *My connection*. Click OK, and the Connect To dialog box opens.

In the Connect To dialog box, you can select the COM port you are using. It will default to COM 1, which is fine because most computers have only one COM port these days. Click OK, and the COM1 Properties dialog box opens.

The COM1 Properties dialog box is the final box you receive before the connection goes live, and it is very important. The settings in each one of these boxes must be as shown in Figure 12.7. The settings may or may not default to these options, but clicking the Restore Defaults button should apply these settings. If you can't make a connection, this dialog box is the first thing to check.

If your device is already on, when you click OK, the router prompt will appear and you will be ready to start working with the device, as shown here:

```
troy>
```

If you turn on your device and it is new or has no configuration, you will see output similar to the following, which is asking whether you want to proceed:

```
A summary of U.S. laws governing Cisco cryptographic products may be
found at:
http://www.cisco.com/wwl/export/crypto/tool/stqrg.html
```

If you require further assistance please contact us by sending email
to
export@cisco.com.
Cisco 1841 (revision 5.0) with 114688K/16384K bytes of memory.
Processor board ID FTX0947Z18E
M860 processor: part number 0, mask 49
2 FastEthernet/IEEE 802.3 interface(s)
191K bytes of NVRAM.
63488K bytes of ATA CompactFlash (Read/Write)
Cisco IOS Software, 1841 Software (C1841-ADVIPSERVICESK9-M), Version
12.4(15)T1, RELEASE SOFTWARE (fc2)
Technical Support: http://www.cisco.com/techsupport
Copyright (c) 1986-2007 by Cisco Systems, Inc.
Compiled Wed 18-Jul-07 04:52 by pt_team
    --- System Configuration Dialog ---
Continue with configuration dialog? [yes/no]:

If you want to use the menu-based setup program (covered later in this chapter),
you type **yes**. If you want to escape from the menu-based setup and use the Cisco
command-line interface, you type **no**.

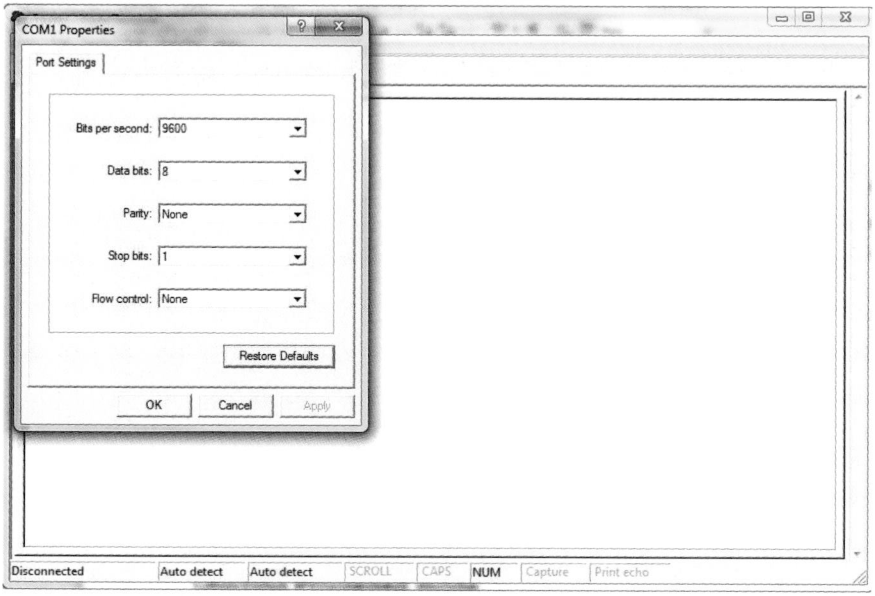

FIGURE 12.7 The COM1 Properties dialog box

Network Connection Using Telnet

If the device has an IP address, you can connect to the device from a computer by using Telnet. Telnet is a command-line program that is included in most operating systems, but in many, such as Windows 7, it is not installed by default. To install it, choose Control Panel ➢ Programs And Features and then select Turn Windows Features On And Off from the menu on the left side of the Programs And Features dialog box. When the list of programs that are installed or not installed appears, scroll down to Telnet Client and select it. Click OK, and the program will install.

After the program is installed, it is used from the command line. Go to the command line and type **telnet** and the IP address of the Cisco router or switch to which you would like to connect. If you connect, you will be prompted for a username and password. If no username and password have been set for the terminal connection (which is called a *line password* and is covered in Chapter 13, "Configuring Routers"), you will not be allowed to connect.

After you are authenticated, the prompt of the device will appear, and from that point forward, everything operates just as if you were connected with the console cable. This is the most common way to access and manage a device, because it doesn't require physical access to the device. A Telnet connection can also be established from one router to another at the IOS CLI.

Accessing User, Privileged, and Global Configuration Modes

There are two levels of access in the IOS, and you must proceed through the lower security level to get to the higher level. It is somewhat like passing through a series of logical doors, with each allowing access to more-sensitive procedures. After you have been authenticated at the privileged access level, you can access global configuration mode, which is called an *operational mode*. The two access levels are as follows:

▶ User mode

▶ Privileged mode (sometimes called enable mode)

You will be prompted for a password only at the privileged mode, but because you must proceed through privileged mode to get to global configuration mode, this password controls access to that level as well.

The relationship between these modes is illustrated in Figure 12.8.

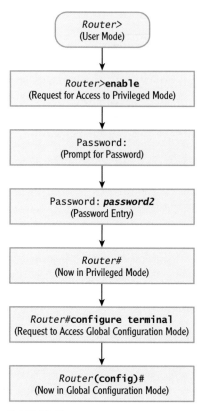

FIGURE 12.8 Access modes

The commands used to proceed through the three modes as they would look in the console are shown here:

```
troy>enable
Password:
troy#config t
Enter configuration commands, one per line.  End with CNTL/Z.
Troy(config)#
```

Note that the password was typed on line 2 but does not appear on the screen for security reasons. It is important to understand the types of things you can do in each of these modes, but it is not necessary to memorize which commands are available at a certain level. You can use the ? command at any time to see the commands available at whatever level you are at. The output at each level is shown next.

The following is the output for user mode:

```
troy>?
Exec commands:
<1-99>      Session number to resume
connect     Open a terminal connection
disable     Turn off privileged commands
disconnect  Disconnect an existing network connection
enable      Turn on privileged commands
exit        Exit from the EXEC
logout      Exit from the EXEC
ping        Send echo messages
resume      Resume an active network connection
show        Show running system information
ssh         Open a secure shell client connection
telnet      Open a telnet connection
terminal    Set terminal line parameters
traceroute  Trace route to destination
```

This is the output for privileged mode:

```
troy#?
Exec commands:
<1-99>      Session number to resume
auto        Exec level Automation
clear       Reset functions
clock       Manage the system clock
configure   Enter configuration mode
connect     Open a terminal connection
copy        Copy from one file to another
debug       Debugging functions (see also 'undebug')
delete      Delete a file
dir         List files on a filesystem
disable     Turn off privileged commands
disconnect  Disconnect an existing network connection
enable      Turn on privileged commands
erase       Erase a filesystem
exit        Exit from the EXEC
logout      Exit from the EXEC
mkdir       Create new directory
more        Display the contents of a file
no          Disable debugging information
ping        Send echo messages
reload      Halt and perform a cold restart
resume      Resume an active network connection
```

```
rmdir         Remove existing directory
setup         Run the SETUP command facility
show          Show running system information
ssh           Open a secure shell client connection
telnet        Open a telnet connection
terminal      Set terminal line parameters
traceroute    Trace route to destination
undebug       Disable debugging functions (see also 'debug')
vlan          Configure VLAN parameters
write         Write running configuration to memory, network, or
terminal
```

The output for global configuration mode is as follows:

```
troy(config)#?
Configure commands:
aaa                 Authentication, Authorization and Accounting.
access-list         Add an access list entry
banner              Define a login banner
boot                Modify system boot parameters
cdp                 Global CDP configuration subcommands
clock               Configure time-of-day clock
config-register     Define the configuration register
crypto              Encryption module
do                  To run exec commands in config mode
dot11               IEEE 802.11 config commands
enable              Modify enable password parameters
end                 Exit from configure mode
exit                Exit from configure mode
hostname            Set system's network name
interface           Select an interface to configure
ip                  Global IP configuration subcommands
ipv6                Global IPv6 configuration commands
line                Configure a terminal line
logging             Modify message logging facilities
login               Enable secure login checking
mac-address-table   Configure the MAC address table
no                  Negate a command or set its defaults
ntp                 Configure NTP
parser              Configure parser
policy-map          Configure QoS Policy Map
priority-list       Build a priority list
privilege           Command privilege parameters
queue-list          Build a custom queue list
```

radius-server	Modify Radius query parameters
router	Enable a routing process
secure	Secure image and configuration archival commands
security	Infra Security CLIs
service	Modify use of network based services
snmp-server	Modify SNMP engine parameters
spanning-tree	Spanning Tree Subsystem
tacacs-serer	Modify TACACS query parameters
username	Establish User Name Authentication
vpdn	Virtual Private Dialup Network
vpdn-group	VPDN group configuration
zone	FW with zoning
zone-pair	Zone pair command

To make using the CLI easier, you should know the following:

► If you type enough of a command for the command interpreter to distinguish that command from any other command, the interpreter will accept the command. This is why typing copy run start will be accepted by the CLI as copy running-config startup-config and why config t will be accepted for configure terminal.

► The CLI will remember the last 10 commands you have typed. If you want to reissue a command without typing it again, you can use the up-arrow and down-arrow keys to scroll through the last 10 commands and use them again without retyping them.

► Many commands have parameters that are used to include details about the command or to alter the command's function. If you type the command and then type ?, all parameters for the command will appear.

Understanding and Managing the Boot Process

It's not enough to understand where everything is located on Cisco devices. To troubleshoot a device, it is critical to understand the boot process. There is a normal boot process and then there are actions you can take to alter the process. It is important to understand how to do that and in what situation doing so would be beneficial.

This section covers the boot process in detail. The output that you can expect to see at certain points in the boot process is described. This section also explains how to copy a Cisco IOS from a TFTP server, how to set a Cisco device to boot to a Cisco IOS located in a network location, and, finally, how to manage the startup and running configuration files referred to earlier in this chapter.

Understanding the Boot Process

The boot process can be broken down into the following steps:

1. When a Cisco device starts, it first looks for instructions in the ROM chip, just as a computer will look for instructions in the BIOS chip. These instructions are independent of the Cisco IOS and will execute regardless of whether there is an IOS in flash. One of the first instructions executed is a power-on self-test (POST). All of the hardware and software contents are checked for functionality.

2. The bootstrap program loads and is executed. You can tell this has happened when you see output on the screen describing the bootstrap version and information about the hardware described in the POST, as shown here:

    ```
    System Bootstrap, Version 11.0(10c), SOFTWARE
     Copyright (c) 1986-1996 by Cisco Systems
     2500 processor with 6144 Kbytes of main
    memory
     F3: 5593060+79544+421160 at 0×3000060
    ```

3. Next the device looks in NVRAM for settings contained in the configuration register. In the upcoming sections, you will be introduced to the details of these settings and how to change them. For now, understand that the configuration register will tell the system what step to take next and what those steps could be:

    > **Boot to ROM Monitor (ROMmon) mode**—This can be used to edit the startup configuration file on the device and to load another IOS image.

    > **Boot to the ROM IOS**—This is a mini version of the IOS that can be used for a limited set of functions if the IOS is corrupted (such as to download another IOS image).

    > **Look for a startup configuration file in NVRAM**

4. If the settings in this register are set to the default, the system will look next in NVRAM for a startup configuration file. This file is read because it could also contain instructions about the boot order. If there is no boot system command found in the startup configuration

◀

Both ROMmon and the ROM mini IOS are located on the ROM chip.

file, the system will begin a search for an IOS. It will search first in flash, and then it will look for a TFTP server, and if all else fails, it will boot into either ROMmon mode or the ROM mini IOS. When the image is found, the image name will appear on the screen, as in the following example:

```
Cisco Internetwork Operating System Software
 IOS ™ 2500 Software (C2500-I-L), Version 12.0(5)
 Copyright (c) 1986-1999 by cisco Systems, Inc.
 Compiled Tue 15-Jun-99 19:49 by phanguye
 Image text-base: 0x0302EC70, data-base: 0x0000100
```

> **Looking for a startup configuration in NVRAM is an alternate way to manage the boot process rather than using the configuration register.**

5. After the IOS becomes operational, it loads the startup configuration file located in NVRAM, if the file is present. After it is read, system messages will begin to appear on the screen as the settings (such as interfaces being enabled) are executed, as shown here:

```
00:00:22: %LINK-3-UPDOWN: Interface Ethernet0, changed state to up
 00:00:22: %LINK-3-UPDOWN: Interface Serial0, changed state to up
 00:00:22: %LINK-3-UPDOWN: Interface Serial1, changed state to up
 00:00:23: %LINEPROTO-5-UPDOWN: Line protocol on Interface
Ethernet0, changed state to up
 00:03:13: %LINK-5-CHANGED: Interface Serial0, changed state to
administratively down
 00:03:13: %LINK-5-CHANGED: Interface Serial1, changed state to
administratively down
```

6. If the file is not found or if you have configured the device to ignore the file (using the configuration register settings), you will receive a menu-based set of prompts that will allow you to create one. You can choose to either use this method to create the file or answer *no* to the first question in the series, and the system will proceed on to the CLI interface. The first part of the setup menu is as follows:

```
        --- System Configuration Dialog ---


At any point you may enter a question mark '?' for help.

Use ctrl-c to abort configuration dialog at any prompt.

Default settings are in square brackets '[]'.


Continue with configuration dialog? [yes]:
```

7. If a configuration file is found or if you answer *no* to the first question in the setup menu, the router will proceed to the CLI and you will see the following prompt:

```
Press RETURN to get started!
```

THE BOOT DECISION PROCESS

Here is a more visual representation of the boot decision process.

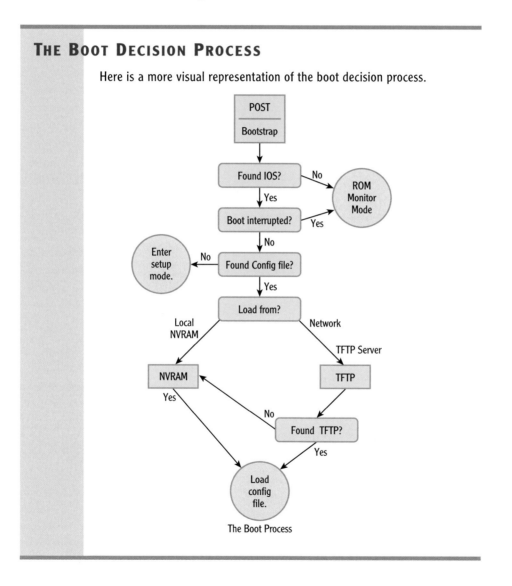

The Boot Process

Managing the IOS

The Cisco IOS image file can be loaded from flash, which is the most common location, but it can also be loaded to the device from a TFTP server. This is a much slower way to load the IOS, but it does offer the benefit of maintaining the image for multiple routers in one location. Operations such as updates and image patches can then be managed in a central location and can help to maintain IOS image consistency across multiple devices.

To set the device to boot from an image located on a TFTP server, a command must be executed (`boot system tftp://ip_address/filename`) and saved to the startup configuration file. When that file is read as indicated in step 3 of the boot process (as shown in the previous section), it will instruct the device to skip looking for the image in flash and proceed to load the image from a TFTP server. Because the command will also include the IP address of the TFTP server and the name of the image file on the server, it will greatly speed the process as the default TFTP location method will be broadcast for the TFTP server.

A more common use of a TFTP server is as a platform to transfer IOS images to the router and to store images for backup and maintenance. The TFTP server can be used to store startup configuration files as well. This offers the same benefits as does centrally locating IOS images, that is, the files can be managed and edited offline in a central location and then loaded to the devices when desired.

To load an image from a TFTP server to a router, conceptually the steps are as follows:

1. You must ensure that at least one interface on the router is enabled and has an IP address in the same subnet as the TFTP server. You should test this by ensuring that you can execute the `ping` command successfully from the router to the TFTP server.

2. Place the IOS image on the TFTP server in the outbound directory. This will be the default location that the TFTP server will look to when the file is requested by the router.

3. Make your connection to the router by using a Cisco console cable.

4. Enter privileged mode on the router.

5. Execute the command **copy tftp flash**. This tells the router you want to copy an image *from* a TFTP server *to* flash memory.

6. The system prompts you first for the IP address of the TFTP server, and then for the name of the image file.

7. The system asks whether you want to erase the current image file. If you have sufficient room in flash, you can keep both the old and the new file. If you are unsure of the room, you can check the available space in flash by using the show flash command. The output you receive will tell you the name of the current IOS file, its size, and the amount of space that remains available:

```
File          Length              Name/status
1             10218508            /c2500-js-l_120-8.bin
[10316471 bytes used, 6460745 available, 16777216 total]
16384K bytes of processor board System flash (Read ONLY)
```

8. When you confirm the process, you will see system messages that will keep you apprised of the progress, as shown next. If you chose to erase the existing file, you will see that process take place first, as indicated by the series of lowercase *e*'s shown in the output. When the transfer of the image starts, it will be indicated by a string of exclamation points. When this is complete, the system will reboot.

```
Accessing file 'c2500-js-l_113-3.bin' on 171.71.93.192...
 Loading c2500-js-l_113-3.bin from 171.71.93.192 (via
Ethernet0): ! [OK]
 Erasing device...eeeeeeeeeeeeeeeeeeeeeeeeeeeeeeeeeeeeeeeee
ee ...erased
 Loading c2500-js-l_113-3.exe from 171.71.93.192 (via
Ethernet0): !!!!!!!!!!!!!!!  !!!!!!!!!!!!!!!!!!!!!!!!!!!!!!!!!
!!!!!!!!!!!!!!
 [OK - 8900924/16777216 bytes]
 Verifying checksum... OK (0x8ABE)
 Flash copy took 0:04:57 [hh:mm:ss]
 %FLH: Re-booting system after download
```

Understanding Configuration Files

During our discussion of router storage locations and of the boot process, I have made numerous references to two configuration files. It is important that these files, their contents, and their relationship to each other are approached in an organized manner. These files contain all the settings of a router or switch and are applied to the device every time the device is started or restarted. In this section, the characteristics of both the startup and the running configuration files are explored.

Startup Configuration File

The *startup configuration file* can be created either by using the menu-based setup program or at the CLI. The benefit of using the setup menu, especially for those new to Cisco devices, is that it will prompt you for important settings that may not occur to you otherwise. Having said that, most administrators use the CLI to create the startup configuration file.

This file is consulted briefly at the beginning of the boot process to determine whether it contains boot commands. Then after the IOS is located, the file is loaded into RAM and applied to the device. *Applied* means that if an interface needs to be enabled, it is, that if an IP address needs to be applied, it is, that if a routing protocol needs to be enabled and its settings applied, it is, and so forth.

After the file is copied into RAM, the version that is located in RAM is renamed. It becomes the running configuration, which is covered in the next section. It is important to note that the startup configuration file is copied into RAM, not moved. The startup configuration file is still in NVRAM after the copy process is complete.

Running Configuration File

After the startup configuration file is copied, it is renamed the *running configuration file*. When you use the CLI on a live router to make changes to the router, you are editing the running configuration. The running configuration contains the settings that the device is using *right now*. There is no need to save this file to make the settings effective. They will be effective *immediately*. However, if you want these changes to remain in effect at the next restart, you must copy these changes to the startup configuration file located in NVRAM. This is done by executing the copy running-config startup-config (copy run start for short) command.

If you make changes to the running configuration that you decide you do not want to keep and you have not saved them to the startup configuration file, you can remove them in one of two ways:

> ▶ If it is acceptable to take the device offline, restart the device, and the device will simply copy the startup configuration to RAM as the running configuration when the devices starts.

> ▶ If it is not acceptable to take the device offline, execute the copy startup-config running-config command (copy start run). This may briefly interrupt some of the functionality of the router, but not as severely as restarting the device.

Managing the Configuration Register

Besides containing the startup configuration, NVRAM contains the configuration register. This is a 16-bit field in hexadecimal that contains information about the boot process. Each of the 16 bits can be set either to 1 (on) or 0 (off). When you make changes to the configuration register, it is done in hexadecimal, and the value you enter is preceded by the characters *0x*, which will simply communicate to the device that what follows is in hex.

To make the relationship between the hex and binary clearer, look at Figure 12.9. You can see that there are four sets of 4 bits. The bottom line indicates the current setting in binary. The top line (2 1 0 2) indicates the hex version and is what you would enter at the CLI to make a change to the setting.

Config Register #	2	1	0	2
Bit Number	15 14 13 12	11 10 9 8	7 6 5 4	3 2 1 0
Binary	0 0 1 0	0 0 0 1	0 0 0 0	0 0 1 0

FIGURE 12.9 Configuration register

The two fields that are important for this discussion are the two on the right side (bits 7–0). The far-right field (bits 3–0) is called the *boot field* and controls where the device looks for an IOS during boot. If this last field is set to 2 or higher (in hex), the device will use the settings found in NVRAM. This could mean one of two things:

1. If there are boot commands in the startup configuration file, it will use them.

2. If there are no boot commands in the startup configuration file, it will look for the IOS in flash, and then look for a TFTP server, and finally boot to ROMmon mode.

Because the default setting of the field is 2 (in hex), then if no boot commands have been added to the startup configuration file, the normal operating procedure is as stated in option 2.

The field that contains bits 7–4 doesn't have a name, but it can be used to control whether the device reads or uses the startup configuration file when the device is restarted. This procedure is (most) commonly used when you need to perform a password recovery.

Passwords that are required to enter privileged and global configuration modes of the device are contained in the startup configuration file. By instructing the device to ignore that file, it becomes possible to boot the device, edit the password in the file, or erase the file.

The default setting for the configuration register is 0x2102. The third number (0, which is the setting for the bits 7–4 described earlier) is the number of interest when controlling the use of the startup configuration file. The relevant settings with respect to the startup configuration file are as follows:

▶ 0x2102 instructs the device to read and apply the startup configuration file in NVRAM.

▶ 0x2142 instructs the device to *not* read and apply the startup configuration file in NVRAM.

Changing the configuration register to perform a password recovery could be used to break into a Cisco device. That's why this procedure can be performed only when physically attached with a console cable.

The configuration register can be edited in two ways. If you have access to global configuration mode (meaning you can provide the privilege mode password if required), it can be done from the CLI. In that case, you can use the config-*register* command along with the proper setting in hex preceded by the required 0x. After executing the command, save the changes to the startup configuration file by executing the copy run start command. When the device reboots, it will use the settings you have just applied to the register.

If you are performing a password recovery (meaning the password is unavailable), this approach will not be an option. This operation will have to be performed while booted into ROMmon mode. The default for the device is to *not* boot into ROMmon mode, but rather to look in NVRAM for any boot commands in the startup configuration file, and then if there are none (which is usually the case), to load the IOS from flash and then apply the startup configuration file.

A comprehensive list of break sequences for common operating systems and versions of terminal software can be found at www.cisco.com/en/US/products/hw/routers/ps133/products_tech_note09186a0080174a34.shtml.

Therefore, this default procedure must be interrupted by executing what is called a *break sequence* while the system is booting up, before it has a chance to get to the NVRAM portion of the process. A break sequence is a combination of keys to strike on the keyboard within a certain period of time after restarting the device. What constitutes a break sequence depends on factors such as the operating system of the computer you are using to connect to the Cisco device and the type of HyperTerminal software.

When you have determined the break sequence, follow this procedure to erase or reset the password:

1. Restart the device. Within the first 60 seconds after you have started the device, execute the break sequence.

2. If you have executed the proper break sequence, the prompt of the device will appear as follows: rommon 1>.

3. At this prompt, type the following command: rommon 1>**confreg 0x2142**.

4. When the prompt changes, type the following command: rommon 2>**reset**.

5. When the device restarts, you will get the menu-based setup. Answer no to the first two questions, and the device will proceed to the CLI.

6. At the first prompt, type the following command: router>**enable**. Now you are in privileged mode.

7. The prompt changes, and now you can do one of two things, depending on your ultimate intentions:

   ▶ If you want to wipe out the entire configuration file containing the passwords and all other settings (perhaps because you are redeploying the device for another purpose), execute the command *router#***copy run start**. This will copy the running configuration (which at this point has *no* settings) over the startup configuration. When you restart the device, it will be as if it is new with no settings, and you can create a new configuration by using either the CLI or the setup menu. If you do this, before you restart, you should program the device to look for a startup file (even though it doesn't exist yet) by resetting the configuration register. Otherwise, once you have created a new one, you will find that the device continues to go to setup mode every time you restart. This will be because you have a startup file but the device is refusing to use it. To set the configuration register back to the default, follow step 9.

   ▶ If on the other hand you merely want to reset the password and keep all the other settings, you need to first copy the startup configuration into RAM so you can edit it. If this is the case, execute the command *router#***copy start run**.

8. If you chose the first option in step 7 (wiping out the configuration file), there is no password to erase, and you can create a new configuration and proceed to step 9. If you chose the second option, you now need to change the two passwords that control access to global configuration mode, where changes are made. There may be two of these; one is called the *enable password* (unencrypted), and the other is *enable secret* (encrypted). You can change them both by entering

> ◀
>
> **You are not prompted for a password when you request access to privileged mode because you are in ROMmon mode, where the configurations file containing the password is not read or used.**

global configuration mode, making the changes, and then returning to privileged mode and saving the changes, as follows:

```
router#config terminal
router(config)#enable <new password>
router(config)# enable secret <new password>
router(config)# c#^Z        (this means you hit ctrl+Z on
the keyboard)
router#copy run start
```

9. Finally, before you restart the device, you need to tell the device to use the startup configuration file you just edited. (Remember, you set it to ignore the file earlier.) Do this by executing the following commands:

```
router# config terminal
router(config)# config-register 0x2102
router(config)# c#^Z
router#copy run start
```

(The c#^Z part means you press Ctrl+Z on the keyboard.)

10. When you next restart the device, it will read and use the file that contains the password that you just edited.

The Essentials and Beyond

A Cisco router or switch uses an operating system called the IOS and startup configuration and running configuration files to perform its tasks. Cisco devices also contain four storage locations: RAM, NVRAM, ROM, and flash memory. RAM is an area where the running configuration and the IOS tables are kept, and it is volatile. NVRAM is nonvolatile and is where the startup configuration file is kept. ROM contains the boot code and a mini version of the IOS. Flash memory is used to store the IOS image file.

The startup and running configuration files contain all the settings of a router or switch. The startup configuration file is applied to the device every time the device is started or restarted and resides in NVRAM. After it is copied into RAM at startup, it is renamed the running configuration.

There are two ways to make a connection to a Cisco router or switch: the HyperTerminal program installed on a computer or over the network using Telnet. There are two levels of access to the IOS: user and privileged. The default boot process of a Cisco device is to access the bootstrap code from ROM, locate the IOS in flash, and load and apply the startup configuration file from NVRAM.

(Continues)

ADDITIONAL EXERCISES

1. In this exercise, you will download the free HyperTerminal software, install it, connect to the router with a console cable, and access the router prompt. This exercise requires the following:

- ▶ A computer with Internet access
- ▶ A router or switch
- ▶ A Cisco console cable

Follow these steps:

A. Connect the RJ-45 end of the console cable to the router console port. Connect the serial end of the console cable to the serial port on the computer. Start the router.

B. Use your Internet browser to access the following web URL: `http://download.cnet.com/HyperTerminal-Private-Edition/3000-2155_4-10966768.html`. Click the Download Now button to download the free HyperTerminal software.

C. When the software downloads, make note of the location where it is being saved. Once the software is downloaded, browse to its location and click the `htpe7.exe` file. Click Next to start the installation.

D. Accept the license agreement and the default installation location. Click Finish, and the installation is complete.

E. Choose Start ➢ Programs ➢ HyperTerminal-Private-Edition. Double-click to start the application.

F. In the Area Code section of the Location Information dialog box, enter your area code.

G. In the Phone And Modem dialog box, click OK and accept the default.

H. In the New Connection-HyperTerminal dialog box, name the connection after your first name.

I. In the Connect To Port dialog box, select COM 1.

J. In the COM1 Port properties dialog box, use the following settings:

9600
8
None
1 None

K. Press Enter.

(Continues)

THE ESSENTIALS AND BEYOND (Continued)

2. Match the storage location with the items that are contained in that area of the Cisco device.

Location	Contents
Flash	Startup config/config register
RAM	Bootstrap code
ROM	Running configuration
NVRAM	Cisco IOS

REVIEW QUESTIONS

1. Where are the Cisco IOS tables located after startup?

   A. ROM   C. RAM

   B. NVRAM   D. Flash memory

2. Where is the configuration register located in a Cisco device?

   A. ROM   C. RAM

   B. NVRAM   D. Flash memory

3. Which of the following storage types loses its information when power is lost?

   A. ROM   C. RAM

   B. NVRAM   D. Flash memory

4. Which of the following is *not* required to make a Telnet connection a Cisco device?

   A. IP address   C. Device name configured

   B. Line username and password   D. Router interface enabled
      configured

5. Which of the following correctly describes the ends of a standard console cable?

   A. Serial and USB   C. Serial and RJ-45

   B. USB and USB   D. USB and RJ-45

(Continues)

6. By default, what is the only mode in which you will be prompted for a password?

   A. Global configuration   C. User

   B. Privileged   D. Interface configuration

7. Which of the following prompts is at user mode?

   A. `troy>`   C. `troy(config)#`

   B. `troy#`   D. `troy(config-if)#`

8. What is the first storage location accessed at bootup?

   A. ROM   C. RAM

   B. NVRAM   D. Flash memory

9. What file is loading and being applied when you see this on the screen?

   ```
   00:00:22: %LINK-3-UPDOWN: Interface Ethernet0, changed state to up
   00:00:22: %LINK-3-UPDOWN: Interface Serial0, changed state to up
   ```

   A. Startup configuration   C. Bootstrap code

   B. IOS   D. ROMON

10. What command can you use to determine the size of the existing IOS image?

    A. `show version`   C. `show nvram`

    B. `show flash`   D. `show config`

CHAPTER 13

Configuring Routers

Cisco routers and multilayer switches can be configured to do some pretty amazing things. However, before a router can perform the magic it does so well, some basic configurations (such as configuring IP addresses and enabling the interfaces) must be in place, or the router will not function.

This chapter covers such configurations. Specifically, this chapter covers the following topics:

▶ **Cabling the router**

▶ **Creating a console session**

▶ **Configuring passwords**

▶ **Configuring interfaces**

▶ **Saving configuration changes**

Cabling the Router

In Chapter 9 you learned about the major cable types. The cable covered in that chapter that will most often be used with routers is Ethernet twisted-pair with RJ-45 connectors. These cables can be used to connect routers to switches and to other routers. There are several other cables and connectors you must also be aware of that can be used from router to router and from a router to a WAN connection.

Cisco makes many configurations of interfaces on routers. The trend has been away from routers with fixed-interface configurations, such as the Cisco 2501 shown in Figure 13.1, and toward those hosting slots for function-specific modules. This change enables customization of a router for a specific function while affording the flexibility of updating the router at any point in time. The backplane of the Cisco 2501 in Figure 13.1 has an Attachment Unit Interface (AUI) style Ethernet connector (which uses a female DB-15 connector), two serial connecters (which are using a female DB-60 connector), a console port, and an AUX port (with an RJ-45 connector) used for modem access to the router. This model doesn't have a single RJ-45 Ethernet connector, and because it has no slots for expansion modules, you would have to perform what is called a forklift upgrade to add this capability.

When these models were in use, Cisco made about seven variations of them. Each model had a set configuration of interfaces.

> When you have to completely replace a router because there is no way to upgrade its features, that replacement is called a *forklift upgrade*.

FIGURE 13.1 Cisco 2501 backplane

Some of the smaller Cisco routers still follow the fixed-interface paradigm, such as the Cisco 871 in Figure 13.2. These models are usually designed as a unit for a specific purpose. The 871 is typically the only router in a mid-sized office and also serves as the connection to the Internet for the office. It has two USB connectors, four Fast Ethernet ports (RJ-45s), and a Fast Ethernet port to connect to the WAN connection. The Fast Ethernet WAN connection typically connects to the ISP's DSL broadband modem. A smaller or medium-sized office is much more likely to make its connection to the Internet via DSL broadband than through a CSU/DSU as a larger office might. Finally, as all Cisco products do, this router has the console connector.

CSU/DSU

A *Channel Service Unit/Data Service Unit (CSU/DSU)* is a digital-interface device used to connect a data terminal equipment (DTE) device, such as a router, to a digital circuit, such as a T1 line. The CSU/DSU is usually placed on the customer premises by the provider, and the router connects to it. However, the router can contain a CSU/DSU, in which case the router would plug directly into the T1 line. An example of this is the router in Figure 13.4, which has an expansion module that contains a Cisco T1 DSU/CSU WAN interface card.

FIGURE 13.2 Cisco 871 backplane

The Cisco 1841 is a commonly used enterprise-level router. It comes with two empty slots that can host modules of all sorts. They could be modules providing wireless access; they could host WAN connections, or multiple serial or Ethernet connections. While Ethernet connections are typically used to connect to switches, the serial connections can be used either as a WAN connection or as a connection to other routers in the LAN. Figure 13.3 shows an 1841 with modules installed. In this instance, the slot on the left holds a Cisco T1 DSU/CSU WAN interface card, and the slot on the right holds a four-port Cisco EtherSwitch card, which allows you to add switching capability to the router. Cisco 1841 also comes with a slot on the lower-left side (under the slot holding the Cisco T1 DSU/CSU WAN interface card) to add more flash memory, two Fast Ethernet ports, a console port, and an AUX port. The list of modules that can be purchased and inserted into these two slots is impressive.

For a list of possible expansion modules for the 1841 router, go to www.cisco .com/en/US/ products/ ps5853/ products_ relevant_ interfaces_and_ modules.html. ◄

FIGURE 13.3 Cisco 1841 with modules installed

Regardless of the interfaces that are available on the router that you work with, certain interface types will always be in use and should be discussed. These interfaces may be found fixed on the backplane of the router or they may be found in an expansion module in a slot. The cables used and the way in which the interfaces are used will remain constant.

In the rest of this section, the connections between a router and other common devices are covered, with special attention to the interface types and cables used to ensure proper communication.

Cabling Router to Router

A router-to-router connection can be cabled one of two ways. It can be accomplished with an Ethernet connection or it can be done by using the serial connectors on the routers. The Ethernet connection requires less configuration once cabled, but in many instances Ethernet connections on a router are at a premium because they are typically used to host switches loaded with hosts.

Ethernet

This is a simple connection. Simply plug the end of a twisted-pair Ethernet cable into the Ethernet (or Fast Ethernet) slot (RJ-45) on one router, and the other end of the cable into an Ethernet slot on the other router. Make sure you keep your cable length under 100 feet to ensure no attenuation problems. Also don't forget that a router-to-router connection requires a *crossover* cable, not a straight-through cable! Figure 13.4 shows this connection between two 871 routers.

FIGURE 13.4 Ethernet router-to-router

Serial

There can be numerous types of serial connectors found on a Cisco router. A common type is the DB-60 you saw in the 2501 earlier, but you are also likely to see what is called the *smart serial connector* on newer models. A smart serial is a smaller 26-pin connector but it functions the same as the DB-60.

The serial cable, regardless of the form factor of its connector on the router end, can be connected to another router or it can be connected to a CSU/DSU for WAN access. In either case, it important to understand how serial cables operate with Cisco devices. Each end of the cable plays a distinct role in the communication process.

One end of the cable is called the *data terminal equipment (DTE)*, and the other is called the *data communications equipment (DCE)*. When a router is connected to a CSU/DSU, the CSU/DSU is the DCE, and the router is the DTE. The DCE end of the process provides the clocking for the connection, which must be performed by one end only and followed by the other end.

When two routers are connected with a serial cable, you must designate which router will perform the clocking. You also must ensure that the DCE end of the cable is connected to that router. The DTE and DCE ends are usually clearly marked on the end of the cable.

When two routers are connected back to back, there are two possible cabling options. There is a two-piece cable set with one end of each cable having a DB-60 or smart serial (router-friendly) connector and the other end having a connector called a V.35. One of the cables will have a male V.35 connector, and the other will have a female V.35. The cables coming from each router meet at the V.35 connector. One end of one of these cables is shown in Figure 13.5. The V.35 end is the end *not* connected to the router.

FIGURE 13.5 Serial connection with V.35

There is also a one-cable method for this. A *back-to-back cable* is one in which both ends are router friendly (DB-60 or smart serial), and the ends are marked *DTE* and *DCE*. The cable simply connects from one router to the other, as shown in Figure 13.6.

In the section "Configuring Interfaces," you will learn how to configure the serial interface to ensure that the clocking is enabled on the correct end of the cable.

FIGURE 13.6 Back-to-back

Cabling Router to Switch

Twisted-pair cables with RJ-45 connecters are used between routers and switches. Although some older routers do have an AUI-style Ethernet connector on them, as the 2501 shown earlier does, you will rarely encounter anything but an RJ-45 connector for a Fast Ethernet connection.

To cable the router to the switch, connect one end of an Ethernet cable to the Fast Ethernet port on the router, and the other end to the switch. There are two items you need to take into consideration with this procedure:

▶ Make sure you are using a straight-through cable and not a crossover!

▶ Understand the difference between the types of ports that may be available on the switch and when to use each type. The types available and their uses are as follows:

10BaseT   Use for access devices (computers, printers, and so on).

100BaseT   Use for access devices if a 1000BaseT port is also present, and use for connections to other switches and to routers if the other ports are 10BaseT.

1000BaseT   Use for connection to other switches and to routers, and use for access devices only if all of the ports are 1000BaseT.

Regardless of which combination of port types you have on the switch, you should use the slower ports (10BaseT or 100BaseT) for devices connected to the switch and use the faster ports (100BaseT or 1000BaseT) for connection to routers or to other switches, because those connections are likely to carry more traffic and need the capacity.

In Figure 13.7, an 871 router is connected to a Cisco 1900 access switch. Note that one of the two 100BaseT ports on the right end is used on the switch instead of one of the 10BaseT ports.

◄

Switches are often connected to one to another by using trunk links (see Chapter 14, "Configuring Switches"). Trunk links carry traffic from many VLANs and therefore need to be as high capacity as possible.

FIGURE 13.7 Router to switch

In the section "Configuring Interfaces," you will learn how to configure either end of the connection to ensure proper function.

Cabling PC to Router

There are two ways to cable a PC to a router. You could connect an Ethernet cable from the network card of the PC to one of the Ethernet interfaces on the router. If you did and you ensured that the router interface and the PC had IP addresses in the same subnet and that the interface on the router was enabled, you could create a Telnet connection from the PC to the router for the purpose of managing the router. This connection is shown in Figure 13.8.

Although this type of connection is possible, it is rarely done because the normal way to manage the router is by connecting to it with the console cable, as shown in Figure 13.9. If you do need to make this type of connection, remember that the cable needs to be a crossover cable, not a straight-through cable!

When connecting the console cable, connect the RJ-45 end to the console port on the router, and the serial end to the serial port of the PC, as shown in Figure 13.9.

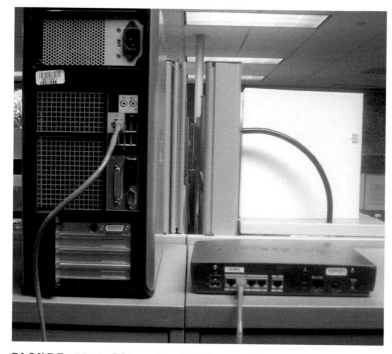

FIGURE 13.8 PC to router with Ethernet cable

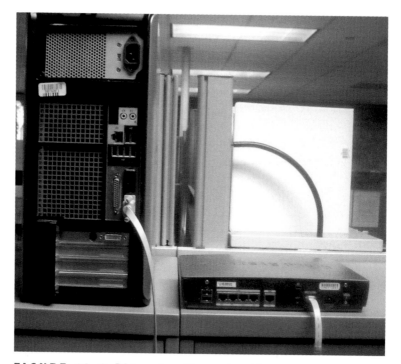

FIGURE 13.9 PC to router with console cable

Cabling Router to CSU/DSU

When connecting a router to a CSU/DSU, various serial connector types could be installed on the CSU/DSU end of the cable. The router end will most likely have either a serial with a DB-60 connector or a smart serial with a 24-pin connector. The CSU/DSU end could have any of the standard types shown in Figure 13.10. This means that you must buy a cable with the correct connector on each end for your specific situation.

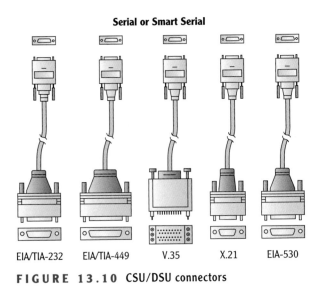

Serial or Smart Serial

EIA/TIA-232 EIA/TIA-449 V.35 X.21 EIA-530

FIGURE 13.10 CSU/DSU connectors

    You need to be aware that in some cases the CSU/DSU function is built into the router. You saw this in Figure 13.3, which shows a Cisco 1841 with a module installed that provided a CSU/DSU T1 interface. This eliminates the need for the service provider to install a CSU/DSU at the site. In this case, you would connect the router's interface (an RJ-48) to an RJ-48 T1 wall outlet from the service provider. The CSU/DSU on the router would talk to the CSU/DSU at the service provider's central office. This connection is shown in Figure 13.11.

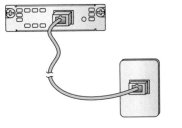

FIGURE 13.11 CSU/DSU in router

In the section "Configuring WAN Interfaces," you will learn how to configure the WAN interface to communicate with a CSU/DSU provided by the ISP as well as how to configure a WAN interface that runs between two of your own routers.

Creating a Console Session

Before you can configure the router, you must create a console session with the router. As you learned in the section on cabling from the PC to the router, this can be done either by directly connecting to the console port with a console cable or by connecting to the router over the network. In this section, you'll review the console connection procedure that you learned in the preceding chapter and explore a more detailed explanation of connecting via the Telnet program. Finally, you will learn about handling the initial screens you will encounter with either method.

Connecting with the Console Cable

After you have the router and the PC cabled together, as shown earlier in Figure 13.9, use the HyperTerminal program to create a terminal or console session with the router. If the computer you are using is Windows XP or later, you will need to install a HyperTerminal program. You can review the procedure in Chapter 12, "Managing the Cisco IOS," on downloading and installing a free HyperTerminal program.

When the program is installed, follow this procedure to establish the session with the router:

1. Choose Start ➤ Programs ➤ HyperTerminal-Private-Edition (the name of your program may be slightly different). Double-click to start the application.

2. Enter the following information in the next dialog boxes you receive:

   ▶ Location Information: In the Area Code box, enter your area code.

   ▶ Phone And Modem: Click OK and accept the default.

   ▶ New Connection-HyperTerminal: Name the connection.

   ▶ Connect To Port: Select COM 1.

   ▶ COM1 Port Properties: Use these settings:
   9600
   8
   None
   1
   None

To review these settings, see Chapter 12.

3. Press Enter. If you have entered the correct settings, you should receive a router prompt or a setup dialog box. The handing of these prompts is covered in the section "Handling Initial Setup."

Connecting through Telnet

Connecting to the router with the Telnet program will not be possible unless the router has an interface enabled with an IP address and you have configured a virtual terminal (vty) or line password. Moreover, attempts to log into a router by using Telnet that are received by a router or switch with no Telnet username or password set are denied by default. If you attempt it, you will receive the following response:

```
Password not set, connection refused
```

The password requirement is a good security feature to leave in place. Moreover, the IP address of the router interface must be reachable by the IP address of the PC. That doesn't necessarily mean that the IP address of the PC must be in the same subnet as that of the router, but if it is not, there must be a router providing routing from the subnet in which the router resides and the subnet in which the PC resides.

If these prerequisites are in place, the next consideration is the Telnet program on the PC. If it has not been installed, it must be, as described in Chapter 12. After the program is installed, it is executed from the command line. The following steps can be used to start a Telnet session with a router that has an IP address of 192.168.5.5:

1. Open a command prompt on the PC and type this command:

   ```
   telnet 192.168.5.5
   ```

   This output will appear:

   ```
   Connecting to 192.168.5.5
   ```

2. If the router is reachable, one of two things will occur:

   ▶ If a Telnet password has been configured, you will be prompted to type the password.

   ▶ If no Telnet password has been created, you will receive the following message:

   ```
   Password not set, connection refused
   ```

3. If you have entered the correct password, you should receive a router prompt or a setup dialog box. The handing of these prompts is covered next.

Handling Initial Setup

Regardless of the method you used to create the session with the router, you will receive either a router prompt (Router>) or an initial setup menu after the session is created. If the router has no startup configuration (for instance, the router may be brand new) or if you have reset the configuration register to ignore the startup configuration file (see Chapter 12) or if someone has simply erased the startup configuration file, an option to enter the initial setup menu will appear, as shown here:

```
--- System Configuration Dialog ---
Would you like to enter the initial configuration dialog? [yes/no]:
```

At this point, you can choose yes. A long series of questions will follow that will allow you to make many of the basic settings required to get the router up and running. However, the focus of this chapter and of this book is how to use the Cisco CLI to configure and manage the router. To proceed on to this interface, type **no** at this prompt.

Configuring Passwords

One of the first things that should be done when configuring the router is to secure access to it by creating passwords. A couple of types of passwords can be used to control access to the functions of the router. These passwords can also be configured per connection type (for example, one password for connecting by console cable, another for Telnet access, another for AUX or modem, and so forth). In this section, the procedure for setting these passwords is explored.

Interpreting Prompts

When you have created the session with the router, the first prompt you will encounter is the user mode prompt:

```
Router>
```

In user mode, you are not allowed to perform any configuration tasks, so it will be necessary to proceed on to privileged mode and then on to configuration mode to do so. Because no passwords have been created yet, you can do this simply by requesting access to the modes and you will not be prompted for a password. To move on to privileged mode, type the following at the user mode prompt:

```
Router>enable
```

Typing enable is tantamount to asking for privileged access to be enabled, which is why the privileged mode password is sometimes referred to as the enable password (and that is exactly how you will refer to it later in this procedure when you create this password). Because you will not be prompted for a password (until you create one), the prompt will change, indicating you are now in privileged mode:

```
Router#
```

Still, you are not at the security level that allows changes to be made. That requires global configuration mode (called *global* because changes made at this level tend to affect the entire router). To move on to this level, type the following at the privileged mode prompt:

```
Router# configure terminal
```

As you may have gathered by now, you really don't need to type out *configure terminal*. You could simply type config t, and the router would understand and apply the command. The prompt will change again, indicating that you are now in global configuration mode, where you can make changes to the router:

```
Router(config)#
```

At this point, there are several password types that you can create. They are covered in the following sections.

Configuring Privileged (Enable) Passwords

As you learned in Chapter 12, the privileged mode or *enable password* controls access to not only privileged mode, but as a result of it being the gateway to global configuration mode, that mode as well. There are two types of these passwords you can create: one is encrypted, and the other is not.

It is important to recognize the modes by their prompts so you understand where you are at all times when configuring the router.

ENCRYPTED?

When a password is *encrypted*, it not only means that it is encrypted as it crosses the network, but also that it is encrypted in the configuration file. For example, if you execute the show start command, an encrypted password can be read in the file output while an enable secret password will not be readable.

To create the unencrypted version, execute the following command at global configuration mode. This example creates a password of *cisco*:

```
Router(config)#enable password cisco
```

At this point, we would normally save this change to the startup configuration by executing the copy run start command. But in this case, let's test it by exiting out to user mode and see if it works:

```
Router(config)# exit
Router# exit
Router>
```

There are two ways to move "backward" in the prompt hierarchy. One way is to use exit, and the other is to use the Ctrl+Z key combination.

Now at user mode, attempt to enter privileged mode. You should be prompted for the password:

```
Router>enable
Password:       <type cisco>
Router#
```

Configuring Enable Secret Passwords

In some cases, the startup configuration file may be located on a TFTP server, meaning that when you provide the enable password to access privileged mode, the password must cross the network. If you configure only an enable password, it will cross the network in plain text, which means it can be can read if the packet is captured with a sniffer.

To encrypt the enable password, you can create an *enable secret password* instead. The only difference is that when you execute the command, you specify that you would like the password to be encrypted by substituting *secret* for password in the command:

```
Router(config)#enable secret cisco
```

If both an enable and enable secret passwords are configured on a router, the router will prompt for the encrypted password instead of the unencrypted password.

Configuring Line Passwords

The two passwords discussed thus far apply to the access of privileged mode after a connection has been made. Passwords can also be configured to authenticate access to connection methods. The most common use of this type of password is to authenticate a user before allowing access to the router through a Telnet or vty session. This is called a *line password*.

vty stands for *virtual teletype terminal*.

To configure a line password, it is necessary to proceed through the access levels to global configuration mode and then proceed from global configuration mode into line configuration mode. The line command also must specify the connection type for which you want to require a password, as shown here:

```
Router>enable
Password:       <type cisco>
Router#config t
Router(config)# line  <type the method>
```

At this point, you type line and specify the connection type. The choices are console (connection through the console cable), vty (connection through Telnet), and aux (connection through a modem connected to the router). Because routers have multiple logical connections of each type that can share the single physical connection, you also need to specify which of those logical connections the username and password applies to.

The number of vty lines varies with the type of router and the IOS version. However, five is the most common number of lines. To determine the number available (so that you secure all of them and not just some of them, which can be done), execute these commands:

```
Router>
Router>enable
Router#config t
Enter configuration commands, one per line.  End with CNTL/Z.
Router(config)#line vty 0 ?
  <1-15>  Last Line number
```

After the execution of the line vty 0 ? command, the output indicates that there are 16 lines numbered 0–15. To set a password for all 16 lines, you first need to enter configuration mode for lines vty 0–15:

```
Router(config)#line vty 0 15
Router(config-line)#
```

Notice that the prompt changed, indicating you are now in the mode that allows you to make changes (such as setting a password) to the 16 lines. Now enter the command password followed by the password you desire, in this example cisco:

```
Router(config-line)#password cisco
```

You also need to instruct the router to prompt for the password with an additional command login:

```
Router(config-line)#login
```

◄

Configuration modes beyond the global mode apply commands only to the specific part of the router (not the entire router). Commands executed in an interface mode affect only that interface.

> ## THE *NO LOGIN* COMMAND
>
> It's not recommended, but if you would like to tell the router to stop prompt-
> ing for a password, the no login command will do this. It will have that
> effect only in the mode where it is executed. For example, if I wanted to
> stop the router from prompting when I connect with Telnet, I would enter
> line vty mode and execute it there.

Configuring Interfaces

After access to the router has been secured, the interfaces can be made functional.
On a Cisco router, that requires two steps:

▶ Configuring an IP address and subnet mask

▶ Enabling the interface

Before those settings can be made, you must navigate to the mode that
accepts and applies them. You also need to know how to verify that the settings
were accepted and that the interface is functional. This section addresses all of
those issues for both WAN and LAN interfaces. Finally, the configuration of a
router to act as a DHCP server will be explained.

Accessing Interface Mode

Earlier you learned that to set a password for the vty lines, you need to proceed
through privileged mode to global configuration mode and on to line vty mode.
To configure an interface, you must also proceed through privileged mode, to
global configuration mode, and on to *interface* configuration mode. The steps in
this process are as follows:

```
Router>
Router>enable
Router#config t
Enter configuration commands, one per line.  End with CNTL/Z.
Router(config)#interface   <interface  identifier>
```

**These are only the
most common media
types.**

The interface identifier refers to the media type, the slot number, and the
port number. The media type could be Ethernet, Fast Ethernet, Gigabit
Ethernet, or Serial.

When you enter the interface numbers, you must keep in mind that interfaces on routers are numbered starting with 0, not 1. Consequently, if you had only a single Fast Ethernet interface on the router, its number would be FastEthernet 0.

Routers without slots that have fixed interfaces, such as the old 2501, will ignore the slot number and use the following syntax:

▶ E0 stands for the first Ethernet interface.

▶ S0 stands for the first Serial interface.

Routers that have interfaces arranged into slots will follow the media type, slot number, and port number syntax as here:

▶ Serial 0/0 is the first serial interface (or port) in the first slot.

▶ Fast Ethernet 0/2 is the second Fast Ethernet interface (or port) in the first slot.

For example, the following command enters the configuration mode required to make changes to the first Fast Ethernet interface located in slot 0 of a router:

```
Router(config)#interface fa0/0
Router(config-if)#
```

Notice that the prompt has changed to indicate that you are now in interface configuration mode. At this point, you can make the settings required in the following sections.

Assigning an IP Address

After you have arrived at the interface configuration prompt, you can assign an IP address and a subnet mask. Remember the following considerations with regard to the IP address and the subnet mask:

▶ The IP address/subnet mask combination must place the interface into the same subnet as the hosts that will be attached to the switch connected to this interface or as the router that is located on the opposite end of this connection.

▶ One of the most common reasons that connections don't work between hosts and their gateway (router) or between routers on either end of a point-to-point connection is an error in the IP address or subnet mask. This is why it is so important to develop the ability to look at two IP addresses and determine whether they are in the same subnet. (See Chapter 8, "Classless IP Addressing.")

◀

Fa is short for *Fast*.

◀

To identify the interfaces on the router, execute the command show interfaces.

To apply the IP address and subnet mask, execute the following IP address command. This example applies the IP address of 192.168.5.5 and the subnet mask of 255.255.255.0 to the fa0/0 interface.

```
Router(config)#interface fa0/0
Router(config-if)#ip address 192.168.5.5 255.255.255.0
```

Enabling the Interface

When you make configuration changes to the router and the changes are accepted, while they are being applied you will many times see what are called *system messages* appear on the screen. These are messages indicating something is changing in the router. For example, when you have successfully completed the configuration of an interface, you will see a message indicating that the interface is becoming operational or "coming up."

You will *not* see such a message after you have executed the command in the previous section. This is not because the command was not accepted or applied. It is because the interface has not been *enabled*. To enable the interface, you must execute the no shutdown command:

> **Yes, it's crazy. To enable the interface, you execute the** no shutdown **command.**

```
Router(config)#interface fa0/0
Router(config-if)#ip address 192.168.5.5 255.255.255.0
Router (config-if)# no shutdown
%LINK-5-CHANGED: Interface FastEthernet0/0, changed state to up
Router(config-if)#
```

Notice what happened after this command was executed. You received a message indicating that the interface state has changed to up. It is important to understand that this message does not indicate that we can now connect to anything on that interface. In fact, it may not even have a cable plugged into it!

In the next section, you will learn how to verify the condition of the interface and gather more-detailed information about its usability.

Verifying the Interface

To verify the interface, you need to use one of the show commands. The show commands, by default, do not work in configuration mode or interface configuration mode.

> **If you add the** do **command at the front of the** show **command, you can execute the** show **command from configuration mode!**

So you need to exit, or back out, to privileged mode:

```
Router(config-if)# exit
Router(config)#exit
Router#
```

The show command used to verify an interface is show interface. If it is executed with no parameter, it will display all interfaces with a section dedicated to each. If you specify the interface after the command, it will display only information regarding that interface. Because we are interested in only the fa0/0 interface, we could execute the following command:

```
Router#show int fa0/0
FastEthernet0/0 is up, line protocol is down (disabled)
   Hardware is Lance, address is 0001.9638.3073 (bia 0001.9638.3073)
   Internet address is 192.168.5.5/24
   MTU 1500 bytes, BW 100000 Kbit, DLY 100 usec,
      reliability 255/255, txload 1/255, rxload 1/255
   Encapsulation ARPA, loopback not set
   ARP type: ARPA, ARP Timeout 04:00:00,
   Last input 00:00:08, output 00:00:05, output hang never
   Last clearing of "show interface" counters never
   Input queue: 0/75/0 (size/max/drops); Total output drops: 0
   Queueing strategy: fifo
   Output queue :0/40 (size/max)
   5 minute input rate 0 bits/sec, 0 packets/sec
   5 minute output rate 0 bits/sec, 0 packets/sec
      0 packets input, 0 bytes, 0 no buffer
      Received 0 broadcasts, 0 runts, 0 giants, 0 throttles
      0 input errors, 0 CRC, 0 frame, 0 overrun, 0 ignored, 0 abort
      0 input packets with dribble condition detected
      0 packets output, 0 bytes, 0 underruns
      0 output errors, 0 collisions, 1 interface resets
      0 babbles, 0 late collision, 0 deferred
      0 lost carrier, 0 no carrier
      0 output buffer failures, 0 output buffers swapped out
```

There is a lot of information displayed. Let's concentrate on the basic information at the first part of the output and discuss how to interpret the information. The part we are talking about is shown here:

```
Router#show int fa0/0
FastEthernet0/0 is up, line protocol is down (disabled)
   Hardware is Lance, address is 0001.9638.3073 (bia 0001.9638.3073)
   Internet address is 192.168.5.5/24
```

The first line tells us the condition of the interface. The first part (on the left) that reads FastEthernet0/0 is up means that the interface has been enabled and has an IP address. The second part, line protocol is down (disabled), indicates that there is no life on the other end of the line because no keep-alives are being received.

Keep-alives are used between the interfaces by Network Access layer protocols to detect when an interface is no longer active.

◀

This could be because it's not plugged in, the cable is bad, or in the case of a serial connection, the encapsulation type is mismatched. You must ensure that both ends of the connection are using the same encapsulation for the connection to work. If an encapsulation mismatch occurs, no communication will occur.

▶

Encapsulation mismatches are covered in the "Configuring WAN Interfaces" section later in this chapter.

There are several informational combinations you could receive with regard to this output. Other combinations and their meanings are as follows:

FastEthernet0/0 is up, line protocol is up—The interface is up and working.

FastEthernet0/0 is down, line protocol is down—There is an interface problem, or the other end has not been configured.

FastEthernet0/0 is administratively down, line protocol is down— The interface is disabled or shut down.

You also can see the IP address for this interface, along with its mask (192.168.5.5/24) and its MAC address (0001.9638.3073). In this instance, we already know the IP and mask. However, in some instances, you may be unfamiliar with the interface and you would like to know its IP address and mask. This command could show you that information.

Enabling DHCP

A Cisco router can be either a DHCP client or a DHCP server. If your router connects to your ISP, and your ISP will issue the router an IP address, then the router interface needs to be set as a DHCP client. This is done with a single command at the interface configuration prompt:

```
Router(config-if)#ip address dhcp
```

It is more likely that the router interface will be functioning as a DHCP server than as a client. The steps to do this are as follows:

1. Enable the DHCP server.

2. Configure a DHCP address pool.

3. Configure the pool options.

Enabling the DHCP server is not done on the interface. DHCP is a service that is enabled at the global configuration prompt. Enabling the service on each interface is done by configuring an address pool that includes the subnet in which the interface resides. To enable the service globally, execute this command:

```
Router(config)#service dhcp
```

Before we can enter the configuration mode for the pool, we need to create and name the pool. After we have executed that command, the prompt will then go to the configuration mode for that pool. If we ever need to go back and make changes to the pool, we can enter its configuration mode by using the same command that created the pool. To create the pool named *our new dhcp pool*, execute the following command at the global configuration prompt. Notice the prompt change to the configuration mode for the pool.

```
Router(config)# ip dhcp pool "our new dhcp pool"
Router(dhcp-config)#
```

To create the addresses and the subnet mask for the pool, you must consider the IP address of the interface on which DHCP will operate. Because we already have set an address and mask on the Fa0/0 interface, let's use that as an example. Its address is 192.168.5.5/24. This interface is in the 192.168.5.0/24 network (see Chapter 8 for more on this). To configure the pool for that network, execute the following command:

```
Router(dhcp-config)# network 192.168.5.0 255.255.255.0
```

At this point, DHCP would be functional, but all the DHCP server would issue to the clients would be an IP address and a mask. They will also probably need to be issued the following:

> ► Default gateway
>
> ► DNS server

These are called *pool options* (or *scope options*, in the Microsoft world). To configure the default gateway option (which in this case would be 192.168.5.5), execute the following command:

```
Router(dhcp-config)#default-router 192.168.5.5
```

To issue the address of the DNS server (for example, 192.168.6.200) to clients, use the following command:

```
Router(dhcp-config)#dns-server 192.168.6.200
```

◄

If you have spaces in the name of the DHCP pool, the name must be surrounded by quotes.

◄

In this case, the router connected to the subnet that this DHCP scope will service has an address of 192.168.5.5, so that should be the default gateway.

There are many more scope options that can be included, many of which are important for more-advanced functions beyond the scope of this book. To read more about these options, see www.cisco.com/en/US/docs/ios/12_2/ip/ configuration/guide/1cfdhcp.html#wp1011532.

Configuring WAN Interfaces

Serial interfaces (WAN interfaces) need all the same settings that Ethernet interfaces do, but they require some additional configuration because they run a different Network Access layer protocol than Ethernet. They still need an IP address and mask, and they still need to be enabled, but they also require you to do the following:

> ▶ Select an encapsulation type (picking the Network Access layer protocol).

> ▶ Specify the end to perform the clocking.

After you have configured these items, there are certainly some additional things that *can* be configured, but the encapsulation type and clocking specifications are required to get the interfaces operational.

Serial lines can use several different Network Access layer protocols. These are also called *encapsulation types*, because they take the original packet and encapsulate it with a different Network Access layer header and trailer. Two of these are designed for point-to-point connections, while the third is designed to operate in a multi-access network. These protocols are as follows:

> ▶ High-level Data Link Control (HDLC)

> ▶ Point-to-Point Protocol (PPP)

> ▶ Frame Relay

Though by no means a hard and fast rule, Frame Relay is typically used to connect to a service provider's Frame Relay network, while HDLC and PPP are the choice when you are connecting two of your own routers with a serial connection. Our focus will be on the use of PPP and HDLC.

The first step to configure a serial line is to specify the encapsulation. If you don't specify this, the default is HDLC, which is fine, but you should be aware that HDLC works only on Cisco routers. Therefore, if you will be connecting to a non-Cisco router, you will need to use PPP. To specify the encapsulation, execute the following command at the interface configuration prompt:

```
Router(config-if)#encapsulation ppp
```

If you want to use HDLC, do nothing, unless the interface was previously configured for PPP, in which case, execute this command:

```
Router(config-if)#encapsulation hdlc
```

You must ensure that both ends of the connection are using the same encapsulation for the connection to work. If an encapsulation mismatch occurs, no communication will occur. After you have set the IP address and mask, you need to specify which end of the connection is performing the clocking. This must be set on the end that is using the DCE end of the cable. If you're unsure about that, execute the following command, and you will see what type of cable is currently attached to the local router (the one you are on). Remember, you need to back out to privileged mode for the show commands. The following command will determine the cable attached to the Serial 0/0 interface:

```
Router# show controllers serial 0/0
Interface Serial0/0
Hardware is PowerQUICC MPC860
DTE V.35 serial cable attached
```

There will be much more output, but the information we are interested in is in line 4, which shows that a DTE V.35 cable is connected. This means that this is the DTE end, which needs no clocking configuration. If the output indicated DCE V.35 serial cable attached, we would need to execute the following command:

```
Router(config-if)#clock rate 64000
```

The value after the clock rate command is the rate in bits per second. The rate selected depends on the interface type. The most common is 64000. For more on clock rates, see www.cisco.com/en/US/docs/ios/interface/command/reference/ir_c2.html#wp1011411.

USING A CSU/DSU

If you were setting up this connection to connect to a CSU/DSU, you would not add a clock rate, because the clock rate would come from the CSU/DSU. Other than that, the configuration is like the one presented in this example.

Saving Configuration Changes

After you have completed all of the basic settings on the router, you need to save these changes to the startup configuration. If you fail to do this, you will find that at the next restart of the router, you have lost all your changes! To save your settings, execute the following command at the privileged mode prompt:

```
router#copy run start
Destination filename [startup-config]?
```

That's correct.
Despite what you
might suspect, you
save in privileged
mode, not configura-
tion mode.

If this is the first time you have saved a configuration, you will be prompted for the name of the startup file, and it will suggest to you the default name startup-config. Press Enter to accept this default. You will be informed that the file is being built:

```
router#copy run start
Destination filename [startup-config]?
```

Press Enter.

```
Building configuration...
[OK]
router#
```

To view the changes or to view the settings on any router for which you are not familiar, use the command show start:

```
Router#show run
```

After you execute this command, the startup configuration file will be displayed, like the partial one shown next. (Parts have been removed for brevity.)

```
Building configuration...

Current configuration : 916 bytes
!
version 12.2
hostname Router
!
interface FastEthernet0/0
 ip address 172.16.13.1 255.255.255.0
 ip helper-address 172.16.10.2
 duplex auto
 speed auto
!
interface FastEthernet1/0
 ip address 172.16.10.1 255.255.255.0
```

```
 duplex auto
 speed auto
!
interface Serial2/0
 no ip address
 shutdown

line vty 0 4
 password cisco
 login
!
```

From the preceding file, you can see the following:

▶ The router name is router.

▶ There are two configured Fast Ethernet interfaces with IP addresses 172.16.13.1/24 and 172.16.10.1/24.

▶ The serial interface has not been configured or enabled.

▶ The password to connect with Telnet is *cisco*.

If you finish your configuration and you have connectivity problems, this command can be used to give you a quick look at what you actually configured, as opposed to what you intended to configure.

THE ESSENTIALS AND BEYOND

Router setup operations and configuration include cabling the router, connecting to the router, configuring passwords, applying IP addresses to the interfaces, enabling the interfaces, and saving the configuration. A router connects to a switch with a twisted-pair cable, to another router with either a twisted-pair cable or a back-to-back serial cable using a smart serial or DB-60 connector, to a PC with either a twisted-pair cable or a console cable, and to a CSU/DSU with connecters dependent on the serial connector present on the router and the CSU/DSU. You create a session with the router on a console or with a Telnet session. After the connection is made, you can configure the router by using the initial setup menu (if no configuration is present) or by using the CLI to build a configuration file. Passwords to control access to privileged and global configuration mode are not required but highly recommended, but default passwords for Telnet access are required. Both Ethernet and serial interfaces require an IP address and subnet mask and must be enabled. Serial interfaces require both ends to be the same encapsulation type (HDLC is the default, with PPP another option), and the DCE end of the serial cable must have a clock rate set. Cisco routers can be either DHCP clients or servers. When operating as a server,

(Continues)

THE ESSENTIALS AND BEYOND *(Continued)*

the DHCP service must be enabled globally, and the interface made operational by creating an address pool that includes the subnet in which the desired interface resides. Changes made during the configuration must be saved, or they will be lost at the next restart.

ADDITIONAL EXERCISES

1. Specify in the following list the cable type that would be used:

   A. Router to router using twisted-pair

   B. Router to switch

   C. Router to PC using HyperTerminal

   D. Router to PC using Telnet

   E. Router to router using serial

2. In this exercise, you will configure a password. This exercise requires the following:

   ► A PC cabled correctly to the router with a console cable

   ► HyperTerminal software installed on the PC

   ► A session created with the router

   Please ensure that these items have been taken care of *before* starting this exercise. The instructions for these items are found in Chapter 12 and earlier in this chapter. Then follow these steps:

   A. If your display is at the initial setup menu, answer no to the prompt.

   B. Proceed through the access levels to global configuration mode by typing the following commands:

   ```
   Router>
   Router>enable
   Router#
   Router# configure terminal
   Router(config)#
   ```

   C. Create an unencrypted password (for this exercise, use mypassword) for access to privileged and global configuration mode by typing the following:

   ```
   Router(config)#enable mypassword
   Router(config)#
   ```

   D. Test it by exiting out to user mode, and attempt to reenter privileged mode:

   ```
   Router(config)# exit
   Router# exit
   Router>
   Router>enable
   ```

   (Continues)

THE ESSENTIALS AND BEYOND *(Continued)*

E. You should be prompted for a password. Enter the password and enter privileged mode:

```
Router>enable
Password:        <type mypassword>
Router#
```

REVIEW QUESTIONS

1. Which of the following is *not* a serial connector type used with a Cisco router?

    A. AUI   **C.** Smart serial

    B. DB-60   **D.** V.35

2. Which port in a Cisco router is used for a modem?

    A. AUI   **C.** Serial

    B. AUX   **D.** Ethernet

3. What setting must be configured on the DCE end of a serial cable that does not need to be configured on the DTE end?

    A. IP address   **C.** Clock rate

    B. Encapsulation type   **D.** Subnet mask

4. In what situation would you receive the following error message?

    ```
    Password not set, connection refused
    ```

    A. When connecting to a router with no enable password set
    C. When connecting to a router with no enable secret password set

    B. When connecting to a router with no vty password set
    D. When connecting to a router with no console password set

5. What of the following is *not* a reason you might see this message when first connecting to a router?

    ```
    --- System Configuration Dialog ---
    Would you like to enter the initial configuration dialog?
    [yes/no]:
    ```

    A. New router
    C. Configuration register set to 0x2102 on a router with an existing startup configuration file

    B. No startup configurations file
    D. Configuration register set to 0x2142 on a router with an existing startup configuration file

(Continues)

THE ESSENTIALS AND BEYOND (Continued)

6. At which prompt will typing enable solicit a password prompt?

   A. Router>

   B. Router#

   C. Router(config)#

   D. Router(config-line)#

7. Which of the following prompts must you be at to make global changes to the router?

   A. Router>

   B. Router#

   C. Router(config)#

   D. Router(config-line)#

8. When using the line command, which of the following is not a connection type that can be specified?

   A. aux

   B. console

   C. vty

   D. tel

9. What command is used to instruct the router to prompt for a password?

   A. login

   B. prompt

   C. auth

   D. secure

10. Which of the following is the second Fast Ethernet port in the first slot on the router?

   A. S0/2

   B. Fa0/1

   C. Fa0/2

   D. Fa1/2

CHAPTER 14

Configuring Switches

Switches can be used in all layers of the Cisco three-layer model—including the distribution and core layers when they operate as multilayer switches. However, this chapter covers switches operating in the access layer. In this role, they provide a connection point to the network for host devices such as computers, printers, network scanners, cameras, or any type of device that needs to be connected to the network. They can also be wired or wireless, as you saw in the discussion of wireless access points that are not routers, but acting as wireless switches (see Chapter 10, "Network Devices").

In many ways, managing a switch is much like managing a router because they both use the Cisco IOS. The differences are most evident in the management of the interfaces and the functions that are possible with the interfaces (which are called *switchports*). Because many of the procedures are no different with a switch than with a router, many of the sections of this chapter are rather abbreviated. The exceptions are the sections on configuring the interfaces and on the features possible with the interfaces, because of the significant difference between router and switch interfaces

Specifically, this chapter covers the following topics:

▶ **Cabling the switch**

▶ **Creating a session with the switch**

▶ **Configuring passwords**

▶ **Configuring interfaces**

▶ **Understanding advanced switch functions**

You can read about switches that can use fiber-optic interfaces at www .hds.com/ assets/pdf/ datasheet -cisco-mds-9134 -multilayer -fabric -switch.pdf.

▶

Cabling the Switch

Cabling an access switch is somewhat simpler than cabling a router. The access switches discussed in this book have only one type of interface, and that is Ethernet, so you won't have to worry about serial ports or cables.

This section explores the cabling considerations for connecting the access switch to other devices.

Cabling Switch to Switch

Switches are often connected to one another. When they are, the links that run between them can be one of two types:

- ► Trunk links
- ► Access links

The only difference between these two types of links is the traffic that is allowed to use them. By default, all ports in a switch are in the same virtual LAN (VLAN). A VLAN is any set of ports on a switch that can communicate with one another without the aid of a router.

VLANS AND SUBNETS

It is also true that the devices that are connected to switchports also must have an IP address in the same subnet to communicate without a router, but VLANs create a Network Access layer boundary, whereas subnets create an Internet layer boundary. Devices must be in the same VLAN and the same subnet to communicate without a router.

VLANs can be configured on a switch, and ports can be assigned to the VLANs (which is covered in detail later in the section "Understanding VLANs"). VLANs can also span two physical switches. For example, VLAN 2 may comprise three ports on switch 1 and three ports on switch 2. When this is the case, the link between the switches must be a trunk link. Trunk links can carry the traffic of multiple VLANs, whereas access links cannot.

When all ports on two switches are in the default VLAN, they are all in the same VLAN (that is, the default VLAN), so an access link works fine between them. It is only when a VLAN other than the default VLAN spans two switches that the link needs to be a trunk link.

Regardless of the link between the switches, by now you can appreciate that the link is probably going to be busy. Therefore, you should use the faster links on the switches for this connection. Figure 14.1 shows a connection between two switches using the 100BaseT ports rather than the 10BaseT ports.

Remember, the cables that run between two switches should be crossover cables!

FIGURE 14.1 Switch-to-switch connection

Cabling Router to Switch

Cabling a router to a switch was already covered from the perspective of the router in the preceding chapter. From the perspective of the switch end, the link can be either an access link or a trunk. If the switch has multiple VLANs, the link going back to the router will have to be a trunk link. If that is not the case, the link can be an access link.

Keep in mind, however, that regardless of the number of VLANs present on the switch, because all hosts on the switch will be using the router interface as the default gateway, any traffic that needs to leave a host's local subnet will need to go to the router. This means that the link will be busy, and you should use a faster link. Figure 14.2 shows the cable running from the 100 Mbps line in the switch to the router.

FIGURE 14.2 Router-to-switch connection

Remember, the cables that run from router to switch should be straight-through cables!

Cabling Hosts to Switch

Hosts can be any devices that need to connect to the network. For these devices, you should use the slower ports, of which there will probably be many more present on the switch.

There is one important consideration. You should ensure that both ends of the connection, the switchport and the NIC on the device, are set for full-duplex. If this is not the case, the device may experience very poor performance. Today, most NICs and switch interfaces are autosensing, which means they take care of this for you, but it can be something worth checking if the performance of a device seems abnormally poor. In the section on configuring interfaces, you will learn how to verify that this is not a problem.

Figure 14.3 show the ports that should be used for the devices.

FIGURE 14.3 Host connections

Remember, the cables that run from host to switch should be straight-through cables!

Creating a Session with the Switch

Just as with a router, a session can be established with a switch either through the console cable by using HyperTerminal or by connecting to the switch over the network via Telnet. The procedures are the same as with a router with respect to using the console cable and HyperTerminal. However, there is one important additional consideration when connecting to the switch for a Telnet session, as you will see in the section "Creating a Session through Telnet."

Creating a Session with the Console Cable

As with a router, this procedure begins by connecting a console cable to the switch. The serial end of the console cable attaches to the PC, and the RJ-45 end connects to the console port on the switch, as shown in Figure 14.4.

FIGURE 14.4 Console cable connection to the switch

After the cabling is in place and you have installed HyperTerminal on the PC, the connection can be established by using the same procedure as with a router:

1. Choose Start ➤ Programs ➤ HyperTerminal-Private-Edition. Double-click to start the application.

2. Enter the following information in the next dialog boxes you receive:

   ▶ Location Information: In the Area Code box, enter your area code.

   ▶ Phone And Modem: Click OK and accept the default.

   ▶ New Connection-HyperTerminal: Name the connection.

   ▶ Connect To Port: Select COM 1.

   ▶ COM1 Port properties: Use the settings

   9600
   8
   None
   1
   None

3. **Press Enter.** If you have entered the correct settings, you should receive a switch prompt or a setup dialog box. The only difference in the outcome of this procedure compared to creating a router session is that when you arrive at the CLI prompt, it will appear as follows, which as you can see indicates that you are on a switch and not a router:

```
Switch>
```

Creating a Session through Telnet

The one huge consideration when connecting to a switch with Telnet is that the switch must have an IP address before you can connect to it. Because a router will always have IP addresses applied to its interfaces, this is not a consideration with a router (you could connect to it by using any of its IP addresses). Switchports don't have IP addresses (remember, all operations are in terms of MAC addresses), and a switch can operate well without an IP address. But if you are going to connect to a switch by using Telnet, it must have an IP address.

When an IP address is applied to a switch, the address is applied to the default VLAN rather than to any interface. The default VLAN is VLAN 1, so to do this you would progress through user, privileged, and global configuration modes first, as shown here:

```
Switch>
Switch>enable
Password:        <enter password if required>
Switch#
Switch#config t
Switch(config)#
```

> **For security reasons, VLAN 1 is usually disabled, and a numbered virtual interface is created to use as the management VLAN—for example, VLAN 100.**

At this point, enter the configuration mode for VLAN 1, as you would enter interface configuration mode on a router:

```
Switch(config)# interface  vlan1
Switch(config-vlan)#
```

Then apply the IP address, just as you would to an interface:

```
Switch(config-vlan)#ip address 192.168.5.5 255.255.255.0
```

You also must enable the interface as you would an interface on a router:

```
Switch(config-vlan)# no shutdown
```

Now the IP address can be used to connect to the switch to use Telnet. Just as a review, the following procedure executed from a PC on the network would establish a Telnet session with the switch. Don't forget that unless you configure a vty password, the connection will be refused.

1. Open a command prompt on the PC and type this command:

   ```
   telnet 192.168.5.5
   ```

   This output will appear:

   ```
   Connecting to 192.168.5.5
   ```

2. If the switch is reachable, one of two things will occur:

   ▶ If a Telnet password has been configured, you will be prompted to type the password.

   ▶ If no Telnet password has been created, you will receive this message:

   ```
   Password not set, connection refused
   ```

3. If you have entered the correct password, you should receive a switch prompt or a setup dialog box. The handling of these prompts is covered in Chapter 13, "Configuring Routers."

Configuring Passwords

Configuring passwords on a switch is no different than on a router, which again makes sense because they both use the Cisco IOS. This section presents a condensed review of the creation of both versions of the privileged mode password (clear text and encrypted) and the line vty passwords.

Configuring Privileged (Enable) Passwords

To create the unencrypted version of the privileged mode password, execute the following command at global configuration mode. The example creates a password of *cisco*.

```
switch>
switch>enable
switch#
switch# configure terminal
switch(config)#

switch(config)#enable password cisco
```

Configuring Enable Secret Passwords

To encrypt the enable password, you can create an *enable* secret password instead. The only difference is that when you execute the command, you specify that you would like the password to be encrypted by substituting *secret* for password in the command, as shown here:

```
switch(config)#enable secret cisco
```

Remember, if both an enable and enable secret passwords are configured on a switch, the switch will prompt for the encrypted password instead of the unencrypted password.

Configuring Line Passwords

Configuring line passwords for switches works pretty much the same as it does for routers, including determining the number of vty lines available, the changing of the prompt, and instructing the switch to prompt for a password. See Chapter 13 for details.

Configuring Interfaces

Interfaces on a switch are called *switchports*. IP addresses are not configured on switchports. In fact, switchports take very little configuration to function. You can simply plug in the devices, and they will work. However, to use some the advanced functions that are discussed later in this chapter or to verify switchports, you must know how to access the ports and how to configure them in port configuration mode.

This section covers accessing a single port or a set of switchports. Enabling and verifying the port status is covered as well.

Accessing Switchports and Using Switchport Mode

Accessing any of the more specific configuration modes in the IOS requires progressing through the user, privileged, and global configuration modes first. That is also the case with accessing switchports in configuration mode. To arrive at this mode, follow these steps:

```
switch>
switch>enable
```

```
Password:  <enter password if required>
switchr#config t
Enter configuration commands, one per line.  End with CNTL/Z.
switch(config)#
```

Among the operations that can be performed with the `switchport mode` command are placing a port or group of ports into a VLAN and setting a port as a trunk link. This `switchport` command is executed after you have entered configuration mode for the port or port group. The following is an example of entering configuration mode for the port Fa0/4:

```
Switch(config)# interface fa0/4
Switch(config-if)#
```

Once in configuration mode for the interface, execute the command with the proper parameter. There are many parameters that can be used. The `shutdown` and `no shutdown` parameters are discussed in the last section of this chapter. As a preview, here is an example of placing the interface into VLAN 2 while also setting it to operate as an access rather than a trunk port:

```
Switch(config-if)#switchport access vlan 2
```

Enabling the Port

◄

The VLAN that all ports are in by default is VLAN 1.

Switchports are normally enabled by default, but if you make a change to the port, such as placing it into a VLAN, the port will need to be enabled again. The command to do this is the `no shutdown` command:

```
Switch(config-if)#no shutdown
```

Verifying the Port

Switchports can be verified by using the `show port status` command. Remember that `show` commands are executed in user mode. When the command is executed and you specify the port number (in the "Accessing Switchports and Using Switchport Mode" section earlier, the port was 0/4), the `show port status` command will display information as shown here:

```
Switch> show  port status 0/4
Port Name Status Vlan  Duplex Speed Type
---- -------------------- ---------- ----------
 0/4       enabled 2     auto  auto 10/100BaseTX
```

The output shows the following:

- ► The port is 0/4.

- ► The port is enabled.

- ► The port has been placed in VLAN 2.

- ► The duplex is set for auto (meaning autosense).

- ► The speed (which can be specified manually) is also set for autosense.

- ► The port can run at either 10 or 100 Mbps and uses an RJ-45 connection (TX).

Understanding Advanced Switch Functions

Creating VLANs is not required for a Cisco switch to operate. By default, all ports on the switch are in the same VLAN and are set to access mode rather than trunk mode. As long as all of the hosts connected to the switch are configured with the IP address of the router interface to which the switch is connected as their default gateway, everything should work just fine by plugging the hosts into the switch.

The frame-forwarding logic discussed in Chapter 11, "LAN Operations," works without any configuration on your part. However, one of the key features that most LAN administrators take advantage of is the ability to organize hosts into VLANs that span multiple switches. This removes the need for hosts to be physically connected to the same switch in order to be in the same network.

This section covers VLANs and trunk ports, which must be created between switches (and between the switch and the router) to allow the transmission of traffic sourced from and destined to multiple VLANs across the link. Although a full VLAN configuration spanning multiple switches is beyond the scope of this book, some of the VLAN commands on the switch are covered. Finally, a more detailed description of Spanning Tree Protocol (STP) ends the chapter. STP, introduced briefly in Chapter 10, is used to prevent the switching loops that become possible when switches are connected in a redundant topology.

Understanding VLANs

VLANs are logical segmentations of a network at the Network Access layer of the TCP/IP model. When hosts are placed into separate VLANs, they cannot communicate with one another without the aid of a router, even if they are connected to the same switch. Routers perform routing based on IP subnets.

Therefore, when a VLAN is created, the VLAN will be assigned an IP subnet number on the router, and all of the devices in the VLAN must have an IP address that resides in that network.

Creating VLANs and assigning a port to them on a switch is a two-step process:

1. Create the VLAN and name it.

2. Assign ports to it.

Consider Figure 14.5. This switch needs to have ports 1–3 assigned to VLAN 2 (which should be named Sales) and ports 5–7 assigned to VLAN 3 (which should be named Accounting). We can't use VLAN 1 because that is the default VLAN, where all of the ports are currently located.

VLAN 2   VLAN 3

FIGURE 14.5 VLANs 2 and 3

To make this configuration, the two VLANs must first be created. Access global configuration mode, as shown here:

```
switch>
switch>enable
Password:  <enter password if required>
switchr#config t
Enter configuration commands, one per line.  End with CNTL/Z.
switch(config)#
```

The command to create a VLAN is simply the following:

```
vlan vlan number name name of the vlan
```

Therefore, the two commands required to create the two VLANs would be as follows:

```
switch(config)#vlan 2 name Sales
switch(config)#vlan 3 name Accounting
```

Now the ports need to be assigned to the VLANs. This requires entering configuration mode for the ports. You learned how to do that earlier, in the section "Accessing Switchports and Using Switchport Mode." This time, however, we are going to enter configuration mode for a group of ports. This is done with the `interface range` command. This command prevents us from having to enter the configuration mode for each port as a separate operation:

```
Switch(config)#interface range fastethernet0/1-3
Switch(config-if-range)#
```

Notice that the prompt has changed to indicate that any operation we perform now will be affecting a range of ports and not a single port. Now we can execute the command that assigns ports 1–3 to VLAN 2, set them as access ports, and commit the changes with the `no shutdown` command:

```
switch(config-if-range)# switchport access vlan 2
switch(config-if-range)# no shutdown
```

To add ports 5–7 to VLAN 3, the operations would be as follows:

```
switch(config-if-range)#exit
switch(config)#interface range fastethernet0/5-7
switch(config-if-range)# switchport access vlan 3
switch(config-if-range)# no shutdown
```

At this point, the devices plugged into the two VLANs would not be able to communicate with one another without a router. The switch would need to be connected to a router, and the link from the router to the switch would need to be a trunk link. That is discussed in the next section.

Understanding Trunk Ports

For more information on ISL and 802.1q, go to www.cisco.com/en/US/tech/tk389/tk689/technologies_tech_note09186a0080094665.shtml.

▶

Access ports on a switch can carry only traffic sourced from or destined to the VLAN of which the port is a member. Trunk ports can carry the traffic of multiple VLANs. To do this, trunk ports need a method for identifying the VLAN to which each frame belongs. This is done with a process called *frame tagging*, which requires an additional protocol to be running on the trunk link.

Two protocols can be enabled on a trunk link to perform this frame-tagging function. One is Cisco proprietary (Inter Switch Link, or ISL), and the other is an industry standard (802.1q). The details and configuration of these protocols is outside the scope of this book, but it is important for you to know that one of these must be configured on the link between the switch and the router, and they *must* match.

These protocols add information (tags) about the frame that the router uses to route the frame to its proper VLAN. A router can be either a separate physical device from the switch or a route card residing in a multilayer switch. In either case, a trunk link must be configured between the routing function or router and the switching function or switch. It is simpler to visualize this relationship by viewing a router connected to a switch, as shown in Figure 14.6. This is sometimes called a *router-on-a-stick*.

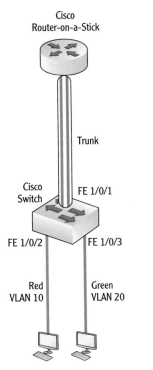

FIGURE 14.6 Router-on-a-stick

Describing STP

Switches should be connected together to provide redundancy if possible. When that is not the case and there is a link failure, hosts become isolated. Consider the network in Figure 14.7.

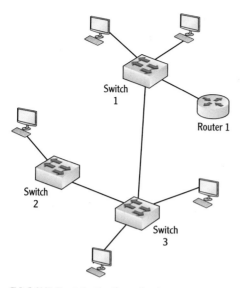

FIGURE 14.7 No redundancy

In Figure 14.7, if something happened to the link between switches 2 and 3 or between switches 1 and 2, hosts in the network would be cut off from the rest of the network. Now look at Figure 14.8.

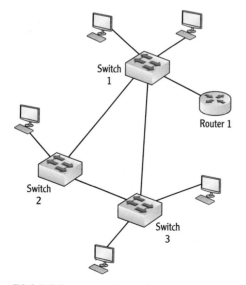

FIGURE 14.8 Redundancy

In this figure, if either of these links went down, there would still be a path (albeit perhaps a longer one) from any device to any device. This was made possible because of the redundant link provided from switch 1 to 2.

The problem with the network now is that a potential switch loop exists from switch 1 to 2 to 3. *Spanning Tree Protocol (STP)* is designed to prevent the loops from happening. STP does not need to be configured; it is already enabled in the switches, although there are some things you can change about its operation if you desire.

What you need to understand at this point is its basic operation. It prevents loops by carrying out the following operations:

▶ The switches elect a root bridge (which is one of the switches that will serve as a reference point for rules to be used on opening and blocking ports).

▶ Based on the root bridge election and the relative position of the nonroot bridges with respect to the root, certain ports on each switch forward traffic and certain other ports on each switch block traffic in such a way that loops are prevented.

Details of these operations are as follows:

Root Bridge Election   The switches exchange packets with one another called *Bridge Protocol Data Units (BPDUs)*. These BPDUs contain information, including the bridge priority. By default, all bridges have the same priority. That can be altered, but if it has not been, the switches compare MAC addresses. The switch with the lowest MAC address number becomes the root bridge.

Root and Nonroot Port Behavior   After the election has taken place, STP rules determine which ports on each switch are allowed to forward and which are blocked. First, the ports on each switch are classified as either root or nonroot. The rules that determine this are as follows:

▶ All ports on the root bridge (switch) are root ports.

▶ On each nonroot switch, the port with the lowest-cost path to the root bridge is a root port. All others are nonroot.

In Figure 14.9, assume that switch 3 became the root bridge. The ports that would be root and nonroot are labeled.

Lowest-cost path means the total of individual costs for each link between the nonroot bridge and the root bridge.

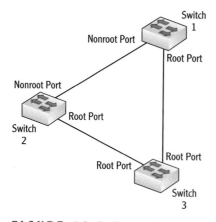

FIGURE 14.9 Root and nonroot ports

Now that the root and nonroot ports are determined, the following STP rules apply to each port:

▶ All root ports forward.

▶ All nonroot ports block.

The STP port operations that would prevent loops after the election of switch 3 as the bridge are shown in Figure 14.10.

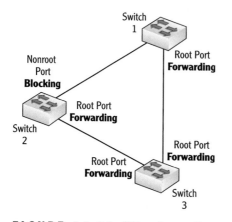

FIGURE 14.10 STP port operations

THE ESSENTIALS AND BEYOND

Access layer switches provide a connection point to the network for host devices such as computers or printers. Managing a switch is much like managing a router, because both use the Cisco IOS. Even password management is the same. One of the biggest differences is the switch interfaces (switchports), but these are easy to configure. Switches can be connected to one another or to routers. A session can be established with a switch by using either HyperTerminal or Telnet. For a Telnet session, the switch must be configured with an IP address. VLANs are logical segmentations of a network at the Network Access layer of the TCP/IP model. When placed into separate VLANs, hosts cannot communicate with one another without the aid of a router. Access ports on a switch can carry only traffic sourced from or destined to the VLAN of which the port is a member. However, trunk ports can carry the traffic of multiple VLANs. Switches should be connected together to provide redundancy. When switches are connected, switching loops are automatically prevented by Spanning Tree Protocol (STP).

ADDITIONAL EXERCISES

In this exercise, you will create two VLANs, name them, assign ports to them, and verify your work. This exercise assumes that your PC is connected to your switch with a console cable and has created a session with the switch. You have been assigned the following tasks to fulfill:

▶ Create two VLANs named Marketing and Management.

▶ Place ports 4–12 in the Marketing VLAN and place ports 17–22 in the Management VLAN.

▶ Verify the status of one port in each VLAN.

REVIEW QUESTIONS

1. In what VLAN are all ports located by default?

    A. VLAN 0   C. VLAN 2

    B. VLAN 1   D. VLAN 3

2. VLANs are segments at what layer of the TCP/IP model?

    A. Application   C. Network Access

    B. Transport   D. Internet

3. What type of cable should be used between a host and a switch?

    A. Straight-through   C. Rolled

    B. Console   D. Crossover

(Continues)

THE ESSENTIALS AND BEYOND *(Continued)*

4. Which of the following situations is the *only* time you would use a crossover cable?

   A. Host to switch   C. Router to switch

   B. PC to console port   D. Switch to switch

5. To which of the following must an IP address be applied to telnet to the switch?

   A. Any switchport   C. VLAN 1

   B. The uplink port to the router   D. A newly created VLAN for Telnet access

6. Which of the following actions are required for a switchport to operate?

   A. Enable it.   C. Assign an IP address.

   B. Assign it to VLAN 1.   D. None of the above.

7. What command should be executed under the switchport configuration mode after changes have been made?

   A. copy run start   C. no shutdown

   B. copy start run   D. enable

8. What command produced the following output?

   ```
   Port Name Status Vlan  Duplex Speed Type
   ---- -------------------- ---------- ---------
    0/4      enabled 2     auto  auto 10/100BaseTX
   ```

   A. show port status 0/4   C. show port status

   B. show port 0/4   D. show ports

9. Which of the following is *not* correct about VLANs?

   A. VLANs provide segmentation at the Internet layer.   C. VLANs can span multiple switches.

   B. VLANs provide segmentation at the Network Access layer.   D. Communication between VLANs requires a router.

10. Which of the following protocols is used to prevent switching loops?

    A. VTP   C. RSTP

    B. STP   D. RSVP

CHAPTER 15

Configuring Static Routing

Cisco routers use routing tables to maintain the information required for them to direct the packets they receive to the proper destination. These routes are categorized as follows:

- ▶ Network routes (routes that identify the location of entire subnets of hosts)

- ▶ Host routes (routes that identify the location of a single host)

- ▶ Directly connected routes (routes to which the router is directly connected via an interface address in the same subnet)

- ▶ Default routes (routes to which all traffic that does not have an existing route in the table is sent).

Regardless of the type of routes present in the table, the routes must be placed into the routing table (except for directly connected routes, which automatically appear in the table). This can be done in one of two ways:

- ▶ Static routing, in which an administrator using the CLI to execute the ip route command places the route into the table

- ▶ Dynamic routing, in which a routing protocol enabled on the router communicates with other routers running the same routing protocol to share routes and populate the tables automatically

Only when routing tables are complete can routers perform the job for which they were designed. This chapter covers static routing, and the final chapter covers the configuration of dynamic routing protocols. Specifically, this chapter covers the following topics:

- ▶ **Populating the routing table**

- ▶ **Configuring inter-VLAN routing**

Populating the Routing Table

Static routing requires that routes be added to the routing table by using the ip route command. Maintaining the routing table manually has advantages and disadvantages. The disadvantages, which may be more obvious than the advantages, include the following:

▶ The additional administrative effort required to create the routes by using the ip route command

▶ The need to manually react to outages and changes in the network by manually editing the routing table when problems arise

There is really only one advantage to static routing: it eliminates routing update traffic. As you will learn in Chapter 16, "Configuring Dynamic Routing," the amount and frequency of routing update traffic varies from routing protocol to routing protocol—but just as an example, when using Routing Internet Protocol (RIP), the entire routing table is sent in each update, and updates are sent every 30 seconds. This is true even if the routing table has not changed in five years!

Therefore, if a network topology is very small, changes rarely if ever occur, and the system is very stable (meaning infrequent link outages), static routing may allow the network to perform better by eliminating the routing update traffic that competes with the regular traffic for bandwidth.

This section explains the use of the ip route command to build the routing table as well as the commands required for viewing and verifying the table.

Using the *ip route* Command

Entries are added to the routing table by using the ip route command. It is executed at the global command prompt, as shown here:

```
Router(config)#
```

The command has parameters that can be added to alter its function, but the syntax of the command in its simplest form is as follows:

```
ip route <network ID> <subnet mask> <next hop ip address>
```

These are the parameters:

<network ID> is the network ID or network number of the destination network.

<subnet mask> is the subnet mask of the destination network.

<next hop ip address> is the IP address of the interface of the next directly connected router to which a packet should be sent to reach this network.

ROUTING LOGIC REVIEW

Remember that a routing table does not store a full set of directions to the destination. The table stores only the IP address of the next router in the path. This is why the `ip route` command references the next hop address at the end of the command and not the address of the last router in the path. This is also why every router in the path needs to know its part of the directions, or the routing process breaks down. Each router in the path knows only how to get the packet to the next router.

Consider the network in Figure 15.1.

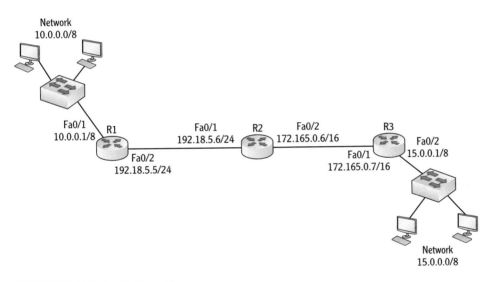

FIGURE 15.1 Static routing

To configure R1 with the route to the 15.0.0.0/8 network on the other end of the diagram (it's a network directly connected to R3), the command would be executed as follows:

```
R1(config)#ip route 150.0.0.0 255.0.0.0 192.168.5.6
```

Notice that the next hop is the directly connected interface on the next router in the path to R3, which is the Fa0/1 interface on R2. It is *not* an interface on R3! Also realize that for routing to work, every router along the path to the 15.0.0.0/8 network must also know the route. The preceding executed command would simply get the packet to R2. If a route for 15.0.0.0/8 did not exist in R2's routing table, the packet would be dropped right there.

To place the route in the table of R2, the command would be as follows:

```
R1(config)#ip route 150.0.0.0 255.0.0.0 172.165.0.7
```

Notice that the next hop is the directly connected interface on the next router in the path to R3, which is the Fa0/1 interface on R3. At this point, the configuration would be complete. Because the 15.0.0.0/8 network is directly connected to R3, R3 will have the route to 15.0.0.0/8 in its table.

You Can't Ping Yet!

If you attempted a ping from a host in the 10.0.0.0/8 network to a host in the 15.0.0.0/8 network, at this point it would fail. Why? Because ping packets have to go to the destination, and the replies must come back. Just because the routers know how to get the packet to the destination doesn't necessarily mean they know how to get the replies back to the source. In this example, we would have to put a route to the 10.0.0.0/8 network in the routing tables of R3 and R2 for the replies to be successfully routed back to the host in the 10.0.0.0/8 network.

Verifying the Route Table

To verify the completion of the ip route command or to verify the existence of a route in the routing table, the table can be viewed with the show ip route command. The command is executed in user mode. The following output of the command for R1 is displayed as it would look with the commands executed to this point. The first part of the output is the *legend*, which indicates the meaning of the letters placed next to the route. Some of the output of the legend is omitted in this example.

```
R1>show ip route
Codes: I - IGRP derived, R - RIP derived, O - OSPF derived,
       C - connected, S - static

       <output omitted>

C    10.0.0.0 is directly connected, FastEthernet 0/1
C    192.168.5.0 is directly connected, FastEthernet 0/2
S    15.0.0.0/8 via  192.168.5.5
```

You can see that the two directly connected routes are present for the two local interfaces on the router. The static route to 15.0.0.0/8 is also shown as available via 192.168.5.5, which is the local exit interface on the router, not the next hop.

THE LEGEND CODES

The legend codes shown in the output of the show ip route command that we have covered are C for directly connected and S for static. The other codes are for routes placed in the table by routing protocols (some of which are covered in the next chapter). Some of the codes have been cut from the output to save space. To see the full legend and read more about the codes, go to www.cisco.com/en/US/docs/ios/12_2/iproute/command/reference/1rfindp2.html#wp1022511.

Configuring Inter-VLAN Routing

In Chapter 14, "Configuring Switches," you learned that when switches are configured with VLANs, hosts in different VLANs cannot communicate without the help of a router. Consider the router and switch in Figure 15.2.

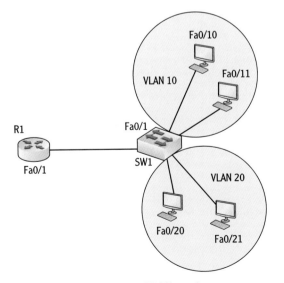

FIGURE 15.2 Inter-VLAN routing

SW 1 is configured with two VLANs: VLAN 10 and VLAN 20. The switch ports Fa0/20 and Fa0/21 have been added to VLAN 20. The switch ports Fa0/10 and Fa0/11 have been added to VLAN 10.

The computers connected to those switch ports will *not* be able to communicate with one another until inter-VLAN routing is configured on R1. The first step is to connect the router to the switch with a straight-through cable, connecting the Fa0/1 interface on the router to the Fa0/1 interface on the switch, as shown in Figure 15.2.

To configure the router to route between the VLANs, the following steps must be taken:

1. Create a trunk link between the router and the switch and configure an encapsulation protocol on the trunk link.

2. Create subinterfaces for each VLAN on the physical link.

These steps are explained in the following sections.

Creating a Trunk Link with Encapsulation

The link that exists between the switch and the router must be specified as a trunk link, because it will be carrying traffic from both VLAN 10 and VLAN 20. Starting on the switch end of the connection, at the interface configuration prompt for the Fa0/1 interface, two commands need to be executed. The first command is as follows:

```
SW1(config-if)switchport trunk encapsulation isl
```

This command instructs the router to set the interface as a trunk link and to use the Inter-Switch Link (ISL) encapsulation protocol. This is one of two trunking protocols available. The other is IEEE 802.1q. Either will work fine, but the same protocol must be set on both the switch end and the router end. Keep these factors in mind when you choose between the two:

▶ 802.1 q is an IEEE standard and works on all routers.

▶ ISL works on only Cisco devices.

The second command to execute on the switch will set the trunking mode of the interface to *trunk*, which will prevent it from acting in any other mode. This command is executed while still in interface configuration mode, as shown here:

```
SW1(config-if)switchport mode trunk
```

When configuring the trunk link for 802.1q, the command is executed as follows: SW1(config-if) switchport trunk encapsulation dot1q.

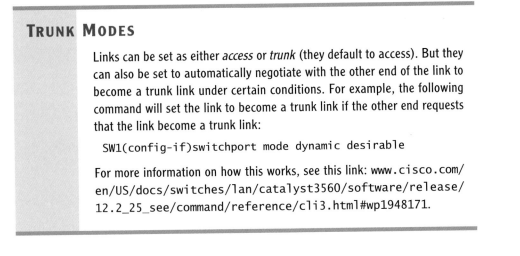

TRUNK MODES

Links can be set as either *access* or *trunk* (they default to access). But they can also be set to automatically negotiate with the other end of the link to become a trunk link under certain conditions. For example, the following command will set the link to become a trunk link if the other end requests that the link become a trunk link:

```
SW1(config-if)switchport mode dynamic desirable
```

For more information on how this works, see this link: www.cisco.com/ en/US/docs/switches/lan/catalyst3560/software/release/ 12.2_25_see/command/reference/cli3.html#wp1948171.

The router end of the connection must be set as a trunk link with the correct encapsulation as well. However, this step cannot be completed without first creating subinterfaces for each VLAN. The next section explains what subinterfaces are and how to configure them on the router.

Creating and Configuring Subinterfaces

When traffic from multiple VLANs will traverse the same physical connection, there must be some way to segregate the VLANs for the purpose of assigning a default gateway to each. Remember that VLANs create Network Access layer segmentation, but the devices will also need to be segregated at the Internet layer with IP subnets.

IP addresses are applied to interfaces on a router. Therefore, to apply two IP addresses (in different IP subnets) to the same physical interface, the interface must be logically subdivided. This is done with *subinterfaces*. Then one IP address (located in one IP subnet) can be applied to one subinterface, and another IP address (located in a different IP subnet) can be applied to the other subinterface.

When subinterfaces are created, they are named after the physical interface of which they are a part, and then a dot is added, followed by a number to identify the subinterface. For example, a subinterface of the Fa0/1 physical interface might be Fa0/1.1 or Fa0/1.2.

After the subinterface has been created, you will immediately be placed into subinterface configuration mode for that subinterface. While you are in that mode, you should do the following:

▶ Set the encapsulation type and associate the subinterface with a VLAN.

▶ Apply an IP address.

Before we get started, consider Figure 15.3. It has been labeled with the IP addresses that the computers in each VLAN will have and the IP address that will be applied to the router interface for each subinterface. There will be a sub-interface for each VLAN. Note that computers must be set with the IP address of the router subinterface that has been associated with the host's VLAN as their default gateway.

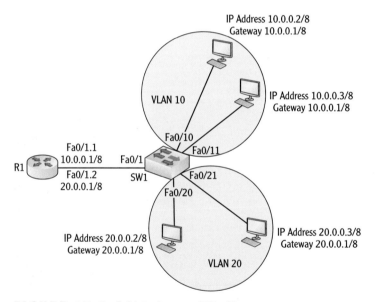

FIGURE 15.3 Subinterfaces and IP addresses

To create the first subinterface, execute the following command at the global configuration prompt on the router:

```
R1(config)#interface Fa0/1.1
R1(config-subif)#
```

Notice that the prompt changed, indicating that you are now in configuration mode for the subinterface Fa0/1.1. Now set the encapsulation to match what was set on the switch (ISL). The 10 that follows identifies the VLAN:

```
R1(config-subif)# encapsulation isl 10
```

Finally, set the IP address just as you would on any other interface:

```
R1(config-subif# ip address 10.0.0.1 255.255.255.0
```

The complete set of commands for the other subinterface is as follows:

```
R1(config)#interface Fa0/1.2
R1(config-subif)# encapsulation isl 20
R1(config-subif# ip address 20.0.0.1 255.255.255.0
```

Because the two networks are directly connected to the router, the routes will automatically be placed in the routing table of R1. Its table is shown here:

```
R1>show ip route
Codes: C - connected, S - static, I - IGRP, R - RIP, M - mobile, B - BGP
       <output omitted>

C    10.0.0.0/8 is directly connected, FastEthernet0/1.1
C    20.0.0.0/8 is directly connected, FastEthernet0/1.2
```

When a host in one of the VLANs needs to send something to a host in the other VLAN, the host will send the packet to its default gateway, which will be the IP address that was assigned to the subinterface associated with its VLAN. The router will then locate the network in its table and route the packet back out the interface to the VLAN on which the destination machine is located.

THE ESSENTIALS AND BEYOND

Cisco routers use routing tables to maintain the information required for them to direct the packets they receive to the proper destination. Routes can be placed into the routing table in one of two ways: static routing and dynamic routing. Entries are added to the routing table by using the ip route command. To verify the completion of the ip route command or the existence of a route in the routing table, the table can be viewed with the show ip route command. To configure a router to route between VLANs, you create a trunk link between the router and the switch, configure an encapsulation protocol on the trunk link, and create subinterfaces for each VLAN on the physical link.

(Continues)

THE ESSENTIALS AND BEYOND *(Continued)*

ADDITIONAL EXERCISES

In this exercise, you will create static routes that link the networks in Figure 15.4. It assumes that you have connected three routers, as shown in the diagram. The interfaces must also be assigned the IP addresses as shown, and the interfaces should be enabled.

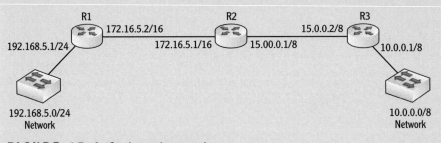

FIGURE 15.4 Static routing exercise

For router R1, perform these steps:

1. Log into the router and access global configuration mode, as shown here:

```
R1>enable
R1>Password:        <enter password>
R1#config t
R1(config)#
```

2. Use the ip route command to add the route to the 10.0.0.0/8 network with a next hop address of 172.0.16.5.1, which is the address of the next router (R2) on the path to R3:

```
R1(config)#ip route 10.0.0.0 255.0.0.0. 172.16.5.1
```

3. Verify that the route is present in the table by backing out to user mode and executing the show ip route command. You should see an entry in the table, as shown in the following output.

```
R1>show ip route
Codes: C - connected, S - static, I - IGRP, R - RIP, M -
mobile, B - BGP
        <output omitted>
C    192.168.5.0 is directly connected, FastEthernet0/1
C    172.16.0.0  is directly connected, FastEthernet0/2
S    10.0.0.0/8 via 172.16.5.2
```

(Continues)

THE ESSENTIALS AND BEYOND *(Continued)*

Note that for FastEthernet0/1 and FastEthernet0/2, your interface may be different.

For router R3, perform these steps:

1. Log into the router and access global configuration mode, as shown here:

```
R3>enable
R3>Password:        <enter password>
R3#config t
R3(config)#
```

2. Use the ip route command to add the route to the 192.168.5.0/24 network with a next hop address of 15.0.0.1/8, which is the address of the next router (R2) on the path to R1:

```
R3(config)#ip route 192.168.5.0 255.255.255.0 15.0.0.1
```

3. Verify that the route is present in the table by backing out to user mode and executing the show ip route command. You should see an entry in the table, as shown in the following output.

```
R1>show ip route
Codes: C - connected, S - static, I - IGRP, R - RIP, M -
mobile, B - BGP
        <output omitted>
C    10.0.0.0  is directly connected, FastEthernet0/1
C    15.0.0.0  is directly connected, FastEthernet0/2
S    192.168.5.0/24 via 15.0.0.2
```

Note that for FastEthernet0/1 and FastEthernet0/2, your interface may be different.

REVIEW QUESTIONS

1. Which of the following routes are placed into the routing table automatically?

   A. Network routes   C. Directly connected routes

   B. Host routes   D. Default routes

2. Where is traffic sent if it does not have an existing route in the table?

   A. A network route   C. A directly connected route

   B. A host route   D. A default route

(Continues)

THE ESSENTIALS AND BEYOND *(Continued)*

3. Which of the following is an advantage of static routing?

    A. Reduced administrative effort required to create the routes

    B. Automatic reaction to outages and changes in the network

    C. Elimination of routing update traffic

    D. Reduction of routing update traffic

4. In which of the following situations would static routing be advisable?

    A. The network topology is very large, changes rarely if ever occur, and the system is very stable.

    B. The network topology is very small, changes frequently occur, and the system is very stable.

    C. The network topology is very small, changes rarely if ever occur, and the system is very unstable.

    D. The network topology is very small, changes rarely if ever occur, and the system is very stable.

5. What command is used to place routes into the routing table?

    A. `ip route`

    B. `route add`

    C. `route`

    D. `insert route`

6. In the following command, what does the IP address 192.16835.6 represent?

    `R1(config)#ip route 150.0.0.0 255.0.0.0.0 192.168.5.6`

    A. The address of the local exit interface

    B. The exit interface on the destination router

    C. The address of the next hop router in the path to the destination network

    D. The address of the destination host

7. What command produced the following output?

    ```
    Codes: I - IGRP derived, R - RIP derived, O - OSPF derived,
           C - connected, S - static
           <output omitted>
           C   10.0.0.0 is directly connected, FastEthernet 0/1
           C   192.168.5.0 is directly connected, FastEthernet 0/2
           S   15.0.0.0/8 via  192.168.5.5
    ```

    A. `show run`

    B. `show ip route`

    C. `show network`

    D. `show interfaces`

(Continues)

THE ESSENTIALS AND BEYOND *(Continued)*

8. Which of the routes in the following table was manually added?

   ```
   C    10.0.0.0 is directly connected, FastEthernet 0/1
   C    192.168.5.0 is directly connected, FastEthernet 0/2
   D    25.0.0.0/8 via  17.6.0.0
   S    15.0.0.0/8 via  192.168.5.5
   ```

   A. 10.0.0.0   **C.** 25.0.0.0/8

   B. 192.168.5.0   **D.** 15.0.0.0/8

9. Which of the following components is *not* required for inter-VLAN routing?

   A. A trunk link   **C.** An encapsulation protocol

   B. Subinterfaces   **D.** Multicast IP addresses

10. Which of the following steps in configuring inter-VLAN routing is *not* done in subinterface configuration mode?

    A. Set the link to *trunk*   **C.** Associate the subinterface with a VLAN

    B. Apply an IP address   **D.** Set the encapsulation type

CHAPTER 16

Configuring Dynamic Routing

Cisco routers can be configured with static routes and will work quite well and do an impressive job of acting as the traffic directors of the network. But perhaps the most impressive and robust feature that can be enabled on a Cisco router is *dynamic routing*.

When a dynamic routing protocol is enabled on the routers in a network, much of the work of managing the network is done automatically by the routers themselves. In this final chapter, the enhancements that dynamic routing provides are covered and the basic configuration of the interior gateway protocols are discussed. Specifically, this chapter covers the following topics:

▶ **Understanding routing protocols**

▶ **Configuring routing protocols**

Understanding Routing Protocols

There are two basic types of routing protocols: interior and exterior. *Exterior routing protocols* such as Border Gateway Protocol (BGP) are used between autonomous systems and are beyond the scope of this book.

An *autonomous system (AS)* is a group of routers under the management of the same entity, usually a corporation or enterprise. An AS will use at least one, and maybe more, interior routing protocols. *Interior routing protocols*, such as the ones discussed in this chapter, are used within an AS.

Interior routing protocols can be further categorized by their routing logic or architecture. Cisco defines three types of interior routing protocols that function on their routers:

> ▶ Distance-vector
>
> ▶ Link-state
>
> ▶ Hybrid

For more information on Border Gateway Protocol (BGP), go to http://docwiki.cisco.com/wiki/Border_Gateway_Protocol.

These three types differ in a number of ways:

▶ The metric used to determine the best route

▶ The number of tables or components used in the routing process

▶ The speed of convergence

▶ The amount of routing traffic generated

▶ The complexity of configuration

The following list provides definitions of these concepts as well as a comparison of the protocol types with respect to these characteristics.

Metric   A metric is a value used to describe the relative desirability of a route to a network. All dynamic routing protocols have the ability to choose the best route from multiple possible routes to the same destination network. The metric is a value used to make the choice of one route over another. With a distance-vector protocol, that metric is hop count, which is simply the number of routers in the path to the destination. In link-state and hybrid protocols, the metric is a value generated by a mathematical algorithm that takes several factors into consideration.

Tables   Routes are not the only routing information stored in tables or databases. Depending on the routing protocol, other tables and databases may be used, such as neighbor tables or topology databases. Distance-vector protocols use fewer tables than hybrid and link-state, but are incapable of making the more sophisticated types of routing decisions of which link-state protocols are capable.

Convergence   Convergence is the time that it takes for all routers to be informed of a change in the network such as a link outage. Link-state and hybrid routing protocols converge faster than distance-vector protocols because of their use of more tables of information. As you will learn in the sections on EIGRP and OSPF (which take different approaches to arrive at the same result), the end result is that a replacement route is determined and distributed faster with link-state and hybrid routing protocols.

Routing Traffic   Distance-vector protocols generate larger amounts of routing traffic and they generate it more often. Because less information is retained about the state of the network, more-frequent communication between the routers is necessary. Link-state and hybrid routing protocols do not send information between routers as frequently, and when they do, it usually relates to changes in the network only, resulting in smaller transmissions.

Complexity of Configuration As you might expect, with functionality comes complexity. Distance-vector protocols take little more than enabling to function. Hybrid routing protocols are somewhat more complex, while link-state routing protocols can become very complex very quickly. The very features that reduce the amount of routing update traffic and speed convergence require more configuration, care, and maintenance.

This chapter covers the three main interior routing protocols. Each is presented in detail in the following sections.

Exploring RIP

Routing Internet Protocol (RIP) is the only distance-vector routing protocol we will discuss. This industry standard protocol operates on non-Cisco routers as well. RIP routers use only routing tables to store information. RIP can store multiple routes to the same destination and uses as its metric a value called *hop count*. Hop count is the number of routers that are in the path to the destination network using that route. If two routes are available, one with a hop count of two and the other with a hop count of three, the route with the hop count of two will be chosen without regard to other factors such as the bandwidth of the links.

When redundant pathways exist among the routers in a network (which is a good design feature for the same reason it is a good design feature between switches: fault tolerance), the possibility of routing loops exists. Routing loops occur when packets that cannot be routed circle the network, eating up bandwidth. Distance-vector protocols use various techniques to prevent routing loops. These features do not need to be enabled; they operate automatically:

Maximum Hop Count Although maximum hop count is not technically one of the route loop-prevention mechanisms, it is an important characteristic to understand and does play a role in some of the mechanisms. The maximum hop count is the maximum number of routers a packet can traverse before it is dropped and no longer routed. In RIP, the maximum hop count is 15, which is a reason why RIP is only good for small networks. This means that a network that is advertised with a metric of 16 is considered unreachable in RIP.

Split Horizon Split horizon is a rule to which all RIP routers adhere that prevents the router from ever advertising (sending a routing update) back in the direction from which it came. Consider Figure 16.1. If R2 learns the route to the 192.168.60.0/24 network from R1, the split horizon rule will prevent R2 from advertising the same route back to R1 as a router reachable through R1.

Network 192.168.60.0/24

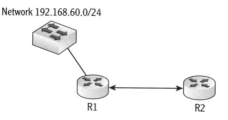

FIGURE 16.1 Split horizon

Poison Reverse This rule states that when a router learns that a route is no longer valid because of a link failure, that router will advertise the network in the direction from whence it was originally learned (actually violating the split horizon rule in that case) with an unreachable metric (in RIP, that is 16). Consider Figure 16.2. If R3 learns about the 192.168.60.0/24 network from R1 and then later learns from R2 that the network is unreachable, R3 will advertise the network to R1 with a metric of 16.

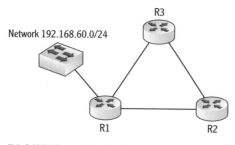

FIGURE 16.2 Poison reverse

Hold-Down Timer Hold-down timers are used to introduce stability into a network at locations where a link may be experiencing transient connection loss (called a *flapping link*). Hold-down timers enforce a period of time that the router must wait, (called the hold-down timer value), before reacting to information that a link is down.

RIP is the slowest of the three routing protocols we will discuss with respect to convergence. This is partly a function of the hold-down timer. However, the more significant factor is that unlike hybrid and distance-vector protocols, RIP does not use any resources to prepare for link outages in advance of the outage.

RIP also creates more routing traffic than EIGRP and OSPF. RIP routers send routing updates to adjacent RIP routers every 30 seconds. When these updates are sent, they include the entire routing table. EIGRP and OSPF routers (with some exceptions), send updates only when something changes in the network, and they usually send only information regarding the change and not all routing information.

The good news about RIP is that it is the simplest of the three to configure. As you will see in the "Configuring Routing Protocols" section, it really consists of two steps:

- ▶ Enabling the protocol
- ▶ Defining the networks (and thus the interfaces) on which it will operate

Exploring EIGRP

Enhanced Interior Gateway Routing Protocol (EIGRP) is an improved version of an older Cisco routing protocol called Interior Gateway Routing Protocol (IGRP). Both are Cisco proprietary and will function only on Cisco routers. EIGRP is considered a hybrid protocol because it has characteristics of both distance-vector and link-state routing protocols.

It uses a composite metric (one that takes multiple factors into consideration) as does OSPF, and it uses some features of distance-vector routing such as a maximum hop count (255) and loop avoidance techniques such as split horizon and poison reverse.

EIGRP uses a metric that takes into consideration the bandwidth on each link along the route and the delay that is occurring on each link. A mathematical algorithm uses this information to arrive at a numerical value that is used to compare routes.

EIGRP converges very fast because of its approach to preparing for losing routes due to link outages. To do this, it makes use of these additional tables:

Neighbor Table   The neighbor table contains information on the other EIGRP routers with which the local router has established a neighbor relationship. *Neighbors* are other EIGRP routers that are located on the same local network.

Routing Table   EIGRP maintains a routing table as do all three of the protocols. This table contains the current best route for each destination network.

Topology Table   The topology table contains all routes to all networks received from its EIGRP neighbors. This includes the best routes and the less favorable routes as well. It also includes the metric attached to each route as advertised by the neighbor from which the route was learned.

The best route for each destination in the topology table is called a *successor route* and is placed into the routing table. The second-best routes are called *feasible successors* and are marked as such and held in the topology table.

EIGRP achieves its speed of convergence by determining in advance the feasible successor route. Then if a successor route becomes unavailable, the feasible successor is immediately placed into the routing table, speeding the convergence process.

EIGRP sends routing updates only when changes occur. It does, however, send hello packets every 5 seconds on fast links and every 60 seconds on slower links. These packets are used to determine when links with neighbors are down.

As you will see in the "Configuring Routing Protocols" section, for all the features it brings to the table, EIGRP is relatively simple to configure. Although many options are available, the basic steps are simply as follows:

1. Enable the protocol.

2. Define the networks (and thus the interfaces on which it will operate).

Exploring OSPF

Open Shortest Path First (OSPF) is an industry-standard protocol that operates on non-Cisco routers as well. It is designed to operate more efficiently than RIP or EIGRP in very large networks. It does this by maintaining more information, as EIGRP does, but its goes a step further by using a concept called *areas*.

Detailed routing information about an area is confined to that area, and only a summary of information is advertised to other areas. This has the benefit of keeping OSPF routing tables smaller. In OSPF, certain routers are designated to perform certain functions on behalf of all routers in an area or all routers in an OSPF AS.

Most of the details of these concepts are covered in Chapter 11, "LAN Operations." A simple OSPF configuration is presented in the next section.

Configuring Routing Protocols

There are some variations in the application, but each of the routing protocols we have covered is configured by using the same basic steps:

1. Enable the routing protocol.

2. Define the interfaces on which the protocol is operational.

3. Verify the routing table.

Enabling a Routing Protocol and Accessing Router Mode

Enabling a routing protocol is a matter of using the `router <routing proto-col>` command at the global configuration prompt. It also worth noting that this also is the way to enter configuration mode for that routing protocol should you need to make changes or additional settings to the protocol. An example of this is the specification of the networks or interfaces where the routing protocol will be operational. This would be done at the routing protocol configuration prompt.

In this section, the steps for enabling the routing protocol and entering configuration mode for that routing protocol are explained.

Enabling RIP

To enable RIP, proceed to global configuration mode and execute the following command:

```
Router(config)#router rip
Router(config-router)#
```

Notice that you are also now in configuration mode for the RIP protocol, and you would use this same procedure to arrive at the prompt required to make any additional settings to RIP.

Enabling EIGRP

To enable EIGRP, the process is the same as with RIP, except that you must also specify what is called an *EIGRP autonomous system number*. This is a number that can be of your own choosing—but it must match with the neighboring routers, or neighbor relationships will not form. Proceed to global configuration mode and execute the following command:

```
Router(config)#router eigrp < autonomous system number>
Router(config-router)#
```

Notice that you are also now in configuration mode for the EIGRP protocol, and you would use this same procedure to arrive at the prompt required to make any additional settings to EIGRP.

Enabling OSPF

To enable OSPF, the process is the same as with EIGRP, except that instead of specifying an AS number, you specify what is called an *OSPF process ID*. This is a number that can be of your own choosing, and it *need not* match with the neighboring routers.

DON'T CONFUSE THE OSPF PROCESS ID AND OSPF AREA ID!

The *OSPF process ID* and *OSPF area ID* are two different concepts and are configured in two different places. The process ID does *not* need to match between OSPF neighbors. It is used to allow you to run multiple instances of OSPF on the same router. The area ID *must* match between the OSPF routers in the same area, for the routers to form an intra-area neighbor relationship. The process ID is defined in the same command that enables EIGRP, whereas the area ID is defined in the same command that defines the networks.

Proceed to global configuration mode and execute the following command:

```
Router(config)#router ospf <process ID>
Router(config-router)#
```

Notice that you are also now in configuration mode for the OSPF protocol, and you would use this same procedure to arrive at the prompt required to make any additional settings to OSPF.

Defining the Interfaces on Which the Protocol Is Operational

Defining the interfaces or networks is usually done before leaving the routing protocol configuration prompt, but it can be done later if desired.

To define the interfaces, you would use the following procedures to access the router configuration prompt.

Defining Interfaces in RIP

Defining the interfaces in RIP is done with the network command, at the protocol configuration prompt, by using the following syntax:

```
Router(config-router)#network  <network ID>
```

▶

Although you can wait until later to define the networks, keep in mind that until you define a network for RIP, EIGRP, or OSPF, no routing will occur!

For example, to make RIP operational on an interface with an IP address of 192.168.5.5/24, the command would be as follows:

```
Router(config-router)#network  192.168.5.0
```

Defining Interfaces in EIGRP

Defining the interfaces in EIGRP is done with the network command, at the protocol configuration prompt, by using the following syntax:

```
Router(config-router)#network  <network ID>
```

For example, to make EIGRP operational on an interface with an IP address of 192.168.5.5/24, the command would be as follows:

```
Router(config-router)#network  192.168.5.0
```

Defining Interfaces in OSPF

Defining the interfaces in OSPF is done with the network command, at the protocol configuration prompt, by using the following syntax:

```
Router(config-router)#network  <network ID> <wildcard mask> <area ID>
```

WILDCARD MASKS

A *wildcard mask* is a mask used to determine the range of networks on which OSPF will operate. When creating a wildcard mask, any octets that are 0s must match the network ID specified to be included as an interface (and thus a network) on which OSPF will operate. Those with 255s need not match. For example, if the network ID is 192.168.5.0, and the wildcard mask is 0.0.0.255, any interfaces on the router from 192.168.5.1–192.168.5.254 would be enabled for OSPF.

For example, to make OSPF area 0 operational on an interface with an IP address of 192.168.5.5/24, you would use this command:

```
Router(config-router)#network  192.168.5.0 0.0.0.255. area 0
```

Verifying the Routing Table

The preceding configurations are the simplest possible to get routing working and are not meant to imply that many more functions cannot be adjusted and set. The best way to determine whether routing is working is to view the routing tables to see if the routers are learning routes from one another. Let's look at some examples for each protocol.

Verifying in RIP

Consider the network displayed in Figure 16.3.

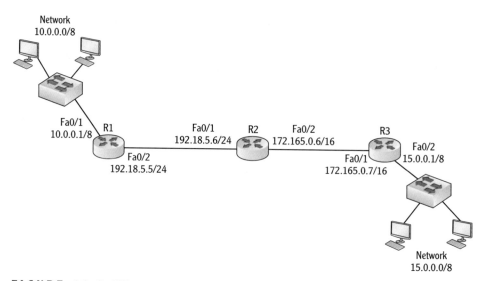

FIGURE 16.3 RIP example

Just as a review, let's look at the commands that would set all three routers up to run RIP successfully.

```
R1(config)#router rip
R1(config-router)#network 10.0.0.0
R1(config-router)#network 192.168.5.0

R2(config)#router rip
R2(config-router)#network 192.198.5.0
R2(config-router)#network 172.165.0.0

R3(config)#router rip
R3(config-router)#network 172.165.0.0
R3(config-router)#network 15.0.0.0
```

That should get routing working. To verify this, execute the show ip route command on each router. All four routes should be in all tables.

```
R1>show ip route
Codes: I - IGRP derived, R - RIP derived, O - OSPF derived,
       C - connected, S - static D - EIGRP

       <output omitted>

C    10.0.0.0 is directly connected, FastEthernet 0/1
C    192.168.5.0 is directly connected, FastEthernet 0/2
R    172.165.0.0/16 [120/1] via  192.168.5.5
R    15.0.0.0/8 [120/2] via  192.168.5.5

R2>show ip route
Codes: I - IGRP derived, R - RIP derived, O - OSPF derived,
       C - connected, S - static D - EIGRP

       <output omitted>

C    172.165.0 is directly connected, FastEthernet 0/2
C    192.168.5.0 is directly connected, FastEthernet 0/1
R    10.0.0.0/8 [120/1] via  192.168.5.6
R    15.0.0.0/8 [120/1] via  192.168.5.5


R3>show ip route
Codes: I - IGRP derived, R - RIP derived, O - OSPF derived,
       C - connected, S - static D - EIGRP

       <output omitted>

C    172.165.0 is directly connected, FastEthernet 0/1
C    15.0.0.0/8 is directly connected, FastEthernet 0/2
R    10.0.0.0/8 [120/2] via  172.15.0.7
R    192.18.5.0/24 [120/1] via  172.15.0.7
```

As you can see, all routes are present because the routers have shared their tables. The routes that were learned via RIP are marked with an R. The information in the brackets after each RIP route is the administrative distance and the metric (hop count).

Verifying in EIGRP

Consider again the network that was displayed in Figure 16.3.

Just as a review, let's look at the commands that would set all three routers up to run EIGRP successfully. The EIGRP AS is 1.

```
R1(config)#router eigrp 1
R1(config-router)#network 10.0.0.0
R1(config-router)#network 192.168.5.0

R2(config)#router eigrp 1
R2(config-router)#network 192.198.5.0
R2(config-router)#network 172.165.0.0

R3(config)#router eigrp 1
R3(config-router)#network 172.165.0.0
R3(config-router)#network 15.0.0.0
```

That should get routing working. To verify this, execute the show ip route command on each router. All four routes should be in all tables.

```
R1>show ip route
Codes: I - IGRP derived, R - RIP derived, O - OSPF derived,
       C - connected, S - static D - EIGRP

          <output omitted>


C    10.0.0.0 is directly connected, FastEthernet 0/1
C    192.168.5.0 is directly connected, FastEthernet 0/2
D    172.165.0.0/16 [90/156600] via  192.168.5.5
D    15.0.0.0/8 [90/177303] via 192.168.5.5

R2>show ip route
Codes: I - IGRP derived, R - RIP derived, O - OSPF derived,
       C - connected, S - static D - EIGRP

          <output omitted>


C    172.165.0 is directly connected, FastEthernet 0/2
C    192.168.5.0 is directly connected, FastEthernet 0/1
D    10.0.0.0/8 [90/156660]via  192.168.5.6
D    15.0.0.0/8 [90/156660]via  192.168.5.5


R3>show ip route
Codes: I - IGRP derived, R - RIP derived, O - OSPF derived,
       C - connected, S - static D - EIGRP
```

```
<output omitted>
```

```
C    172.165.0 is directly connected, FastEthernet 0/1
C    15.0.0.0/8 is directly connected, FastEthernet 0/2
D    10.0.0.0/8 [90/156660]via  172.15.0.7
D    192.18.5.0/24 [90/177303]via  172.15.0.7
```

As you can see, all routes are present because the routers have shared their tables. The routes that were learned via EIGRP are marked with a D. The information in the brackets after each EIGRP route is the administrative distance and the metric.

Verifying in OSPF

Consider the network displayed in Figure 16.4.

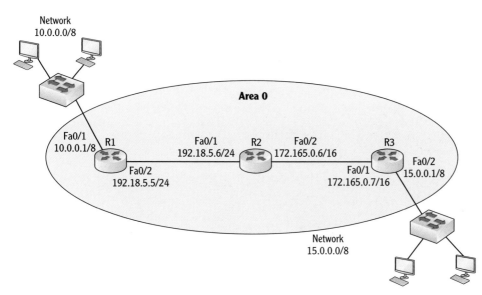

FIGURE 16.4 OSPF example

Just as a review, let's look at the commands that would set all three routers up to run OSPF successfully. The OSPF process ID is 1, and the area ID for all routers is 0.

```
R1(config)#router ospf 1
R1(config-router)#network 10.0.0.0 0.255.255.255 area 0
R1(config-router)#network 192.168.5.0
0.0.0.255 area 0
```

```
R2(config)#router ospf 1
R2(config-router)#network 192.198.5.0
0.0.0.255 area 0
R2(config-router)#network 172.165.0.0
0.0.255.255 area 0

R3(config)#router ospf 1
R3(config-router)#network 172.165.0.0
0.0.255.255. area 0
R3(config-router)#network 15.0.0.0
0.255.255.255 area 0
```

That should get routing working. To verify this, execute the show ip route command on each router. All four routes should be in all tables.

```
R1>show ip route
Codes: I - IGRP derived, R - RIP derived, O - OSPF derived,
       C - connected, S - static D - EIGRP

       <output omitted>


C    10.0.0.0 is directly connected, FastEthernet 0/1
C    192.168.5.0 is directly connected, FastEthernet 0/2
O    172.165.0.0/16 [110/1] via  192.168.5.5
O    15.0.0.0/8 [110/2] via 192.168.5.5

R2>show ip route
Codes: I - IGRP derived, R - RIP derived, O - OSPF derived,
       C - connected, S - static D - EIGRP

       <output omitted>


C    172.165.0 is directly connected, FastEthernet 0/2
C    192.168.5.0 is directly connected, FastEthernet 0/1
O    10.0.0.0/8 [110/1]via  192.168.5.6
O    15.0.0.0/8 [110/1]via  192.168.5.5


R3>show ip route
Codes: I - IGRP derived, R - RIP derived, O - OSPF derived,
       C - connected, S - static D - EIGRP

       <output omitted>
```

```
C    172.165.0 is directly connected, FastEthernet 0/1
C    15.0.0.0/8 is directly connected, FastEthernet 0/2
O    10.0.0.0/8 [110/2]via  172.15.0.7
O    192.18.5.0/24 [110/1]via  172.15.0.7
```

As you can see, all routes are present because the routers have shared their tables. The routes that were learned via OSPF are marked with an 0. The information in the brackets after each OSPF route is the administrative distance and the metric.

THE ESSENTIALS AND BEYOND

There are two basic types of routing protocols: interior and exterior. Exterior routing protocols are used between autonomous systems, and interior routing protocols are used within an AS. Cisco defines three types of interior routing protocols that function on their routers: distance-vector, link-state, and hybrid. These interior routing protocols differ in their metric, number of tables or components used, speed of convergence, amount of routing traffic generated, and the complexity of configuration. Routing Internet Protocol (RIP) is a distance-vector routing protocol that uses only routing tables to store information. RIP can store multiple routes to the same destination and uses a metric called hop count. Distance-vector protocols such as RIP use a number of techniques to prevent routing loops, including split horizon, poison reverse, and hold-down timers. Enhanced Interior Gateway Routing Protocol (EIGRP) is Cisco proprietary and is considered a hybrid protocol because it has characteristics of both distance-vector and link-state routing protocols. While it uses a composite metric, it uses some features of distance-vector routing such as a maximum hop count (255) and loop avoidance techniques such as split horizon and poison reverse. Open Shortest Path First (OSPF) is an industry-standard protocol designed to operate more efficiently than RIP or EIGRP in very large networks. It uses areas. It contains detailed routing information about an area to that area and sends only a summary of information to other areas, which keeps OSPF routing tables smaller. Routing protocols are configured by enabling the routing protocol and defining the interfaces on which the protocol is operational.

ADDITIONAL EXERCISES

1. In this exercise, you will configure a set of three routers to operate using the EIGRP protocol. The process ID is 1. This exercise assumes that you have cabled and configured the three routers using the IP addresses shown in Figure 16.5. Your interface numbers may be different, so take that into consideration.

(Continues)

THE ESSENTIALS AND BEYOND *(Continued)*

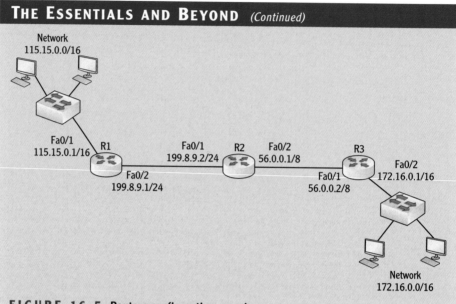

FIGURE 16.5 Routers configuration exercise

2. Use the show ip route command and the ping command to verify the routing tables.

REVIEW QUESTIONS

1. Which of the following is *not* an interior routing protocol?

   A. BGP   **C.** EIGRP

   B. RIP   **D.** OSPF

2. A _____ protocol uses only hop count as a metric.

   A. Link-state   **C.** Hybrid

   B. Distance-vector   **D.** Spanning tree

3. Which of the following has the slowest convergence?

   A. STP   **C.** EIGRP

   B. RIP   **D.** OSPF

4. Which of the following is the most complex to configure?

   A. STP   **C.** EIGRP

   B. RIP   **D.** OSPF

(Continues)

5. Which of the following has a maximum hop count of 255 by default?

    A. BGP   C. EIGRP

    B. RIP   D. OSPF

6. Which loop avoidance measure prevents the router from ever advertising (sending a routing update) back in the direction from which it came?

    A. Spanning Tree Protocol   C. Split horizon

    B. Poison reverse   D. Count to infinity

7. How often do RIP routers send routing updates to adjacent RIP routers ?

    A. Every 10 seconds   C. Every 30 seconds

    B. Every 15 seconds   D. Every 45 seconds

8. Which if the following is *not* a table used by EIGRP?

    A. Routing   C. Neighbor

    B. Topology   D. Link-state

9. Which table contains the feasible successor?

    A. Routing   C. Neighbor

    B. Topology   D. Link-state

10. After the routing protocol is defined, at which of the following prompts is the interface on which it is operational defined?

    A. Router(config)#   C. Router(config-if)#

    B. Router(config-router)# D. Router #

Answers to Review Questions

Chapter 1

1. **B** Security is *increased* when computers are networked because data can be transferred securely between computers.

2. **B** A directory services server forms a security association between network members and helps to locate resources.

3. **B** Only two computers are required to form a network.

4. **True** Telecommuting helps save gas and commuting time by allowing work from home or another location remote from the LAN.

5. **C** A protocol, an agreement on how the data is packaged, forms a communications agreement between the computers.

6. **A** *Proprietary* refers to any process or way of doing something that works only on a single vendor's equipment.

7. **B** A LAN is a high-speed data network covering a small geographical area.

8. **False** A de facto standard is one that becomes the standard simply by being the method all parties gradually choose to use over a period of time, without a formal adoption process.

9. **C** A peer-to-peer network is also sometimes called a workgroup.

10. **D** Because of broadcast traffic, a peer-to-peer network will experience network congestion.

Chapter 2

1. **B** Networking reference models encourage standardization but they do not in and of themselves ensure any particular performance level for a network.

2. **C** The Department of Defense (DoD) created a four-layer model in the early 1970s based on the protocol that eventually became the protocol of the

Internet and later the de facto standard for LAN protocols, called the TCP/IP, or Internet, model.

3.   **B, C, D** The Application, Presentation, and Session layers map to the Application layer of the DoD, or TCP/IP, model.

4.   **C, D** The Data-Link and the Physical layers map to the Application layer of the DoD, or TCP/IP, model.

5.   **B** The Session layer of the OSI model is responsible for coordinating the exchanges of information between the layer 7 applications or services that are in use.

6.   **C** IP addresses are used on layer 3 (the Network layer) of the OSI model.

7.   **C** TCP 23 communicates the transport protocol (TCP) and the port number (23).

8.   **A** The port numbers 1–1,023 are standardized and are called well-known port numbers.

9.   **C** A unicast is used from one device to another device, on a one-to-one basis.

10.   **C** Broadcast and multicast traffic both use UDP.

Chapter 3

1.   **C** By 1983, it was mandated that all machines that connected to the ARPANET use this protocol. When this mandate was handed down, it set in motion the adoption of TCP/IP as the protocol of the coming Internet and of any LANs that wanted to connect (without using any protocol conversion) to the Internet.

2.   **B** The Presentation layer is not found in the four layers of the TCP/IP model.

3.   **C** The parts of the TCP/IP suite dedicated to using information provided by the port numbers are located in the Transport layer.

4.   **B** The IP address of the source and destination devices are determined and placed on the package at the Internet layer.

5.   **D** The six protocols in the suite are TCP, UDP, IP, ARP, ICMP, and IGMP.

6.   **A** In TCP/IP, session management is performed at the Transport layer.

7.   **B** At the Transport layer, the PDU is called a segment.

8.   **A** At the Network Access layer, the PDU is called a frame.

9.   **C** UDP is stateless, non-connection-oriented, and nonguaranteed. It is *not* used for unicast.

10.   **D** ARP identifies and places the source and destination MAC address in the frame.

Chapter 4

1. **A** The layer on which a protocol operates is dependent on the type of information that it uses in the process of carrying out its job. For example, if a protocol uses Transport layer information (port numbers) to perform its job, it will be a Transport layer protocol. If it uses MAC addresses, it would be considered a Network Access layer protocol.

2. **B** NetBEUI, an early Microsoft protocol, was designed as a protocol for small workgroups of computers that were located on the same physical segment. NetBEUI is not routable.

3. **C** DNS resolves computer names to IP addresses and operates at the Application layer.

4. **B** File Transfer Protocol (FTP) is a connection-oriented protocol dedicated to moving files from one computer to another. FTP operates at the Application layer.

5. **C** The port number is UDP 69 to begin the connection, but the client and server may change to random ports for the transfer afterward.

6. **C** TFTP is used to transfer a router operating system (called the Cisco IOS) from a TFTP server to a route.

7. **D** Queries are used in DNS, not SNMP.

8. **B** TCP is responsible for sequencing the packets.

9. **B** The three steps are SYN, SYN-ACK, and ACK.

10. **C** The protocol number is found in the IP header.

Chapter 5

1. **C** A point-to-multipoint topology is an example of a WAN topology.

2. **False** A token ring topology is a physical star but is logically a ring topology.

3. **B** Each end of the bus topology must have a special connector called a terminator installed.

4. **D** A ring topology does not require terminators.

5. **A** A star topology uses either switches or hubs.

6. **D** Although it is expensive to implement and maintain, the mesh topology provides the best fault tolerance.

7.   **C** The point-to-multipoint topology requires that a physical interface be divided logically into multiple subinterfaces on the router.

8.   **C** A Token Ring is physically a star topology with the devices all connected to a central device called a Media Access Unit (MAU).

9.   **C** A Fiber Distributed Data Interface (FDDI) ring uses a double ring for fault tolerance.

10.   **A** The contention method used in an Ethernet star is called Carrier Sense Multiple Access/Collision Detection (CSMA/CD).

Chapter 6

1.   **D** MAC addresses use hexadecimal, not binary.

2.   **B** Any number to the zero power is 1.

3.   **C** The Unicode system represents multiple language characters with 2-byte, or 16-bit, patterns.

4.   **D** Hex is used in MAC addresses and in memory addressing.

5.   **C** IPv6 uses hexadecimal.

6.   **C** Because hex uses powers of 16 for each place in the number, it can represent very large numbers concisely.

7.   **B** A MAC address is also called a burned-in address (BIA).

8.   **A** The Organizationally Unique Identifier (OUI) identifies the manufacturer.

9.   **D** The right half is called the Universally Administered Address (UAA) and identifies the network card.

10.   **B** 00/50/56/C0/00/08 is *not* an accepted representation of a MAC address.

Chapter 7

1.   **C** Segmentation yields all of the listed benefits except requiring less hardware. It may even require more hardware.

2.   **False** With smaller LANs segmented by routers, network problems are easier to isolate.

3.   **D** The value of the first octet (the octet to the far left) determines the class in which an IP address resides. The range for Class B is 128–191.

4. **D** The most significant bits of the three classes are as follows:

        Class A—000

        Class B—100

        Class C—110

5. **C, D** 127.0.0.1 is the IPv4 loopback address, and ::1 is the IPv6 loopback address.

6. **C** The first three octets make up the network portion of a Class C address.

7. **B** The private IP address ranges are as follows:

      ▶ 10.0.0.0–10.255.255.255

      ▶ 172.16.0.0–172.31.255.255

      ▶ 192.168.0.0–192.168.255.255

8. **C** When you can ping a computer by its IP address but you can't connect to a service running on the computer, you can ping the port number of that service to see whether the port is blocked or the service is not functioning. Port numbers are on the Transport layer.

9. **C** The command `arp -a` displays all the current ARP entries for all interfaces.

10. **C** The order is DHCPDiscover, DHCPOffer, DHCPRequest, and DHCPAck.

Chapter 8

1. **A** The design flaws resulted in three main issues:

      ▶ Exhaustion of the Class B network address space

      ▶ Unmanageable routing tables

      ▶ Exhaustion of the 32-bit IPv4 address space

2. **B** A is *not* an issue resulting from classful subnetting. C and D were addressed by the introduction of Classless Inter-Domain Routing (CIDR). B was partially addressed but was not fully addressed until the development of IPv6.

3. **B** Classful IP addressing not only resulted in the overuse of the Class B space, but also resulted in many wasted IP addresses in most cases.

4. **C** Network summarization reduces the number of networks in the routing table and allows routers to make quicker routing decisions.

5. **B** When an organization with 5,000 computers requiring Internet access can be represented by a single public IP address as is possible with NAT, it helps to save public IP addresses.

6.   **A** Breaking a larger network into a number of smaller subnets increases performance by reducing the number of computers per subnet, thereby lowering the chances of collisions and reducing the amount of broadcast traffic produced.

7.   **C** With 20 bits in the subnet mask, the subnet mask in binary is 11111111.11111111.11110000.00000000, which in dotted decimal is 255.255.240.0.

8.   **D** For 39 subnets, 6 bits must be added for subnets. When added to the 16 bits for a Class B address, the result is /22.

9.   **A** To have subnets large enough for 78 hosts, 7 bits must be left for host bits, leaving 25 bits in the mask.

10.   **B** With a /23 mask, the interval, or block size, is 2. If the network ID is 172.168.8.0, the next network ID will be 172.168.10.0, so the range is 172.16.8.1/23–172.168.9.254/23.

Chapter 9

1.   **D** Stolen login passwords can just as easily occur on a wired network as a WLAN. Rogue access points could occur in only a WLAN. Wireless transmissions and the data they contain can be captured by anyone in the transmission area, and while it is easy to make a connection to an unauthenticated WLAN, physical access to a port is required on a cabled LAN.

2.   **D** 1 Gbps to the desktop is almost 10 times what wireless can currently deliver at its best to the desktop.

3.   **B** The SSID is displayed in transmissions between legitimate users and the AP. It is not displayed in beacon frames, it is not the MAC address of the AP, and no channels are hidden.

4.   **D** Port-scanning software is not required, although it could be used as part of the peer-to-peer attack after the highjack has occurred. The highjack attack requires an AP, DHCP, knowledge of the SSID and the channel, and a jammer.

5.   **A** A cabled LAN is always more secured than a WLAN. The WLAN is more convenient, cheaper, and easier to install.

6.   **B** The loss of energy as an electrical signal travels down a wire or an optical signal travels down a glass tube is called attenuation.

7.   **A** Electromagnetic interference is called EMI.

8.   **C** Coaxial cabling is familiar to anyone who has had cable TV. It has either a solid copper wire or a stranded copper wire in the center.

9.   **C** 10Base5 coaxial transceivers are connected to cable segments with either N-connectors or a vampire tap.

10.   **C** The twisting mitigates a behavior called crosstalk that occurs when the twisting is not in place. Crosstalk occurs when the signals on one wire interfere with those on another wire.

Chapter 10

1.   **B** Repeaters operate at the Network Access layer.

2.   **D** A repeater takes the original signal and amplifies, or boosts, the signal. After the signal has traversed a certain length of cable, the signal strength is gradually weakened by the resistance in the cable (which is called attenuation).

3.   **D** Routers operate at the Internet layer of the TCP/IP model and make routing decisions based on IP address information.

4.   **A** On hubs, all of the ports are on a shared network. They all exist in one collision domain.

5.   **A** Both bridges and switches perform MAC address learning.

6.   **A** Switches do not use IP address information for filtering.

7.   **C** Multilayer switches perform routing and switching and thus operate on both the Network Access and the Internet layer.

8.   **B** There are no multicast routes in a routing table.

9.   **A** If a router is configured with a default route and you issue the command to show all routes (show ip route), this route will be referred to as the gateway of last resort.

10.   **A** Dynamic routing protocols create more network traffic, because they send routing updates.

Chapter 11

1.   **A** A routing table entry will consist of network, population method, next hop, exit interface, and metric.

2.   **B** Route tables cannot be populated using DHCP.

3.   **D** The method is indicated by a letter next to the network ID. *C* indicates directly connected, *S* indicates static, and if the route came from another router, a letter

that represents that particular routing protocol (such as *R* for Routing Internet Protocol, or RIP) will be used.

4.   **C** The section 0:01:50 states the time in terms of hours: minutes: seconds.

5.   **D** Border Gateway Protocol (BGP) is an exterior routing protocol.

6.   **B** RIP uses hop count as its sole metric.

7.   **A** The default AD of EIGRP is 90.

8.   **D** Static routes have an AD of 1, which is a lower AD than any of the routing protocols listed.

9.   **C** RIP sends regular routing updates every 30 seconds.

10.   **B** Split horizon is a routing rule built into the protocol (no need to enable it or anything) that prevents a router from advertising a route to the same interface on which it was learned. The assumption is that if a router is attempting to advertise a route back in the direction from whence it came, a loop is occurring.

Chapter 12

1.   **C** The Cisco IOS tables and the running configuration are located in RAM after startup.

2.   **B** NVRAM contains both the configuration register and the startup configuration.

3.   **C** Only RAM loses its information when power is lost.

4.   **C** It is not required that the device have a name configured.

5.   **C** A console cable has a serial connector on one end and an RJ-45 connector on the other.

6.   **B** By default, the only mode in which you will be prompted for a password is privileged.

7.   **A** The > prompt indicates user mode.

8.   **A** The bootstrap code is loaded from ROM first.

9.   **A** Once the IOS becomes operational, it loads the startup configuration file located in NVRAM. After that file is read, system messages will begin to appear.

10.   **B** If you are unsure of the room, you can check the available space in flash by using the show flash command. The output you receive will tell you the name of the current IOS file, its size, and the amount of space that remains available.

Chapter 13

1. **A** An Attachment Unit Interface (AUI) connector is Ethernet.

2. **B** The AUX port is used for a modem.

3. **C** The DCE end of the process provides the clocking for the connection.

4. **B** Connecting to the router with the Telnet program will not be possible unless the router has an interface enabled with an IP address and you have configured a virtual terminal (vty) or line password.

5. **C** If the configuration register is set to 0x2102 on a router with an existing startup configuration file, you would *not* receive this message. This setting tells the router to use the file.

6. **A** Typing enable is tantamount to asking for privileged access to be enabled, which is why the privileged mode password is required at the Router> prompt before you can get to the Router# prompt.

7. **C** The global configuration prompt is Router(config)#.

8. **D** The choices are console (connection through the console cable), vty (connection through Telnet), and aux (connection through a modem connected to the router).

9. **A** To instruct the router to prompt for the password, use the login command.

10. **C** Fa0/2 is the second Fast Ethernet port in the first slot on the router.

Chapter 14

1. **B** By default, all ports in a switch are in VLAN 1.

2. **C** VLANs are segments at the Network Access layer of the TCP/IP model.

3. **A** Cables that run from host to switch should be straight-through cables.

4. **D** Cables that run between two switches should be crossover cables.

5. **C** An IP address must be applied to VLAN 1 to telnet to the switch.

6. **D** By default, switchports are enabled, assigned to VLAN 1, and need no IP address.

7. **C** After changes have been made, no shutdown should be executed under the switchport configuration mode.

8. **A** The output was produced by the show port status 0/4 command.

9. **A** VLANs provide segmentation at the Network Access layer, not the Internet layer.

10. **B** Spanning Tree Protocol (STP) is designed to prevent the loops from happening.

Chapter 15

1.　**C** Only directly connected routes are placed into the routing table automatically.

2.　**D** A default route is a route to which all traffic that does not have an existing route in the table is sent.

3.　**C** Elimination of routing update traffic is the only advantage of static routing. All of the other options are advantages of dynamic routing.

4.　**D** When the network topology is very small, changes rarely if ever occur, and the system is very stable, static routing may be advisable because it eliminates the routing update traffic that competes with the regular traffic for bandwidth.

5.　**A** The ip route command is used to place routes into the routing table.

6.　**C** 192.168.5.6 is the address of the next hop router in the path to the destination network.

7.　**B** The output shown was produced by the show ip route command.

8.　**D** Only static routes, indicated with an S, are manually added.

9.　**D** Multicast IP addresses are not required for inter-VLAN routing.

10.　**A** Setting the link to *trunk* is done in interface configuration mode.

Chapter 16

1.　**A** Exterior routing protocols such as Border Gateway Protocol (BGP) are used between autonomous systems.

2.　**B** A distance-vector protocol uses only hop count as a metric.

3.　**B** RIP is the slowest to converge.

4.　**D** OSPF is the most complex to configure.

5.　**C** EIGRP has a maximum hop count of 255 by default.

6.　**C** Split horizon, a rule to which all RIP routers adhere, prevents the router from ever advertising (sending a routing update) back in the direction from which it came.

7.　**C** RIP routers send routing updates to adjacent RIP routers every 30 seconds.

8.　**D** Link-state tables are used by OSPF.

9.　**B** The topology table contains all routes to all networks received from its EIGRP neighbors, including the feasible successor.

10.　**B** Defining the interfaces is done with the network command, at the protocol configuration prompt, using the following syntax:

```
Router(config-router)#network  <network ID>
```

INDEX

Note to the Reader: Throughout this index **boldfaced** page numbers indicate primary discussions of a topic. *Italicized* page numbers indicate illustrations.